12342363

S0-BII-475

WITHDRAWN

INNOVATORS
AND
PREACHERS

INNOVATORS
AND
PREACHERS

The Role of the Editor
in Victorian England

Edited by JOEL H. WIENER

Contributions to the Study of Mass Media and Communications,
Number 5

Greenwood Press
Westport, Connecticut • London, England

Library of Congress Cataloging-in-Publication Data

Main entry under title:

Innovators and preachers.

(Contributions to the study of mass media and
communications, ISSN 0732-4456 ; no. 5)
"Based on the proceedings of the fifth CUNY
Conference on History and Politics . . . held at . . . the
City University of New York on October 29-30, 1982 . . .
sponsored by the Research Society for Victorian
Periodicals and by the CUNY Center for European
Studies"—CIP pref.
Bibliography: p.
Includes index.
1. Journalism—Great Britain—Editing—History—19th
century—Congresses. I. Wiener, Joel H. II. Research
Society for Victorian Periodicals. III. City University
of New York. Center for European Studies. IV. CUNY
Conference on History and Politics (5th : 1982)
V. Series.
PN5124.E34I56 1985   070.4 '1 '0941   85-17658
ISBN 0-313-24164-3 (lib. bdg. : alk. paper)

Copyright © 1985 by Joel H. Wiener and CUNY Conference
on History and Politics

All rights reserved. No portion of this book may be
reproduced, by any process or technique, without the
express written consent of the publisher.

Library of Congress Catalog Card Number: 85-17658
ISBN: 0-313-24164-3
ISSN: 0732-4456

First published in 1985

Greenwood Press
A division of Congressional Information Service, Inc.
88 Post Road West
Westport, Connecticut 06881

Printed in the United States of America

The paper used in this book complies with the
Permanent Paper Standard issued by the National
Information Standards Organization (Z39.48-1984).

10 9 8 7 6 5 4 3 2 1

Copyright Acknowledgments

Grateful acknowledgment is given for permission to use excerpts reprinted from: Six
letters to William Makepeace Thackeray, editor of *Cornhill Magazine* in the
Beinecke Rare Book and Manuscript Library, Yale University; Quotations from
Charles Lever's Notebook and Correspondence, courtesy of The Piermont Morgan
Library, New York.

For Suzanne

Contents

Preface

This volume is based on the proceedings of the fifth CUNY Conference on History and Politics that was held at the Graduate Center of the City University of New York on October 29-30, 1982. The conference was also sponsored by the Research Society for Victorian Periodicals (its fourteenth annual conference) and by the CUNY Center for European Studies. I am grateful to these organizations for their support and to the CUNY Academy for the Humanities and Sciences, which provided financial support for the conference.

This book is a group effort in the best sense. I am particularly indebted to my colleague Professor George Schwab for his unstinting help and encouragement. Professor Michael Wolff shared with me his considerable knowledge of Victorian journalists and editors. Professor Robert A. Colby was a constant source of creative stimulation. I am also very grateful to the following scholars for their indirect contributions to this book:

Scott Bennett, Norman Kelvin, Helene Roberts, Marcia Allen-
tuck, Vineta Colby, Malcolm Woodfield, David Roberts, Joseph
Hamburger, Barbara Bellow Watson, Frederic Hunter, Merrill
Distad, and Charmazel Dudt.

I wish also to thank Miss Edwina McMahon for her skillful
editing, Diana Graham and Miriam Rodriguez for setting the
manuscript into type, Paul Wiener for his editorial assistance,
and my wife, Suzanne, who aided me in ways too numerous to
record. Finally, a special tribute is owed to George Spater, a contributor to this volume, whose untimely death has deprived Victorian scholarship of one of its most fertile minds.

Joel H. Wiener
City College of New York
and the CUNY Graduate Center

Joel H. Wiener

Introduction

"Wagg's white waistcoat spread out . . . with profuse brilliancy;
his burly red face shone resplendent over it, lighted up with the
thoughts of a good joke and a good dinner. He liked to make his
entree into a drawing-room with a laugh, and, when he went
away at night, to leave a joke exploding behind him. . . .
Whatever his griefs might be, the thought of a dinner rallied his
great soul; and when he saw a lord, he saluted him with a pun."[1]
The portly editor in *Pendennis* contrasts with the autocratic "Tom
Towers" in Trollope's *The Warden:* "No one could insult him; no
one could inquire into him. He could speak out withering words,
and no one could answer him: ministers courted him, though
perhaps they knew not his name; bishops feared him; judges
doubted their own verdicts unless he confirmed them; and

generals in their councils of war did not consider more deeply what the enemy would do than what the 'Jupiter' would say."[2]

Similarly, outside the world of fiction, the contemporary image of the Victorian editor varied. To Thomas Carlyle, "the true Church of England, at this moment, lies in the Editors of its Newspapers," while W.T. Stead, a leading practitioner of the craft, described editors as "the uncrowned kings of an educated democracy."[3] William Hazlitt took a more caustic view: "Some editors are scrubs, mere drudges, newspaper-puffs: others are bullies or quacks: others are nothing at all—they have the name, and receive a salary for it!"[4] And then there is the well-known anecdote about Mark Twain who, in a moment of gratitude for having been spared the indignity of becoming an editor, once confided to his readers: "I am not an editor of a newspaper, and shall always try to do right and be good so that God will not make me one." Perhaps Henry Labouchere, who edited *Truth,* was most accurate in his assessment: "I have now been connected with newspapers over thirty years and I have never yet discovered what an editor is."[5]

In the hope of making the discovery that eluded Labouchere for more than thirty years, about seventy-five scholars gathered at the Graduate Center of the City University of New York in October 1982 to discuss the "Victorian Editor" in a conference sponsored jointly by the CUNY Conference on History and Politics, the CUNY Center for European Studies, and the Research Society for Victorian Periodicals. The event was a lively academic undertaking, which spawned many disagreements and much enlightenment. The bulk of the conference papers, slightly revised for publication, are presented in this volume, with additional essays by Derek Fraser and Joel H. Wiener.

Editing is at the core of the Victorian experience. In an age characterized by the proliferation of print, the editor acted as a conduit between text and audience. He communicated ideas and values to a multiple readership. He enriched Victorian political and cultural life in diverse ways. And, perhaps of most importance, he helped create the modern newspaper and magazine, without which life for our Victorian forebears and ourselves would be considerably duller. In brief, the editor was situated at the nucleus of the Victorian world: He typified both the transformations that were making Britain an urban nation and a stable society.

As has been suggested by two historians of journalism, "the press [in all its manifestations] became during the Victorian period the context within which people lived and worked and thought, and from which they derived their (in most cases quite new) sense of the outside world."[6] In recent years the publication of a large number of books and articles about journalism, the appearance of successive volumes of *The Wellesley Index to Victorian Periodicals* and the *Victorian Periodicals Review,* and the sponsorship of research projects by organizations such as the Research Society for Victorian Periodicals have made this statement almost a truism. Yet the most important element in journalism, its editors — "ungrown, unshaped, ungroomed thing[s]" in the words of Frederick Greenwood[7] — has not been adequately studied. Admittedly, there are major biographies of Victorian editors such as Thomas Barnes, John T. Delane, James Knowles, Mark Lemon, and A. G. Gardiner. Likewise, histories of leading newspapers and magazines, including *The Times,* the *Manchester Guardian,* the *Saturday Review,* and the *Pall Mall Gazette,* have been published. These yield a treasure trove of material about editors. There are also general histories of the press and specialized studies of aspects of journalism — some of recent vintage, others published in the nineteenth century — which include useful information about editors and the problems of editing.[8]

As yet, however, no history of the Victorian editor has been written. *Innovators and Preachers: The Role of the Editor in*

Victorian England, though limited in scope, is intended to pave the way for such a history. It does not purport to be comprehensive. Political editing is inadequately discussed, as is the "new journalism" of the late nineteenth century with its many editorial innovations. Many influential Victorian editors such as John Black, Frederick Greenwood, T. P. O'Connor, and Ernest Parke — about whom little has been written so far — are not represented. There is insufficient coverage of the technical aspects of editing with the exception of its legal framework. None of the essays deals specifically with the professional status of editors, with their relationships to subeditors and reporters, or with editing in specialized areas such as sports or foreign news. Nor do any of the essays focus on the distinctive problems faced by editors in Wales, Scotland, or Ireland. These are not insignificant gaps, and though some of them can be filled by a close reading of the essays in this book, most will have to await the outcome of additional research before being repaired. Nonetheless, these essays do make available for the first time important work on Victorian editors and illuminate avenues for future study and debate.

Innovators and Preachers is divided into three sections. Part One, "Editor and Audience," is concerned with the interaction between editors and readers. Anne Humpherys analyzes the career of G. W. M. Reynolds, a major mid-Victorian editor, and concludes that his interest in both sensational fiction and political radicalism reflected the inclusiveness of popular culture. Stephen Elwell's discussion of the successive editors of *Once a Week,* a rival of Dickens's *All the Year Round,* shows how these editors failed to develop a successful marketing strategy to take into account a changing readership. Hartley S. Spatt deals with the problems encountered by editors of art periodicals in trying to give effect to their diverse aesthetic philosophies. Sheila R. Herstein traces the collective editorial history of the *English Woman's*

Journal, a periodical that helped create the first effective feminist network by its advocacy of employment for women and other issues of concern to women. Barbara Quinn Schmidt's study of Leslie Stephen, as the editor of the *Cornhill Magazine,* demonstrates his ethical concerns for and sensitivity to the religious and moral feelings of his audience.

Part Two, "The Context of Editing," places the editor in a social and a journalistic context. Christopher Kent analyzes the complex web of legal and informal restraints that limited the freedom of editors throughout much of the nineteenth century. Derek Fraser shows how provincial editing differed from its London counterpart in its increased political commitments and the opportunities it provided for upward mobility. Josef L. Altholz analyzes the totality of the persons involved in the editing process (what he defines as its redaction) in its Roman Catholic setting. Joanne Shattock examines the role and the status of several leading mid-Victorian quarterlies and documents the ways in which traditions of editing, such as that of the amateur scholar, developed and underwent changes. Charlotte C. Watkins, focusing on the *Queen,* discusses special problems involved in editing a "class" journal, in this instance one written for educated women.

Part Three, "Some Leading Practitioners," provides several case studies of editors and attempts to shed light on their objectives and the reasons for their successes or failures. Robert A. Colby discusses the interaction of periodical journalism and fiction in the careers of four famous novelist-editors — Anthony Trollope, William Makepeace Thackeray, Harrison Ainsworth, and Charles Lever. Ann P. Robson and John M. Robson investigate the private and the public motives that led John Stuart Mill to become the editor of the *London and Westminster Review,* and they assess his limited success in that role. Joel H. Wiener evaluates the career of Edmund Yates as a "veteran gossiper" and an examplar of the new journalism. Mary Bostetter describes how Thomas Wakley used his editorship of the *Lancet* to pioneer investigative journalism and advance a variety of medical reforms. The late George Spater explores the contentious relationship between the radical editor William Cobbett and the Whig *Edinburgh Review*.

The fifteen essays in *Innovators and Preachers* not only raise many questions but also go some way toward imposing a form and a solidity on Greenwood's "unshaped" and "ungroomed" editors. A pattern emerges from the careers of the editors discussed in these essays. It is of men and women overcoming the ambivalence of earlier decades and taking on full-fledged professional status. The proprietor/printer/editor of the late eighteenth century (James Perry, William Woodford, Daniel Stuart, John Walter II); the autodidact of the early nineteenth century (William Cobbett, Richard Carlile, James Watson); and the semiamateur of the mid-Victorian decades who conceived of editing as a branch of the "profession of letters" (Douglas Jerrold, Angus Reach, James Hannay) gave way slowly to the "classic" Victorian editor (Leslie Stephen and Edmund Yates are among this type) who ran their newspapers or journals in a strong fashion.[9] By means of powerful leadership, a tough-minded cutting of literary essays and political contributions, an intuitive grasp of what the market would bear, and a willingness to take risks, they became dominant personalities in the world of print (even, curiously, when they remained anonymous). In the words of an Edwardian observer, these editors "managed to imprint (their) personality on everything permitting of the expression of personality that appears in (their) paper."[10]

Yet, as is made clear in many of the essays, the material on which editors worked was often intractable. As a result of competing personalities, the mechanization of the press, the continual expansion in the size of the audience, and the complicated administrative and financial arrangements needed to conduct a newspaper or a journal in the late-Victorian period, even the "classic" editors sometimes played a less powerful role than they would have liked. Henry Wickham Steed commented that by the early twentieth century, "autocratic editorship (had become) an anachronism"[11] and that notwithstanding some great journalists, the heyday of Victorian editorship was over. It had ended almost as quickly as it began. Journalism was becoming a business, and the reading public no longer formed an identifying relationship with the editor. The mediating role of the editor, as between ideas and audience or proprietor and reader, had once again to undergo a series of transformations. Such changes form the basis for another book in the same way that the history of twentieth-century journalism differs in important ways from its Victorian predecessor.

Many more questions remain to be answered before a complete assessment of the role and the influence of the Victorian editor can be attempted. To what extent, for example, did editors reflect public opinion, shape it, or, as has been said about Delane, do both simultaneously?[12] Likewise, what kinds of relationships did they have with staffs, management, and editorial boards particularly in the later decades of the nineteenth century? Were they considered a collective relationship? Autocratic ones? Or primarily passive connections? How did the breakdown of the convention of anonymous writing and its replacement by signed articles affect editors? To what extent did editors take charge of more than one journal at a time, and if so, how was this accomplished?

Finally, there is the most basic question: that concerning the function and the role of editors. Was Arnold Bennett speaking for many editors when he maintained that "Safety first . . . (is) the watchword of all editors to-day, and it will be the watchword of all editors to-morrow and eternally?"[13] Or was the more aggressive W. T. Stead closer to the mark in imploring editors to become missionaries and apostles instead of "eunuchs of the craft"?[14] Was the Victorian editor the "helmsman of a crew" (Gardiner), the "conductor of a concert" (Thackeray), or the sponsor of a "fair field" (Knowles)? If the essays in *Innovators and Preachers* help us answer some of these questions and understand better the decisive role played by editors in diffusing Victorian culture, they will have performed a valuable service.

NOTES

1. The description is taken from chapter 34 of Thackeray's *Pendennis*. "Wagg" is based on Theodore Hook, the editor of *John Bull*, who also put in a cameo appearance as "Lucian Gay" in Disraeli's *Coningsby*.

2. "Tom Towers" closely resembles the famous editor of *The Times*, John T. Delane. The quotation is from chapter 14.

3. Thomas Carlyle, "Signs of the Times," as reprinted in *The Emergence of Victorian Consciousness*, ed. George Levine (New York: The Free Press, 1967), p. 34; W. T. Stead, "Government by Journalism," *Contemporary Review* 49 (1886): 664.

4. William Hazlitt, "On Editors," *Complete Works*, ed. P. P. Howe (London: J. M. Dent and Company, 1913), p. 461.

5. Algar Labouchere Thorold, *The Life of Henry Labouchere* (London: Constable and Company, 1913), p. 510.

6. Joanne Shattock and Michael Wolff, eds., *The Victorian Periodical Press: Samplings and Soundings* (Leicester: Leicester University Press, 1982), p. xv.

7. Greenwood, a very great editor of the *Pall Mall Gazette* and the *St. James's Gazette*, was allegedly the prototype of "Rockney," the fictional journalist in Meredith's *Celt and Saxon*.

8. References to these works will be given in the bibliographical essay at the end of the volume.

9. Benjamin Pote, the "mad Editor" of the *Foreign Quarterly Review*, wrote: "I had fancied Editors shortened, altered or varied, & curtailed always: in truth I had . . . so acted myself, in every case." *The Wellesley Index to Victorian Periodicals, 1824-1900* (Toronto: University of Toronto Press, 1972), vol. 2, p. 138; Frederick Harrison berated John Morley, the editor of the *Fortnightly Review*, after sending him an article: "Tyrant, take your pound of flesh. . . . You are the best of masters and yet the hatred I feel for you at these moments enables me to realise the enmity between workmen and employers all over the world." Harrison to Morley, 24 April 1871, cited in Royden Harrison,

Before the Socialists: Studies in Labour and Politics, 1861-1881 (London: Routledge and Kegan Paul, 1965), p. 266.

10. "E. T. Raymond" (Edward Raymond Thompson), *Portraits of the Nineties* (London: T. Fisher Unwin, 1921), p. 240.

11. Henry Wickham Steed, *The Press* (Harmondsworth, Middlesex: Penguin Books, 1938), p. 144.

12. Sir Edward Cook, *Delane of The Times* (London: Constable and Company, 1915), p. 298.

13. Arnold Bennett, *The Savour of Life: Essays in Gusto* (London: Cassell and Company, 1928), p. 144.

14. Stead, "Government by Journalism," p. 664.

Part One

EDITOR AND AUDIENCE

Anne Humpherys

G. W. M. Reynolds: Popular Literature and Popular Politics

G. W. M. Reynolds has been called the most popular writer in England,[1] and indeed in a decade of issue and reissue and simultaneous issue, his mammoth novel *The Mysteries of London* sold over a million copies. He was also an important editor of several journals that played a significant role in the development of the popular press in the 1840s and the 1850s. The nature of his life and work in fact makes him a figure critical to our under-standing of how the radical weeklies of Cobbett, Hetherington, and others modulated into the commercially successful mass market newspaper.

Reynolds — as a person, an editor, and a politician — was full of contradictions; this piece might well have been titled The Mysteries of G. W. M. Reynolds. For example, he was an upper-middle-class Englishman who was strongly republican in his sentiments. The most interesting in the context of this volume, however, is the paradoxical mixture of politics and pornography, sentiment and sensationalism, rules of behavior and calls to political action in his fiction and journals. These mysterious contradictions were also elements in Victorian popular culture, and so we may be able to understand futher that partially charted sea of readership as well by looking at Reynolds's work.

Despite his enormous popularity in his own time, Reynolds has suffered the fate of many best-selling writers: He is now almost unknown to many Victorian scholars. Therefore some pertinent biographical information may be helpful in coming to terms with his work. George William MacArthur Reynolds was born in 1814, the son of a postcaptain in the Royal Navy. He was educated at Ashford Grammar School and at the Royal Military College, Sandhurst, but in 1830, at the death of his mother (his father having died in 1822), he inherited some £12,000. At that point he left Sandhurst and went to Paris, where he encountered the revolutionary politics that were to shape his political consciousness for the rest of his life and where he gained his lasting interest in French literature. Not much is known about his years in Paris; according to Louis James and John Saville, he "temporarily" became a French citizen and served in the National Guard. In about 1833 he married an Englishwoman, Susanna Frances Pearson, in France. During the next few years he was involved in various English-language newspapers through which, he later said, he lost most of his fortune. In 1836 he was declared bankrupt and returned to England. He moved into the world of London journalism and during the next ten years established a pattern of interchange between his fiction and his journalism. Over half his novels first appeared as serials in journals that he was editing; the first series of his grand novel, *The Mysteries of London,* was published in weekly parts by the publishers of the *London Journal,* which he was editing. In the twenty years between 1840 and 1860, Reynolds wrote approximately thirty-five or forty million words, published fifty-eight novels, eleven works of translation, plus a good number of political pieces.[2]

His career as an editor was equally varied. While in France in the 1830s he edited the *London and Paris Courier* (1835) and was literary editor for the *Paris Literary Gazette* in which he published the first pieces of Thackeray for which the novelist received payment.[3] After Reynolds returned to England, he edited the old *Monthly Magazine* for over a year (1837-1838). In the magazine he published his first big literary success — *Pickwick Abroad* (a continuation of Dickens's novel as a sort of travel guide to France) — and published initially his critical work *Modern Literature of France.* In 1840 he began an association with the radical *Weekly Dispatch,* for which he acted as the foreign intelligence editor, and began a somewhat breathlessly polemical journal *The Teetotaller,* which was published for about a year. One of the more startling contradictions in Reynolds's career is associated with this otherwise predictable journal. A fortnight before he began publishing *The Teetotaller* Reynolds "had become Director-General of the United Kingdom Anti-Teetotal Society" and under this hat had "published one or more issues of an anti-teetotal magazine."[4]

Not until Reynolds took the editorship of the new *London Journal* in 1845, however, was his career as an editor of the popular press really launched. The *London Journal* was one of the first "mass market" publications, and its initiation was made possible by technological advances such as high-speed presses and cheaper paper and by an increasingly literate working class. Also, a shift in the economic assumptions of publishers such as John Vickers, the publisher of the *London Journal,* occurred, as Sally Mitchell has pointed out, when they "recognized that the same profit could be made by selling a magazine to thirty thousand people at a penny each instead of to three thousand at sixpence and that a lot more people could afford to spend a penny than could part with a larger sum."[5] Two journals, *The Family Herald* and the *London Journal,* soon controlled most of this market, the latter generally considered the more low brow and sensational of the two. A decade after the founding of these two journals in the midforties, their "combined sale was at least three quarters of a million copies per week."[6]

Though Reynolds's association with the *London Journal* was brief, lasting only from its start in March 1845 to November 1846, he played a decisive role in establishing the pattern that made this magazine so successful. Basically the formula was simple: Appeal to every taste represented by an audience of lower-middle-class and working-class readers. Each issue contained an adventurous serial, some short fiction, occasionally a "true-life" adventure story, and a page of answers to correspondents on various problems and concerns. The editors also liked to include an educational piece such as one on history or a biography of a model figure. Nor were they shy about including discussions of contemporary problems. And like the editors of daily newspapers, the editors of magazines filled out their columns with household hints, recipes, and cases of odd events.[7].

After a year Reynolds and Vickers had some sort of disagreement, and Reynolds left the *London Journal.* (Vickers's involvement in publishing *The Mysteries of London* is probably the reason Reynolds changed the name of that serial to *The Mysteries of the Court of London* after he and the *London Journal* parted ways.) Reynolds's affairs were in disarray in 1848, and he had to sell his assets and declare bankruptcy for the second time. But about 1847 he had made a business association with John Dicks, a clerk in his office, that eventually gave him financial security, even wealth. Dicks acted as publisher and Reynolds as editor for all Reynolds's subsequent journalism; out of this association finally came their greatest success, *Reynolds's Weekly Newspaper,* founded in 1850 and lasting until 1967.

The first enterprise that Dicks and Reynolds began, however, was modeled on the *London Journal* and was meant to compete with it for the new mass readership. *Reynolds's Miscellany* (1846-1869) underwent some modifications in format in its early years—increasing both the page size and the number of pages—but the nature and the quality of its contents remained fairly consistent. Like the *London Journal, Reynolds's Miscellany* combined escapist fantasy and lessons of improvement. The *Miscellany* differed from the *London Journal,* however, in at least two important ways, both of which reflected Reynolds's personal tastes and enthusiasms. First, the serialized novel, which began each number and from which the cover engraving was taken, tended to be somewhat more sensational than even those in the *London Journal,* particularly when those serials were written by Reynolds himself. The first such serial, for example, *Wagner, the Wehr-Wolf,* was a horrific Gothic tale by Reynolds. Second, Reynolds's politics was much more in evidence in this "family" magazine than in the *London Journal.* For example, in the first volume Reynolds contributed a series of "Letters to the Industrious Classes" in which he tried to educate cotton spinners, needlewomen, schoolmasters, and governesses about the ways in which an aristocratic hierarchy oppressed them. In later volumes the popular "Notices to Correspondents," in which the editor answered all kinds of questions, provided additional opportunity for Reynolds to propagandize his readers. This seeming paradox of an increased sensationalism and a more overt radical political content in *Reynolds's Miscellany* is an emblem of Reynolds's peculiar place in the history of the popular press.

In any case, the formula for *Reynolds's Miscellany* was immediately successful. Within a year the weekly *Miscellany* had reached what Sally Mitchell and others consider the economically crucial circulation number of 30,000, a number that allowed a penny weekly to meet fixed expenses.[8] This success soon recouped Reynold's financial losses, gave him an outlet for his literary productions, and assured him a place in the history of the popular press.

But in 1848 something happened to him that redirected some of his energies. Reynolds became an active Chartist. Though an outspoken republican from his youthful days in France, in 1848 he was catapulted into active politics by his apparently spontaneous speech at the Chartist demonstration at Trafalgar Square on March 6. His performance there led to his being carried home on the shoulders of a cheering crowd and subsequently to an intense involvement in the Chartist movement as a speaker and a writer. This period of activism lasted only four years, however, and ended in acrimony and libel suits involving other Chartist leaders, particularly Ernest Jones, who Reynolds found too soft and accommodating. But it was during the years of his political activism that *Reynolds's Weekly* was founded, a journal that is not only important in the history of the press but also, as James and Saville say, significant in the development of the working-class movement itself.[9]

The story of *Reynolds's Weekly* has been told not finally but generally and is not my focus here. Instead, I shall look at Reynolds's career just before that final endeavor, for *Reynolds's Weekly Newspaper* grew out of another weekly that Reynolds tried in the first flush of success of the *Miscellany* and his new career as a political activist, namely, *Reynolds's Political Instructor* (November 1849-May 1850).

In the title of this weekly political journal, one of whose purposes was to propagandize for the Charter, lies another emblem of the contradictory nature of Reynolds's career as an editor. The *Political Instructor* echoed if it did not repeat the name of one of the most important radical newspapers of the 1820s, the *Political Register* of William Cobbett. I think the echo is more significant than the slightly condescending implications of being an "instructor" to the working classes. It calls attention to the serious political nature of the work. However, by prefixing his name to the new journal, Reynolds connected it to his widely read family magazine, *Reynolds's Miscellany* (often referred to simply as *Reynolds's),* with its successful blend of sensational fiction, woodcuts of full-bosomed ladies, lessons of improvements, and practical advice. And in the connection between these two essentially working-class journals lies the problem of G. W. M. Reynolds and the popular press in general. The elements of popular literature and popular politics do not always mix very comfortably. The often prurient fascination with the private lives of the high and mighty, the normative values of melodrama, and the escapism of romance and fantasy undercut the call to action and realism of practical politics. That Reynolds linked the two raises questions about intent. To what degree was his invocation of the association with Cobbett's newspaper a courageous reflection of political belief and to what degree was it a cynical exploitation to gain sales? This is the central question about Reynolds's work as an editor. It was asked and answered variously in his own day and continues to perplex modern commentators.[10]

I shall outline the problem another way. From the very beginning of his career as a successful editor, that is, from 1844 and the publication of *The Mysteries of London* to the end of his life, the expressed opinion about Reynolds seems strangely at odds with his enormous popularity among lower-middle-class and lower-class readers. "Respectable" commentators abhorred him as much for his sensationalism as for his espousal of republican sentiments. Dickens indirectly referred to Reynolds as one of the "Bastards of the Mountain, draggled fringe on the Red Cap, Panders to the basest passions of the lowest natures" in the opening number of *Household Words.*[11] Another reviewer scorned his work as "poison," full of "fire and brimstone" and madeup, "terrific" views. [12] At the same time important elements of the working classes rejected him. Many Chartists did not credit his role in the movement. W. E. Adams wrote of him later that "it was rather as a charlatan and a trader than as a genuine politician that G. W. M. was regarded by the rank and file of Chartism."[13] Marx called him a scoundrel,[14] while acknowledging the special role that *Reynolds's Weekly* played in the consciousness of the working class. Marx did not trust Reynolds; in a letter to Engels in 1858 he said that Reynolds was a "rich and an able speculator. The mere fact that he has turned into a Chartist shows that this position must still be a 'bearable' one. . . ."[15] Meanwhile the working classes bought hundreds of thousands of Reynolds's serialized novels and weekly publications.

Marx was referring to Reynolds in his role as political agitator both on the hustings and in the pages of the *Weekly* and not to his role as the editor of the *Miscellany* or as the author of *Wagner, the Wehr Wolf.* But surely Reynolds's career as a writer of slightly salacious tales of adventure and romance made him suspect in the eyes of the more radical elements of the working class, as did the financial success these fictions brought him. And though the anonymous reviewer who called his work poison was referring primarily to his sensational stories, he was likely to have found Reynolds's virulent republican sentiments just as revolting. I think finally all these critics were talking about the same element—that all were reacting, from quite opposed positions, to the same thing in Reynolds's work; his coming to rest, as it were, on the fine point in the popular mind where escapism and activism touch. Reynolds's work and life are, to change the comparison, like a print by the artist M. C. Escher, in which distant forms are imperceptibly transformed into one another. And as in an Escher print, where it is not possible to point to the exact place in which a bird becomes a fish (and vice versa), it is hard to separate sincere political expressions from clever careerism in

Reynolds's work. In the interchange of these two aspects the significance of his success lies, a significance that has importance not only for the study of the press but also for an understanding of the nature of popular culture itself and, not incidentally, for the course of many broad based political movements.

We can see this "problem" most clearly at one particular moment in Reynolds's early career as an editor, the seven months when he was active in Chartist politics and editing both the *Political Register* and the *Miscellany*. The difficulties of coming to terms with Reynolds at this time have been eloquently expressed by Raymond Williams. He has argued that the early nineteenth-century radical journals such as the *Political Register* and the *Black Dwarf* were popular in a good sense in that they were truly "for the people" and embodied a "style of genuine arousal."[16] Running counter to these political journals, however, was the "established popular reading" of the lower classes, the chapbooks, dying speeches, and other "street literature," as Henry Mayhew referred to it, material that dosed up crime, scandal, romance, and sport in crude and, from one point of view, politically irresponsible ways.

As Williams points out, when the political climate changed, the nature of the popular journals did too. Less official opposition lessened the intense focus and tone, and the introduction of the profit motive into the popular press, when technological developments in printing and distribution became practical, aborted any expansion of those early radical journals. Instead, a new kind of popular press emerged at midcentury, the Sunday newspaper, which combined "general political attitudes" with the more senstational elements of popular reading, particularly, as it developed, sports news. This movement culminated in a popular press that was not "for the people" but for the money—amoral and apolitical—that used, in Williams's words, "apparent arousal as a cover for an eventual if temporary satisfaction."[17] He thinks of the *Daily Mail;* we think of the *Daily News* or, perhaps even more poignantly, the *New York Post.* Williams sees *Reynolds's Weekly* as one of the journals in which the shift took place, and in his gentle censure of the commercialism of the *Weekly,* he comes down on the side of Marx on Reynolds.

I see it a little differently. In Reynolds's work we do indeed see limned the point at which the ingredients for the shift that Williams deplores have been brought together, but they were not perfectly mixed — in fact not mixed at all. Further Reynolds's disposition to leave unblended the various elements of the popular mind is what made him successful both as fiction writer and as an editor. To borrow a term from an earlier English poet, I think Reynolds as an editor possessed a kind of "negative capability" — an ability to absorb the contradictory impulses and desires of the populace without making any "irritable" effort at resolution. His instinct for doing so may have been at bottom commercial — one group of his critics certainly thinks so — but the result was the creation of a form that was popular in the best sense of the word because it was inclusive.

We can see signs of this "negative capability" in Reynolds's first important editorial enterprise, the *London Journal.* In its first year Reynolds contributed a few characteristic tales, either uplifting or romantic, but his major contribution as a writer was a seventeen-part series on "Etiquette for the Millions." The various topics covered included proper table manners, dress, correct forms of address, hints about proper behavior in different social situations. In all of these pieces Reynolds took the most conventional line; as he said in the introductory piece: "No man has a right to consider himself entitled, as a unity in the millions which constitute a society, to act entirely for himself and by himself. He must pay deference to the interests of others."[18] And although this sentiment out of context could receive a nod of approval from the most devoted socialist, in context it was used to justify adherence to the most restrictive surface behavior.

Reynolds's series on etiquette fit right in with the general tone of the *London Journal,* which appealed to a "mass reader-ship . . . made up of people with aspirations for respectability," as Sally Mitchell puts it,[19] but it struck an odd note coming as it simultaneously did with Reynolds's calls for revolutionary political changes in the columns of the *Weekly Dispatch.* We can charge him with hypocrisy, a willingness to do anything that paid, or we can see in this juxtaposition a straightforward, perhaps unconscious expression of two paradoxical elements in the popular mind: the desire for a better life defined predominant-ly by what the populace perceives as better in the lives of those "above" them and a contradictory tendency to want to destroy that very desired life because those that had it were seen as exploiting those that didn't.

A similar series of paradoxes was reflected in the contrasting pages of *Reynolds's Political Instructor* and *Reynolds's Miscellany.* The two journals were issued simultaneously over a period of seven months, after which time Reynolds abandoned the *Political Instructor* for *Reynolds's Weekly Newspaper.* The *Political Instructor* itself was an outgrowth of his personal involvement in Chartist politics. Eight months after his triumphal appearance at the Trafalgar Square demonstration, Reynolds issued the first weekly number of the *Instructor.* Though a political platform for Chartism, it took its formal aspects from the *Miscellany.* For example, each issue began with a handsome woodcut. Though in the *Instructor* these were of "eminent Political Characters," in the *Miscellany* they were of exciting scenes from the current sensational serial. The two journals also advertised the same things, including each other.

The contents of the two were, of course, different in tone but surprisingly not very much in content. The *Political Instructor* ran articles that addressed current social and economic issues; the *Miscellany* frequently referred to the same events. In the *Instructor,* Edwin Roberts, a minor journalist of the period, was contributing a "New History of England," while in the *Miscellany* the same author was represented by romanticized historical fiction. The Stamp Act prohibited overtly political articles in journals such as the *Miscellany,* but in the "Notices to Correspondents" (of which more later) there were many short "essays" on political economy and politics. There was frequently, however, a real difference in attitude in these articles. Take, for example, the different approaches to the aristocracy. In the *Political Instructor* attacks on the aristocracy constituted the fundamental statement of Reynolds's politics after his assertion of the Chartist program with the added demand for the elimination of primogeniture. But at the same time that he was running in the *Political Instructor* a series on "The Aristocracy: Its Origins, Progress and Decay," in the *Miscellany* he was featuring a series on famous aristocratic ladies, dosing up large numbers of titillating tales of intrigue and scandal and sometimes selfless sacrifice. Thus the aristocracy provided for his readers, as it always has, the target for abuse and the source of escapist fantasy.

A juxtaposition of simultaneous issues of the two journals will further demonstrate the contradictions of popular literature and politics. The December 1849 *Political Instructor* ran a woodcut of Thomas Cooper, the poet-shoemaker, plus articles on Manchester, a segment of the series on the aristocracy, an article "The Cry of the Poor," and short items on "The People" (antioligarchy) and "The Colonies" (antiimperialist). The corresponding issue of the *Miscellany* for December 8, 1849, featured a very exciting woodcut showing a diaphanously clothed maiden about to be subjected to some machine of torture, an illustration for Reynolds's romantic historical novel *The Bronze Statue or the Virgin's Kiss,* derived ultimately from the notorious eighteenth-century Gothic novel *The Monk* by Matthew Lewis.[20] There was another serial on "The Beauties of the Court of Charles the Second," and the featured article on social conditions was entitled "The Evil Consequences of Tight Lacing." The reader of both the *Instructor* and the *Miscellany* could have it any way he wanted it: He could blame the aristocracy for every social ill and feed on the imagined pleasures their money and position brought them; he could be shocked by living conditions in Manchester or be soothed into thinking that tight lacing was a major cause of ill health among women.

While editing both journals and attending Chartist meetings and rallies, Reynolds's own contributions to the *Miscellany* diminished in number. But two of his fictions were serialized after February 1850, and they too demonstrate Reynolds's ability to take the popular pulse. The first was "The Pixy; or, the Unbaptized Child," a tale containing much folklore and superstition. The other was a politically relevant piece called in the first installment "The Slaves of England" but which became in one of the next installments "The Seamstress: A Domestic Tale." In the quick change of title we see again that frustrating blend of calculation and politics that marked his work. "The Slaves of England" as a title must have seemed a bit strong for the readers of the *Miscellany,* though presumably many of them were reading at the same time in the *Political Instructor* a famous series by Bronterre O'Brien on "The Rise, Progress and Phases of Human Slavery." (James and Saville think Reynolds was closest in his political attitudes to O'Brien.[21]) So Reynolds changed his title to emphasize that sentimental and safe iconology of the early Victorian period, the victimized seamstress.[22]

To me Reynolds's "negative capability" as an editor was most interesting in his "Notices to Correspondents," a department in the *Miscellany* that served the readers of both the *Political Instructor* and the *Miscellany* since there was no room in the

Instructor for a "notices" column. He announced in the *Instructor* that queries sent to that journal would be answered in the *Miscellany.*

A "Notices to Correspondents" column was a very popular department in the family periodicals of the 1840s and 1850s. *Lloyd's* had one, and so did the *London Journal.* The readers of these journals asked similar questions. In *Reynolds's Miscellany* they wanted to know about etiquette and medical and legal matters. The answers to their queries about political and historical concerns became a hallmark of all Reynolds's journals. There were also many questions regarding jobs as clerks and ways to emigrate. And almost every issue of *Reynolds's Miscellany* included the answer or answers to one or more requests for Reynolds to evaluate a correspondent's handwriting.

There seems little doubt to me that Reynolds, albeit with help, wrote most of the responses, maintaining his role as the respondent even when he did not have time for other writing for the *Miscellany.* There are several reasons for his devotion to this department, which grew from a couple of columns when the journal started in 1846 to several pages in 1849. For one thing, the "Notices" provided one place in which political issues could be addressed without calling too obvious attention to them. But more important, I think, was the intimacy of the relationship that developed between Reynolds and his readers through the personal nature of many of the requests. They wrote to ask him about specific doctors; Reynolds in turn recommended various medical men by name. He gave advice on love and legal matters, and in these concerns no question seemed too personal. For example, a characteristic response to a personal question was "To Robert — the young lady is perhaps only a little inclined to flirtation, and you must not judge her too severely. It is out of our power, being unacquainted personally with the party, to determine whether you are suited to each other. Study the lady's character and watch her disposition closely; after six months have elapsed let us know the result, that is to say, if our advice is then required."[23] The next week's "Notices" began with an essay decrying the exploitation of needlewomen, followed by short pieces of medical and legal advice, and some job counseling: "Your handwriting is very good, but if you had read our Notices in previous numbers, you would have had your mind disabused of the fallacious idea, that a clerk's situation is to be got for the mere asking, whereas, in point of fact, it is most difficult to obtain," and (to a dyer) "there will soon be a good opening for your trade in Australia, but at present we could hardly recommend you to emigrate."[24]

The harshness in Reynolds's response to the query about getting a clerk's job was a frequent tone in the "Notices": for example, "E.H.B. You cannot claim any relationship: your mother was not married: your father's wife being still alive, he committed bigamy, and you are consequently illegitimate."[25] But he could be encouraging as well: "There is no need ever to apologize for the looseness of the writing, we are always happy on hearing from our friends from the working classes, and never scrutinize, unless asked, their style of penmanship."[26] In addition to these sorts of responses, Reynolds gave advice about proper behavior—when to wear white gloves—and hundreds of recipes for making everything from hearty soup to silver paint. These recipes, which he published with the aid of his wife, were so popular that when he indexed the volume, he included "Useful and Practical Receipts (sic) in the Notices to Correspondents," which was the longest single section in the index. His wife subsequently published under her own name a collection entitled *The Household Book of Practical Receipts*. (She also wrote a number of popular romances, such as *Gretna-Green; or, All for Love*, written with "a high moral purpose," according to the advertisements for it in the *Miscellany*.)

We cannot know which queries were originally sent to the *Instructor* as opposed to the *Miscellany*. There were a few direct references to the *Instructor,* and some of the longer "essays" that appeared in the "Notices" on social questions are likely to have been in response to questions addressed to the political journal. The audience for both journals, though, seems fairly consistent: for the most part an upwardly mobile working class concerned, even obsessed with respectability.

The complex relationship between Reynolds and his readers, which enabled him to act like a stern adviser, a knowledgeable informant, an avuncular domestic manager, is surely one of the reasons for the *Miscellany's* success; by 1855 it had a circulation of 300,000. Yet in the "Notices" we can see the same contradictory mixture of social conformism and political radicalism that was evident elsewhere in Reynolds's work. Although he was nearly always hard-nosed about careers in the respectable trade of clerking, he never challenged the desires of his readers to fit into the established order of things by getting these jobs and hence moving up the class scale. The political inclusiveness of the "Notices" in fact raised the same questions about Reynolds's seriousness as a political radical. Some critics have charged that he was unthinking and just repeated the old-fashioned republicanism he had learned in Paris in the 1830s. It is true that he usually blamed all social and economic injustice on the aristocracy's control of land; he seems to have believed that the elimination of that class plus the achievement of the Charter would usher in a political Utopia. Yet every now and again, Reynolds said something that suggests that he knew as well as Marx did that feudalism had already been replaced by industrial capitalism. For example, in the conventional little essay in the "Notices" on the "contrasts of London" trope, Reynolds substituted the labels *labour and capital* for the more cliched *rich and poor* and remarked that "land was at first the capital that swept everything before it, then came capital, and now must come labour—the only real and permanent capital—the only currency upon which society can with safety calculate for its endurance, and, which must before long assert its supremacy and independence."[27]

Reynolds's political understanding was more complicated than he has been given credit for by later critics such as Raymond Williams who criticized him for his outdated views and the role they played in misdirecting the political energies of the working class. Reynolds's politics, his editorial stance, and the contents of his fiction reflect the inclusiveness of popular culture. His contradictions were the contradictions of the audience he was writing for. We social and literary historians have the same difficulty in coming to terms with the one as with the other. Each time that Virginia Berridge, in her study of *Lloyds* and *Reynolds's Weekly,* attacked these Sunday papers for their commercialism and their dissipation of working-class radicalism, she qualified her censure in judging *Reynolds's Weekly.* Nevertheless, her final judgment of G. W. M. Reynolds as insincere and politically expedient is harsh.[28] This contradiction in her own text remains unresolved, as does my own disconcerted reaction to seeing advertisements for Chartist meetings cheek by jowl in the *Weekly* with others promising to make the buyer more respectable with a patent medicine to grow more luxuriant whiskers. But unless we take into account these contradictions in the popular mind, unless we are able to exercise our own negative capabilities as literary historians, we will not be able to understand fully either popular literature or popular politics. G. W. M. Reynolds as an editor and a writer is a good place to begin our task.

NOTES

1. *Bookseller* (July 1868), p. 447; (July 1879), p. 660.

2. The source for most of the biographical material on Reynolds is Louis James and John Saville, "G. W. M. Reynolds," in the *Dictionary of Labour Biography* (London: Macmillan, 1976), III: pp. 146-151. E. F. Bleiler, in his "Introduction" to the Dover reprint of Reynolds's novel *Wagner, the Wehr-Wolf* (New York: Dover, 1975), gives some additional biographical information and also a seemingly complete bibliography of Reynolds's works.

3. Robert A. Colby, *Thackeray's Canvas of Humanity: An Author and His Public* (Columbus: Ohio State University Press, 1979), p. 272 n. 67.

4. James and Saville, p. 147.

5. Sally Mitchell, "The Forgotten Woman of the Period: Penny Weekly Family Magazines of the 1840's and 1850's," in *A Widening Sphere: Changing Roles of Victorian Women,* ed. Martha Vicinus (Bloomington, Indiana: Indiana University Press, 1977), p. 31.

6. Mitchell, p. 31.

7. Mitchell outlines this formula on p. 31.

8. Mitchell, p. 37. See also Louis James, *Fiction for the Working Man* (1963; rpt. Harmondsworth, Middlesex: Penguin, 1979), chapter 2, "Currents in Popular Publishing, 1840-1850."

9. James and Saville, p. 149.

10. Richard Altick, for example, remarks in *The English Common Reader* that it is very hard "to decide which motive—principle or policy" governed Lloyd and Reynolds as editors. (Chicago: University of Chicago Press, 1957), p. 344.

11. Cyril Pearl, *Victorian Patchwork* (London: Heinemann, 1972), p. 73, identifies Reynolds as the source of Dickens's diatribe.

12. Quoted in *Bookseller* (July 1868), p. 447.

13. W. E. Adams, *Memoirs of a Social Atom* (1903; Rpt. New York: A.M. Kelley, 1968), p. 235.

14. Karl Marx in a letter to Ferdinand Lassalles, 28 April 1862. *The Letters of Karl Marx,* ed. Saul K. Padover (Englewood Cliffs, N.J.: Prentice-Hall, 1979), p. 465.

15. Karl Marx in a letter to Frederick Engels, 8 October 1858, quoted in Virginia Berridge, "Popular Sunday Papers and Mid-Victorian Society," in *Newspaper History: From the Seventeenth Century to the Present Day,* ed. George Boyce, James Curran, and Pauline Wingate (London: Constable, 1978), p. 254.

16. Raymond Williams, "Radical and/or Respectable," in *The Press We Deserve,* ed. Richard Boston (London: Routledge and Kegan Paul, 1970), pp. 16-23.

17. Williams, p. 21.

18. *London Journal,* 12 April 1845.

19. Mitchell, p. 30.

20. The source was first noted by Montague Summers in *The Gothic Quest* (1938; rpt. London: The Fortune Press, 1968), p. 248.

21. James and Saville, p. 148.

22. See T. J. Edelstein, "They Sang 'The Song of the Shirt': The Visual Iconology of the Seamstress," in *Victorian Studies* XXIII (1980): 183-210.

23. *Reynolds's Miscellany*, 24 November 1849.

24. *Reynolds's Miscellany*, 30 November 1849.

25. *Reynolds's Miscellany*, 8 December 1849.

26. Ibid.

27. *Reynolds's Miscellany*, 24 November 1849.

28. Berridge, pp. 254-261, passim.

Stephen Elwell

Editors and Social Change: A Case Study of *Once a Week* (1859-80)

Once a Week is particularly appropriate for an editorial case study for a number of reasons, some having to do with its status as one of the earliest and best examples of the popular illustrated magazines of the "sixties" period and others with aspects of its publishing history.[1] Although the magazine has been largely ignored in the recent resurgence of interest in Victorian periodicals, in its own day it played a pioneering role in establishing illustration as an important feature of the popular magazine. And as the principal competitor of Dickens's *All the Year Round, Once a Week* clearly occupied a prominent place in Grub Street in the 1860s and represents a valuable source of information concerning the magazine trade during the mid-Victorian period.

But beyond the characteristics and associations that establish *Once a Week's* pedigree among popular middle-class magazines, there are other considerations that have weighed equally in my decision to use it as the focus of this paper. The two decades during which it was published were a time of accelerating social and economic change. Although it is impossible to prove that *Once a Week* was responding directly to these broad changes, examinations of its five distinct series, of the work of its five different editors, and of the concerns of its three owners suggest that those who oversaw its editing and production were sensitive to the market. That they not only ultimately lost the solidly middle-class audience to which the magazine had originally appealed but also failed to engage the less easily characterized and more marginal lower-middle-class audience that was emerging during the period is symptomatic of the difficulty that many magazines of the period had in making the transition from a class-based journalism to a "new" journalism designed to appeal to a mass audience. That transition had a powerful effect on the evolution of popular journalism during the second half of the nineteenth century. I will conclude then with some comments and speculations about the way in which the new generation of magazines that began to appear in the eighties and early nineties redefined the conception of audience in such a way that they were able for the first time to speak to the mass rather than to a discrete class of readers.

I

Once a Week was created in 1859 by the publishing firm of Bradbury and Evans. It resembled Dickens's miscellany *All the Year Round* in many ways. Indeed, *Once a Week* grew out of a feud between Dickens and Bradbury and Evans. Although that feud is peripheral to the subject of this case study, I think it is important to keep in mind that both competition with and imitation of Dickens played a significant role in the magazine's evolution.[2].

By far the most important distinguishing feature of the magazine was its emphasis on illustration.[3] Bradbury and Evans, in translating that medium from its comic environment in *Punch,* another of their properties, to a more serious magazine context, established a basic model for all the illustrated magazines that broke into the market during the sixties. As a pacesetter, *Once a Week* enjoyed considerable success, but it is impossible to determine whether it drew circulation away from *All the Year Round.* Alvar Ellegards's figures for the period from 1860 to 1870 show that *All the Year Round's* circulation, beginning at an estimated 80,000 copies in 1860, had dipped 20,000 to 60,000 in 1865 and then to 50,000 by 1870. *Once a Week,* beginning with 60,000 in 1860 (at a price of 3d. as opposed to *All the Year Round's* 2d.), maintained that level of circulation in 1865, by which time the price had been reduced, but then circulation dropped to an estimated 40,000 copies by 1870.[4] Surely there was a trade-off between *Once a Week's* illustrations and the fact that *All the Year Round* carried the name of Dickens on its masthead, but each periodical was competing with others as well. *Good Words,* for example, an illustrated magazine similar to *Once a Week,* grew, according to Ellegard, from an initial circulation of 30,000 copies in 1860 to 80,000 in 1870.[5]

Once a Week's first series lasted from July 1859 until December 1865. The editorship of Samuel Lucas during that five-and-a-half-year period followed a rather uncertain line with regard to fiction in particular. Beginning initially with the idea in their prospectus that the magazine should have "effective Tales complete in one number," Bradbury and Evans quickly contradicted themselves by bringing out a number of serialized novels. That about-face is convincing evidence of *Once a Week's* rivalry with *All the Year Round,* in which Dickens obviously intended to push serialized fiction and a clear sign from the publishing market in the early 1860s that the serial would be the stock item in popular weekly and monthly magazines that hoped to succeed with the public. And before long *Once a Week* moved toward sensational fiction, then very much in vogue, as a way of competing successfully with its rivals.

When Lucas left the editorship of *Once a Week,* his position was taken over by Edward Walford, who had been his subeditor, and a new, or second, series began. Walford's tenure was brief and was marked by tension with Bradbury and Evans over the editorial direction of the magazine. In a letter written to Bradbury and Evans shortly before his departure, Walford questioned their tendency to look to "outsiders" or "aspiring talents" for contributions. That Bradbury and Evans were themselves beginning to question this approach is implicit in Walford's reference to their growing desire to "lean strongly to an increased employment of well-known and practised pens," and he committed himself to engaging "a number of gentlemen . . . whose well-known names appearing in the early numbers of your new series will do much to conciliate the confidence of the public. . . ."[6] Walford's real complaint centered on Bradbury and Evans's unwarranted interference with what he saw as his editorial prerogatives:

. . . In order to enable an Editor to do his work satisfactorily either to himself or to his employers, it is necessary that he shd. be free to act, & what is more, should *feel himself free to act.* The proprietors, I submit, should place before him a line of action which they consider advantageous to their magazine, & then leave him free to carry out that line of action. . . . And yet, to speak plainly & honestly, as matters are & have been of late, I do not feel myself free to act in my position as Editor. I constantly find myself controlled, & my judgment overruled in matters of detail, in a way which not only disheartens me, but which also makes it impossible for me to reply to letters which require an answer from the editor, or to write as I could wish in asking the aid of able pens.[7]

It is clear that Walford's principal objection was that Bradbury and Evans were meddling in matters that he considered his own concern, but the statement also seems to suggest that Bradbury and Evans were having difficulty defining their interest in the proprietorship of *Once a Week*. Was it essential to press their challenge of Dickens's conception of a weekly miscellany as a carefully orchestrated product of a small circle of professional writers, with emphasis on first-rate serial novels, or was it more important simply to succeed, even at the expense of conceding the effectiveness of Dickens's strategy? Bradbury and Evans's failure to come to terms with their own ends did not prevent them from producing a literary and art magazine of high quality, but it had a serious impact on their ability to engage a large, loyal audience. Dickens, on the other hand, was both in control of his product and sure of his appeal. William Buckler's statement that Dickens "called out boldly to the great mass of readers" and that "his ends were social ends, the discussion of class questions, and the raising up of the down-trodden" suggests that Dickens was more in touch with the rapidly growing audience of lower as opposed to upper middle-class people.[8]

Walford was succeeded by Eneas Sweetland Dallas, for whom Bradbury and Evans began a new (third) series. *Foul Play,* a collaborative serial by Dion Boucicault and Charles Reade, led off the first issue under Dallas's editorship and was the only fiction to appear in that number. Obviously, Bradbury and Evans felt that the serial, illustrated by George Du Maurier, was a sure draw. There was, to be sure, little else of more than routine interest. Dallas's particular contribution during his short tenure of about a year and a half was "Table Talk," a regular two- to three-page collection of generally humorous miscellanea linked together in stream-of-consciousness fashion.

With the exception of *Foul Play,* the other serials that ran during Dallas's editorship were unillustrated. In fact, the amount of illustration in general was reduced. Dallas, for the first time in the journal's history, introduced what we might call a house illustrator. There were also illustrations by other artists, but they tended to be genre subjects unrelated to any text, an indication that they might have been taken from contemporary paintings. The absence of illustrated poetry, which had traditionally accounted for a high percentage of *Once a Week's* illustrations, tended to emphasize the space-filling nature of the few poems that remained.

The interest in *Once a Week* by this time was almost exclusively on fiction, and even that had lost the competitive edge that illustration had given to all the magazine's features in earlier years. Bradbury and Evans's decision to sell the magazine in 1869 comes as no surprise. But to understand these changes during *Once a Week's* first decade, we need also to consider the magazine's image during that period and, more specifically, to take a closer look at those who were responsible for creating that image.

In beginning *Once a Week* Bradbury and Evans had targeted the professional world of the established middle class as their most likely source of readers. Their choice of Samuel Lucas as the magazine's first editor was consistent with that goal. The son of a Bristol merchant, Lucas had taken his B.A. and M.A. degrees at Queen's College, Oxford, in preparation for a law career. While at Oxford he distinguished himself by winning various literary prizes, and having been admitted to the bar in 1846, Lucas "went the western circuit, where his genial manners made him extremely popular."[9] Sometime in the early 1850s he decided to devote his energies solely to writing. He contributed reviews to *The Times,* published a number of essays on history and colonial government, and was involved briefly with another periodical.

Lucas came to *Once a Week* as a well- and conventionally-educated man with solid professional credentials as a journalist. He had well-defined literary tastes and clear opinions on contemporary novelists. In describing Lucas's critical perspective on literature, Buckler says that he "admired the sober strength and adherence to probabililty that he found in Eliot's *Scenes of Clerical Life"* and found Thackeray's "panoramic plan of novel-writing superior to Dickens's approach," which, along with those of prominent sensational novelists—namely, Charles Reade, Mary Elizabeth Braddon, Mrs. Henry Wood, and Wilkie Collins—depended too heavily on "melodramatic surprises and wonderful secrets" and "[used] accidents too conveniently." Lucas had equally conventional, judicious ideas about things in general, stressing "unity of conception and execution. . . ."[10]

Obviously no Grub Street hack, Lucas was paid a salary of over five hundred guineas per year by Bradbury and Evans for his editorial labors and supplemented his income considerably with earnings from his own writing. He was thoroughly middle class, a gentleman with cultured tastes. Yet the high tone that *Once a Week* assumed initially under his editorship was tempered by the exigencies of the market. Sensational fiction *did* appear, and within a few years illustration had begun to lose ground not so much in quality as in quantity. But Lucas, despite these compromises, established a certain genteel standard for the publication as a literary miscellany.

It seems reasonable to suppose that Edward Walford, Lucas's subeditor and successor, was of a like mind in editorial matters. His personal background was tinged with aristocratic connection, and he was the son of a clergyman.[11] Educated first at Church of England schools, he attended Balliol College, Oxford, winning the Chancellor's Prize for Latin verse in 1843 and taking B.A. and M.A. degrees in 1845 and 1847 respectively. He became an Anglican priest in 1847 but later wavered back and forth between the Church of England and Roman Catholicism. Having assumed a post as assistant master of Tonbridge School in 1846, Walford also tutored private pupils for Oxford between 1847 and 1850. Perhaps Walford's greatest interest—certainly the one that occupied most of his professional life—was in antiquarian and genealogical subjects. He produced in 1855 the first of three "Hardwicke's Shilling" guides to the Baronetage and Knightage, House of Commons, and Peerage, which became annual publications. In 1860 the first annual edition of his *County Families of Great Britain: A Manual of the Titled and Untitled Aristocracy* appeared. In his preface he explained that he had "arranged both these orders under a single alphabet, because I remember the words of James I, that 'the king, though he can make a *noble,* cannot make a *gentleman,*' and because the bearing of arms, not of titles, has ever been considered as the distinctive mark of true *noblesse.*"[12] Numerous other of Walford's biographical and genealogical works catering to the interests of the upwardly mobile middle classes appeared until his death in 1897.

We already have some sense of Walford's concerns as the editor of *Once a Week.* His advice to Bradbury and Evans to engage "practised pens" suggests that he was more sensitive than Samuel Lucas to the importance of engaging reader attention, but there is little evidence that he was any more inclined to pursue the Dickensian line of appealing to the broadest cross section of society. Stories of mésalliances between college men and seamen's daughters and satirical sketches of working-class life obviously were pitched toward a solidly middle-class readership, as were descriptions of European university life, biographical sketches of composers and artists, and continental vacation travelogues that were frequent features of the magazine during his tenure.

Eneas Sweetland Dallas, the last editor under Bradbury and Evans's ownership of *Once a Week,* possessed all the middle-class characteristics of his predecessors.[13] He was the eldest son of a Scottish plantation owner in Jamaica. His mother came from a family of Scottish clergy. Returning to Britain at the age of four, Dallas was later educated in philosophy at the University of Edinburgh. His special interest was in the connection between poetic and "eclectic psychology," and he published several works on the subject, most notably *The Gay Science*. More successful apparently were his biographical, political, and literary articles and reviews for *The Times*, where he was a colleague of Samuel Lucas.

There is little information available concerning the circumstances of Dallas's appointment to the editorship of *Once a Week*.[14] He was paid a total annual compensation of £800 (a figure that apparently included the salary for his subeditor). As my description of Dallas's three volumes of *Once a Week* suggests, there is probably less evidence there of his editorial proclivities than of Bradbury and Evans's own waning interest in carrying the journal.

It is not difficult to see why Bradbury and Evans wanted to dispose of the magazine. It was not competitive; indeed, it had been losing ground from the very beginning. Dickens's own assessment of Bradbury and Evans's action is telling: "What fools they are! As if a mole couldn't see that their only chance was in a careful separation of themselves from the faintest approach to assimilation to *All the Year Round.*"[15] Professional rivalry and a galled sense of pride seduced Bradbury and Evans into shortsighted competition with Dickens that focused more attention on their quarrel with him than on the need to address the desires of the readers they were trying to take away from him.

Where Bradbury and Evans had ambitiously undertaken illustration as their own specialization and succeeded brilliantly in the beginning at least at engaging the best and the brightest talents, they neglected or were very uncertain in their approach to fiction, which was quickly defined as the ingredient most basic to the success of a popular magazine in the 1860s. Furthermore, in capitulating later to fiction yet still insisting on the high visual standards with which they had begun, Bradbury and Evans's expenses soared, drastically eroding the magazine's profitability.

Contrast that with the example of Dickens, who had a sure editorial sense of the market for fiction, understood intuitively the social ferment taking place in mid-Victorian Britain, and was an astute businessman besides.

We have also seen clear indications that there were significant tensions between Bradbury and Evans and their editors. Given what I have described above of that friction, it is difficult to determine whether the publishers or the editors had a better sense of what should be done to attract readership. What does seem fairly clear from Bradbury and Evans's choices of editors, however, is that they were drawn to men whose backgrounds placed them firmly in the ranks of the established middle class. Lucas and Dallas were critics with intellectual pretensions. Their approach to literature was one that looked beyond the immediately popular for enduring value of insight and intelligence. Walford's antiquarian and genealogical interests made him an effective spokesman for the sense of history, tradition, and social connection that many felt were threatened by the increasing anonymity of urbanization and commercial and industrial development.

What I am suggesting about these men is that they represented a very traditional form of middle-class gentility. Their economic and social roots were at least two or three generations deep. Their families occupied secure positions in the social hierarchy. They were well educated. In short, they were not typical. Unlike the great "amorphous strata" about which Richard Altick speaks, their middle-class identity was well-defined.[16] And that clear definition put them out of touch with the mainstream in which a steady influx of "greenhorns" was pushing into the middle class from below. Lucas, for example, might cast aspersions on sensational fiction for its implausibility or its lack of realistic surface, but the mix of fantasy and reality that one often sees in popular magazine fiction during the period nurtured the dream that one's fantastic aspirations could under certain conditions be made real.

Turning now to *Once a Week's* second decade, we will see a sincere but ultimately unsuccessful attempt by the magazine's later owners to reach a wider constituency.

II

Both men who owned and edited *Once a Week* during the 1870s were as much involved in a process of searching for their own identities as they were in seeking a successful formula and marketing strategy for the magazine. That, I think, finally had a great deal to do with its collapse. When James Rice, at the age of twenty-five, purchased *Once a Week* from Bradbury and Evans in the early summer of 1869, he had just left Queen's College, Cambridge, without a degree and was probably already at work on "The Mortimers: A Novel With Two Heroes," whose serialization began a few months after he took over the magazine. It is clear that he was attempting to capitalize on Dickens's effective use of *All the Year Round* as a showcase for his own fiction. After "The Mortimers" came "Mr. Golightly; or, the Adventures of an Amiable Man" (later subtitled "Memoirs of a College Freshman"), which appeared in the next volumes. "Ready-Money Mortiboy," the first of a number of novels that Rice coauthored with Walter Besant, one of the best journalists of the day, began to appear in 1872.

The volume in which "My Little Girl," Rice and Besant's second collaboration, began to appear contained no fewer than six serial stories, numerous short stories, tales, and "first-person" narratives. Yet *Once a Week* was not prospering. The Dickensian formula was not working. Although one can only speculate on reasons for Rice's lack of success, elements in his personality that emerge even from a skeletal outline of his biography suggest some possible explanations.[17] Rice, even as he was beginning his editorship of *Once a Week,* was studying for the bar and was admitted to practice in Lincoln's Inn in 1871. When he sold the magazine in 1873, he also suspended his literary partnership with Besant in order to practice law. But he was unsuccessful there as well and soon returned to literature. "Ready-Money Mortiboy," according to Rice's *DNB* biographer, had "proved a great literary, though not great commercial success." Rice, whose childhood and adolescence had coincided with the apex of Dickens's career, had a clear image of the kind of popular success to which he aspired, but his own work fell short; indeed, his best work was a shared property.

In selling *Once a Week* to take up law, Rice comes across as a man who, like one of his fictional heroes, had a clear image of what he desired in the way of success but was very uncertain as to how it could be achieved. Rice's failure to gain the professional status and security he was seeking at the bar was an echo of his failure, as the owner and the editor of *Once a Week,* to succeed in capitalizing on a formula that characterized the industry on which Dickens had had such an enormous impact.

If Rice's career reveals considerable uncertainty about the nature of his undertaking with *Once a Week,* George Manville Fenn, the magazine's last owner and editor, was absolutely committed to succeeding in Grub Street. More than the biographies of any of the other editors of the magazine, Fenn's is one of a man who raised himself from humble origins and later claimed success as a prolific writer, mostly of boys' books.[18]

Born to a poor family, Fenn did, however, study at the Battersea Training College for Teachers and for a time was master of a national school in Lincolnshire during the 1850s. Intent on breaking into popular journalism, he went to London in the mid-1860s and finally managed to get some work accepted in *All the Year Round.* That small opening apparently gave Fenn entrée into the profession, and his work was accepted by a number of newspapers and magazines. In the midst of this professional flowering, Fenn in 1870 became the editor of *Cassell's Magazine,* published by John Cassell, with whom he had had by that time a connection as a writer for several years.[19] Simon Nowell-Smith, in describing Fenn's association with *Cassell's,* says that "he was one of their most indefatigable authors, writing fiction for every one of their magazines that printed fiction, and articles for periodicals as diverse as the *Working Man* and the *Live Stock Journal*" He adds that Fenn "dressed like Dickens, essayed the intonations and gestures of Dickens, and liked nothing better than to be mistaken for Dickens."[20]

Fenn's vision of himself as an editor was also conceived largely in Dickensian terms. It is important to keep in mind that his experience immediately prior to his purchase of *Once a Week* was with a magazine whose audience — "the 'family' public" — was, as Nowell-Smith describes it,

vast, amorphous, but limited both socially and intellectually to a lower level than the subscribers to *Macmillan's* and *Blackwood's,* the *Cornhill* and *Temple Bar.* That public did not ask for literature: it asked simply for entertainment, and the publishers saw to it that the entertainment should be innocuous and monotonous. . . . The success of a popular magazine rested upon the avoidance of trouble. Safety lay in writers who. . . wrote what suited the greatest number of lower and lower-middle class families and what could with propriety be given to the sons and daughters of those families to read. . . . [21]

Fenn was one of the writers particularly well suited for this audience.

The *Once a Week* that Fenn acquired from Rice, however, was still attempting to appeal to a more socially elevated clientele. True, it was dominated by fiction, but that development or trend was hardly limited to magazines for the working and lower-middle classes in the 1870s. It is evident in many of the well-established shilling monthlies — for example, *Cornhill,* the *Argosy, London Society.* And *Once a Week's* interest in fiction was certainly pitched toward solidly middle-class interests. When

Fenn assumed ownership of *Once a Week* in 1873, he characterized the fourth series that was about to begin as an opportunity "to make the magazine light, bright, and sparkling."[22] That the announcement was euphemistic is an understatement to say the least, for the magazine, far from brightening, took on a decidedly pulpy appearance and character. Although the pages were wider and full-page illustrations reappeared, the paper was of an inferior quality and the pictures were crude caricatures, made all the more so by their ubiquity. Whereas the six-month volumes of the preceding series had averaged 560 or 570 pages, the page count dropped with the first volume of the fourth series to 360 pages. Individual articles were short, seldom more than three quarters of a page in length, and serial installments were also quite short.

As the next volumes appeared, Fenn's use of the magazine as a vehicle for his own fiction was stressed. At least one of the two or three serials being run at any given time was his own. At one point, for example, he was publishing only a skeletal regular volume and then three separately paginated novelettes, two of which were his own. Although the size of the volume was approximately the same, this technique betrayed, I think, a clear break with the idea of the magazine as a true miscellany. Even if one assumes that those novelettes were published in weekly parts, the fact is that they were not integrated into the magazine. And the miscellaneous contents were clearly treated as space filler.

If we look for a prevailing tonality in *Once a Week* under Fenn's direction, we come up against contradiction after contradiction. In one volume, for example, there were not only several color plates of fashions and what might be called garden fantasies but also an assortment of double-page and foldout adventure illustrations of jungle scenes, the American West, and wild animals. Fiction, especially Fenn's own, tended toward high adventure, with a decided preference for colonial escapades and hidden treasure, yet there were also serials and stories about suburban life and middle-class domesticity. "Madame," a regular column that seems incongruous in a magazine largely given over to adventure tales and articles on sport, exploration, and North American Indian lore, was a strange mixture of advice on how to keep hands in good condition in spite of cooking and cleaning, fashion notes, etiquette, the royal calendar, the appropriate treatment of governesses, and so forth.

It is impossible to know for sure the reasoning behind Fenn's choices, but one has an image of him desperately struggling to find a formula that would work.[23] Every volume seems to have introduced a feature or to have recast what was already there. We can get no clear idea of what audience Fenn was attempting to attract. At the same time, there are signs that Fenn did have, at least subconsciously, a faint vision of what was or soon would be marketable. Ironically, though, in beginning a new series in January 1880, he tried to base a comeback on a return to the old miscellany formula.

The appearance of *Once a Week's* fifth series in January 1880 was marked with a self-congratulatory statement claiming credit for the host of famous writers and illustrators whose works had graced the pages of the magazine over the years.[24] Fenn then projected a future of continued greatness that would include something for everyone. What, in fact, appeared was a completely new magazine that established a variety of new features. It was a miscellany formula with series on "Products of the Earth," "Industries of the World," and "Insurance." There would be regular book and theater reviews and two illustrated serials. Unfortunately, even this updating was doomed to fail, and *Once a Week* abruptly ceased publication just two months later.

III

Why was Fenn, a seasoned journalist, unable to discover a successful marketing strategy for *Once a Week?* Given his background and experience at *Cassell's,* it seems safe to assume that he had a clear sense of lower-middle-class taste and that he sought initially to restructure *Once a Week* to attract that audience. At the same time, it is evident that he wanted to hold onto the well-defined middle-class audience the magazine had traditionally served. His failure, I believe, resulted from his equivocations between these two audiences. There can be no doubt that the raw appearance of the fourth series alienated the established middle-class reader who had followed *Once a Week* in the sixties and early seventies. And although Fenn's name must have had an appeal among readers lower on the social ladder, he could not compete with giants such as the *London Journal, Cassell's,* and the *Family Herald,* which had represented those interests for decades.

Ironically, just eighteen months after *Once a Week* ceased publication, a magazine called *Tit-Bits,* under the direction of George Newnes, made its first appearance in Manchester, incorporating many of the ideas that had cropped up here and there in *Once a Week* under Fenn. The squibs and anecdotes, the brief excerpts from books and other magazines and papers, the random jumble of miscellaneous information that Fenn had used as padding were the essential ingredients of *Tit-Bits.* What mattered about *Tit-Bits* was not solely that it was a repository of amusing information and astounding facts but that it became a promotional tool. There was the railway insurance policy that protected the commuter with the magazine on his person as he went to and from work or play, the *"Tit-Bits* Villa," which was the prize of a short story contest, the cryptic clues to the whereabouts of buried tubes of sovereigns, and so forth.[25]

Once a Week began at a time when there was a need for periodicals that could fill the gap between the large working-class audience and the very small intellectual and cultural elite, both of whom were already well served by periodicals by the 1850s. The magazines that came into being throughout the 1860s stressed themes that were consciously middle class in orientation. They sought to establish a viable place for middle-class existence within the emerging professional and social milieus of the city, they used poetry and illustration as a way of framing a moral consensus and a self-image to reinforce middle-class values, and they used fiction to reward their readers for having those values.

But it is obvious that the complexion of the middle class changed during the mid-Victorian period in which *Once a Week* was published. That complexion did not alter in ways that made obsolete the interests, values, and rewards cultivated in the magazines, but it challenged magazine editors to express them in ways that did not create or emphasize divisions or separate layers within the middle class. The case of *Once a Week* shows how difficult it was to negotiate that change. *Once a Week's* failure is noteworthy because it was the result of experimentation in search of the right formula rather than complacency. Other magazines of the sixties survived longer not because their owners and editors discovered the magic combination that would attract a larger and a more diverse audience but because they were either content or could afford to carry on with fewer readers.

The new wave of magazines that began to emerge in the 1890s shared a good many similarities with the illustrated magazines of the sixties, but it is less clear that they were being guided by an editorial strategy based on class interest than that they were responding to a lucrative commercial opportunity. To a certain extent, one can argue that magazine proprietors simply wanted to make more money, but both that decision and its desired results were necessarily contingent on attracting a larger readership.

Editors in the nineties saw that the class consciousness that had characterized the magazine of the sixties and had made it popular was inadequate to accommodate the interests of the new mass of people who looked progressively more and more alike and who were destined to share a similar future based on more or less equal access to education and a job market based on individual competence rather than class or social patronage.

Confronted with a potential middle-class audience less clearly distinguishable from other constituencies moving up into the middle social strata than they had been twenty years earlier, new magazine owners saw that they had to look for and speak to the lowest common denominator that could attract a large readership. They did not abandon middle-class values but subsumed them in less consciously class-oriented features such as detective and adventure fiction and articles and essays on subjects of generalized national interest. Entrepreneurs such as Newnes and Lord Northcliffe stand out now because they discovered in the 1880s and 1890s how to define and exploit the common interest of the middle class in inclusive rather than exclusive terms. We are perhaps culturally poorer for their eagerness to use the magazine as a tool for merchandising rather than as a primary vehicle for moral and social education, but few would dispute the important role that popular magazines play today in reflecting and influencing the interests and the concerns of our society as a whole.

NOTES

1. The following chronology of *Once a Week* has been pieced together from information in the *New Cambridge Bibliography of English Literature*, the *Dictionary of National Biography*, and a variety of other sources:

Dates / Series: vols. 1-13; 2 July 1859-30 December 1865
NS vols. 1-4; 6 January 1866-28 December 1867
3d ser. vols. 1-13; 4 January 1868-29 August 1874
4th ser. vols. 1-11; 5 September 1874-27 December 1879
5th ser.; 3 January 1880-24 April 1880

Owners: Bradbury & Evans, 1859-69
        James Rice, 1869-73
        George Manville Fenn, 1873-80
Editors: Samuel Lucas, 1859-65
        Edward Walford, 1865-68
        Eneas Sweetland Dallas, 1868-69
        James Rice, 1869-73
        George Manville Fenn, 1873-80

2. William Buckler in *"Once a Week* Under Samuel Lucas, 1859-65"
(*PMLA*, 67 [December 1952]: 924), and, more recently, Robert Patten in
Charles Dickens and His Publishers ([Oxford: Clarendon Press, 1978], pp.
261-271), provide full details of the nature and effect of Dickens's quarrel with
Bradbury and Evans. Portions of my argument in this paper owe much to
Buckler's research in the article noted above and two other short notes concern-
ing *Once a Week* editors that he published in the early 1950s.

3. That reputation has been fostered in studies that have treated *Once a Week*
exclusively as an art journal. See Gleeson White, *English Illustration, "The Sixties": 1855-70* (London: Constable & Co., 1897); Forrest Reid, *Illustrators of
the Sixties* (1928: rpt. New York: Dover, 1975); and Joseph Pennell, *"Once a
Week:* A Great Art Magazine" (*Bibliographica*, III [1897]: 60-82).

4. Buckler's figures for *Once a Week* contrast sharply with Alvar Ellegard's
in *The Readership of the Periodical Press in Mid-Victorian Britain* (Göteborg:
Almqvist and Wiksell, 1957), p. 35. Whereas Ellegard suggests that *Once a
Week* maintained a fairly constant circulation, Buckler indicates that the
magazine suffered from a steadily declining readership from 1859 to 1865.

5. See Ellegard, Table 16, p. 35.

6. William Buckler, "Edward Walford: A Distressed Editor," *Notes and
Queries* 198 (December 1953): 537.

7. Ibid.

8. Buckler, *PMLA*, p. 940.

9. Charles William Sutton in *Dictionary of National Biography* (1885-1900;
rpt. in 22 vols. plus supplements [London: Oxford University Press, 1917-],
XII, p. 242). (Cited hereafter as *DNB.*)

10. Buckler, *PMLA*, pp. 927-928.

11. Walford's biography by Edward Irving Carlyle appears in *DNB*, XX, pp.
496-497.

12. Taken from the 32d edition (London: Chatto & Windus, 1892), n.p.

13. Biographical information comes from George Clement Boase's entry for
Dallas in *DNB*, XIII, pp. 394-395.

14. William Buckler, in another *Notes & Queries* piece, reproduces Bradbury
and Evans's offer of the position to him, his written acceptance of their terms,
and a routine letter from him to them after the sale of the magazine, asking them

to be sure that the new owner would publish without interruption the final installments of the current serial. ("E. S. Dallas' Appointment as Editor of *Once a Week,*" *Notes & Queries,* 195 [June 1950]: 279-280.)

15. Walter Dexter, ed., *The Letters of Charles Dickens,* III (London: Nonesuch Press, 1938), pp. 108-109.

16. *The English Common Reader* (Chicago: University of Chicago Press, 1957), p. 82.

17. Biographical information on Rice comes from Richard Garnett's article in *DNB,* XVI, pp. 988-989.

18. George Simonds Boulger in *DNB: Supplement 1901-11* (1912), I, pp. 17-18.

19. *Cassell's Magazine* succeeded *Cassell's Illustrated Family Paper* in 1867. Ellegard estimates its circulation at 200,000 in 1870 (Table 16, p. 32).

20. Simon Nowell-Smith, *The House of Cassell, 1848-1958* (London: Cassell & Co., 1958), p. 123.

21. Ibid., p. 121.

22. See editorial note, *Once a Week,* 3d ser. 13 (29 August 1874), p. 766.

23. For a comparison of this problem of finding an identity, see Sally Mitchell, "The Forgotten Woman of the Period: Penny Weekly Family Magazines of the 1840s and 1850s," in *A Widening Sphere: Changing Roles of Victorian Women,* ed. Martha Vicinus (Bloomington, Indiana: Indiana University Press, 1977), pp. 29-51.

24. *Once a Week,* 5th ser. 1 (3 January 1880), p. 1.

25. See Amy Cruse, "The New Journalism," in *After the Victorians* (London: George Allen & Unwin, 1938), pp. 191-204, for an impressionistic account of the *Tit-Bits* phenomenon.

Hartley S. Spatt

The Aesthetics of Editorship: Creating Taste in the Victorian Art World

Anyone who deals with the world of periodical journalism must continually confront the question of the editor's true power. Within the offices of the publication he or she has tremendous influence not only through the power to rewrite submissions and determine their placement in the magazine but through the very choice of writers and the control over resources. Externally, however, the editor is typically effaced by anonymity, or considered by readers to be merely a mouthpiece for the publisher, or dismissed as a creature bowing to readers' demands. The number of Victorian editors named in the Queen's Honours List, or became a figure worthy of gossip, or made a fortune is small.

The editor's lack of visible influence is even more marked when one turns from periodical politics, where a Walter Bagehot might stand visibly above his staff on *The Economist,* to periodical aesthetics. Reference to aesthetics in nineteenth-century periodicals calls up visions of savage reviewers, not savage editors, of vague charges by the Haydons of the world against an anonymous conspiracy in the art establishment to condemn or, more accurately, to ignore their words and their genius. But it is typically the Royal Academy or the autocratic Thomas Taylor (art writer for *The Times*) that serves as the butt of such criticism. Indeed, to blame the art purchasers and the art critics rather than the editors is to judge the situation correctly. *The Athenaeum* under Norman MacColl (1871-1900) had tremendous power over the reputations of artists reviewed in its columns; but MacColl never wrote a single RA review. It was Frederic G. Stephens, an original member of the Pre-Raphaelite Brotherhood and the official art critic of *The Athenaeum* from 1860 to 1900, whose opinions and predictions controlled the fates of young artists. On *The Art-Journal* much of the day-to-day discussion of art and artists was left to James Dafforne and J. Comyns Carr, not S. C. Hall; and when Hall did at one point suggest that certain artists and exhibitions might receive more favorable notices since their advertisements were keeping the magazine afloat, Comyns Carr quit rather than allow his editor to influence his writing.

What then are the possibilities open to the editor of a Victorian art periodical? Is he to set himself up as the standard-bearer of the art world, exposing the vices and the follies of the less gifted while preaching the gospel of fine art? Should he content himself with the less demanding task of working on public opinion, acting as an exponent of aesthetics but leaving the actual defense of the arts to artists themselves? Or should he eschew both these tasks and restrict himself to the simple reflection of public tastes? As one might imagine, in the Victorian art world all three of these possibilities had their exponents; in the range of their editorial and aesthetic philosophies Victorian editors embody the diversity and exuberance that make Victorian art itself fascinating.

It might be best to set the stage for this discussion by starting a few years before Victoria's accession, with the famous Charles

Wentworth Dilke. As the editor of *The Athenaeum* from 1830 to 1846 and an occasional contributor for twenty years beyond that date, Dilke laid the foundation for his magazine's eminence under later editors such as MacColl. But outside its annual exhibition reviews and occasional book notices, *The Athenaeum* did not specialize in the aesthetics of the early Victorian world; not until after Dilke had relinquished control of the magazine was a "Fine-Art Gossip" column even added. But during his thirty-year association with *The Athenaeum* Dilke contributed more than a dozen separate (anonymous or pseudonymous) items on the fine arts, at first because Henry Chorley (the original art writer) was sickly but later out of a deep concern for at least one role of the arts: "the spread of knowledge."[1] Assuming the role of a concerned observer of the arts impelled to write to *The Athenaeum,* Dilke called for public lectures by Royal Academy members or for more access to museums by the general public: "In this way the public would learn to appreciate Art; and the artist . . . would be forced to work *up* to his public."[2] One month Dilke might be seeking "to educate the eye – to create a sympathy for Art"[3]; a few months later he might call for volunteers in the art community to formulate "laws of proportion, laws of relation, laws of colour, laws of order and arrangement . . . which would offer reasons for our preferences" in art.[4] Yet Dilke remained content with invitations to others; the pages of *The Athenaeum* were clearly not the place where such a set of laws might be promulgated – by the editor or his writers. In this reluctance to engage in rule making he was merely being consistent with the magazine's first pronouncement on the arts in its eighth number: "We pretend not as judges to pass sentence; nor would we plead as advocates."[5] Or, as the matter was put in a continuation article, "to change the taste of the public is the province of the artist, and the artist only."[6]

It is apparently this last argument that seemed to inform the editorial policies of William Luson Thomas forty years later in planning for *The Graphic*. In his "Preface" to the volume collecting the first six months' issue, Thomas wrote of his appreciation for the "numerous distinguished Artists . . . [who] have assisted us, from the belief that we are doing a good work."[7] In an article accompanying one particularly striking engraving in that first volume, the role of the artist as a key contributor to the creation of taste was further adumbrated: "It is he who sees Nature . . . and translates it for the benefit of many good people whose only fault is to go about with their eyes shut."[8] *The Graphic* has often been hailed for its commitment to naturalism in art and social conscience, both of which Thomas summed up in his desire to make it "worthy of preservation as an artistic record of the times in which we live."[9] And one of the first illustrations in the new magazine was Luke Fildes's famous image of the urban poor, "Houseless and Hungry" (Fig.1); *The Graphic* for many years sent artists into areas of poverty and cultural deprivation such as Ireland and the Americas to send back not only written reactions but vivid portraits of noble Indians and destitute famine victims.

Unfortunately, these first efforts were not succeeded by further achievements, except in the area of circulation. *The Graphic* quickly became the largest circulation magazine of its kind, selling as many as 200,000 copies of a single issue; it regularly outsold all the serious journals combined. When one achieves such mass success, however, innovation quickly gives way to formula: A brilliant series on the English poor was followed by a trite series on the Irish poor; extensive coverage of the Franco-Prussian War was followed by jingoistic coverage of the Afghan border conflicts. As a general rule, the sedate and the conventional overtake the daring and the new. Within ten years *The Graphic* settled into the shape that made it the model for the great American magazines of the early twentieth century such as *Life* and *The Saturday Evening Post*.

Fig. 1
Luke Fildes
"Houseless and Hungry"

Fig. 2
Clarkson Stanfield
"Moonlight"

Fig. 3
Matthew W. Ridley
"Leaving Old England"

Fig. 4
Ford Madox Brown
"The Last of England"

Fig. 5
A. Boyd Houghton
"Buried Quick and Unburied Dead"

Fig. 6
F. W. Lawson
"Peasant Girls Tending the Wounded"

Fig. 7
J. Parker
"My Love is like the Melody
that's Sweetly Played in Tune"

Fig. 8
M. J. Bertrand
"Virginia Drowned"

Fig. 9
W. Cave Thomas
"Angels Regarding Men"

Fig. 10
E. Davis
"On the Way to School"

Fig. 11
J. M. W. Turner
"Ulysses Deriding Polyphemus"

Fig. 12
J. E. Millais
"The Pearl of Great Price"

One could not ask for a clearer contrast to *The Graphic* and its philosophy of following the audience than *The Portfolio,* a joint product of the publisher, Richmond Seeley, and the editor, P. Gilbert Hamerton (1834-94). Hamerton, one of the first modern art historians, edited *The Portfolio* by mail from his home in France. In 1890, responding to criticism of his absentee editorship, Hamerton asserted that he "read all articles carefully, and often abridge[d] them," that he settled "all doubtful questions about illustrations," and that he and Seeley would "consult together about our programme" at least once a year.[10] As one might infer from this sketch of his editorial activities, Hamerton's own contributions to his magazine were limited to monographs on individual artists and reviews of art books or exhibitions on the Continent, along with an occasional reattribution of an individual artwork that was the sort of thing a critic was expected to do.[11] Over the years this preference of Hamerton's for the individual study shaped the expectations of the magazine's readership; when he died in 1894 the magazine was given a new subtitle to reflect that change: *The Portfolio: Monographs on Artistic Subjects.*

From the time of the first number in 1869, *The Portfolio* was best known for Hamerton's championship of what he called black and white art, especially etching. The first volume contained an extended topographical essay on the English landscape as seen through the eyes of an etcher; Hamerton followed this in subsequent years with "Examples of Modern Etching" (1872), "Etchings by the Great Masters" (1878), "The Ruined Abbeys of Yorkshire" (1882), and many other essays and reviews. At times Hamerton's emphasis on what he called the Technical Notes of the etcher's art blinded him to precisely those qualities that Thomas's artists focused on. Late in 1871, for example, he reviewed two collections of etchings depicting Paris since the Commune and engaged in an extensive discussion of the two artists' divergent styles and techniques; their subjects, palaces and museums destroyed by Prussian gunfire and French looting, came within his notice only as occasions for metaphor: "The flames have gutted [the *Pavillon de Flore*] . . . and the leaden roof ornaments have trickled down in thin streams, as the melted snow trickles in the sun of March."[12] Hamerton was little concerned with art's ability to yield a "true record" of the world; he tended to shy away from any generalized comment that the paintings he loved so dearly might engender. In an 1890 essay on the subject of "National Supremacy in Painting," for example, Hamerton apologized for his inability to deal with the nominal subject: "I had hoped to [reach] a conclusion about national supremacy in painting, but have found it impossible to avoid some consideration of individual efforts."[13] In fact, he had discussed eight artists (admittedly of different nationalities) and had failed to produce a single extended paragraph on his topic; the French were ultimately granted supremacy merely because they had contributed most of the artists worth discussing.

Hamerton would not, however, have felt it necessary to apologize for these omissions from his aesthetic program. He deliberately rejected "any militant position in art criticism," any "particular doctrine" that might be thought of as aligning him to some "artistic sect" or "party." His vision of *The Portfolio* was of a world pervaded by "a certain serenity, like that which pervades a great national gallery"—the serenity, that is, of a collection that is united solely by the excellence of the individual pictures.[14] "We intend," Hamerton said in 1875, "to get together . . . a record of past and present experience, which may thus form a sort of common fund . . . accessible to every one."[15] Hamerton's only real aim in *The Portfolio,* it seems (apart from assuring himself an outlet for his art historical inquiries), was the passive one of "making the outside public less on the outside."[16] To the extent that he profiled some artists who would otherwise never have received exposure and provided notes on processes of composition and materials, Hamerton must be granted his measure of success: An attentive reader of *The Portfolio* over its more than thirty-year history would undoubtedly have become knowledgeable enough about contemporary art to carry on a superficial conversation with a dealer. Whether that same person would have been able to judge what price to pay that dealer for a given artwork or to judge whether a given piece was worth buying at all is another question entirely, demanding just that application of general standards that Hamerton eschewed. As James Kissane has charitably put it, Hamerton was "not . . . distinctly apt at separating the permanently valuable from what fashion approved."[17] For "a periodical that would often be bound and kept on the shelves of libraries,"[18] however, *The Portfolio* did far more than other middle-brow periodicials to keep alive a sense of quality in art at a time when aesthetics were changing more rapidly than at any equivalent period in history.

The Portfolio did far more, that is, than *The Magazine of Art,* which printed during its twenty-five years (six of them under no less an editor than W. E. Henley) everything it could fit between covers, illustrating, it may be said, the "random walk" principle of art editorship. Founded as a poor man's version of *The Art-Journal,* which will be discussed below, *The Magazine of Art* never succeeded in establishing an independent, coherent philosophy or aesthetic of art or editorship; instead, it tended to be treated as a "Miscellany of Art."

A more serious example of the difficulties a magazine can fall into when it fails to establish a coherent editorial policy is the short-lived *Universal Review,* the brainchild of Harry Quilter. Quilter had gained fame as the art critic for *The Spectator* and as the butt of James Whistler's invective before he attempted to make the transition from writer to publisher in 1888; and when he wrote essays in the *Universal Review* extolling "beauty of colour and line, intensity of emotion, essential truth of feeling or of fact,"[19] his own sensitivity justified his efforts. But he was unable to write the entire issue himself, and hence his magazine suffered from both uneven writing and random makeup. Henry James contributed a fine story, "The Lesson of the Master," to the first number; but it was printed next to an essay "On a Certain Deficiency in Women"; Luke Fildes's "Houseless and Hungry" reappeared in a special issue commemorating twenty years of *The Graphic,* sandwiched between essays on "Germany in 1888" and "The Philosophy of Marriage." It seems that Quilter was willing to let his audience decide what his policy should be; readers responded to the implicit appeal by deciding that he should not publish the magazine any more. By the fourth number Quilter was desperate and started adding articles such as "Palmistry as a Fine Art" or essays condemning the prevalence of nudes in art — fully illustrated with examples. Providing neither consistency nor quality, the *Universal Review* folded after eight numbers and joined a long list of short-lived aesthetic periodicals in Victorian England.

There was only one exception to this seemingly universal pattern of bright promise and tarnished reality — one periodical successfully dedicated to didactic art journalism and run for forty-one years by its founder: *The Art-Journal.* The man who vowed in February of 1839 to "express [his] opinions fully, freely, and without reserve"[20] and kept his promise until he retired in 1880 was Samuel C. Hall. The one thing critics can agree on about Hall is that he was not at all the sort of person one would expect to found, edit, and at times singlehandedly write a journal dedicated to "the fine arts, and the arts decorative and ornamental." He was a teetotaling Irishman born with the century, more given to platitude than profundity, and certainly incapable of the sort of close stylistic analysis that Hamerton specialized in; scanning a listing of the more than five hundred books that he and his wife, the pulp novelist Anna Maria Fielding, wrote and often published themselves, one can see why Hall has often been thought to be Dickens's model for Mr. Pecksniff. Jeremy Maas, who has written a short study of Hall's character, readily admits that Hall's "turgid and rambling prose," his "oleaginous platitudes" justify a "swelling chorus of [personal] abuse."[21]

But it took more than platitudes to inspire the respect of Prince Albert and John Ruskin, more than a toady's personality to address Queen Victoria like a chiding uncle: "Money is found by this wealthy and complaining nation for anything save Literature and Art. . . . These arts we call on the Queen and the Government to support and honour."[22] What Hall dared say when *The Art-Journal* was a struggling magazine seeking to make a name for itself he did not shrink from stating later in his career, when large circulation figures and government patronage were at stake; in the late 1870s Hall's magazine could still be heard proclaiming the need for copyright and trademark protection in industrial designs.

In these last items, in fact, can be found the secret of Hall's influence over the Victorian art world: He was before all a practical aesthete. Like a modern marketing expert, Hall first entered the world of art periodicals because he saw a niche for himself and his product: "[In] the Newspapers . . . a passing remark of praise or censure is frequently all that can be given to a work [of art]. . . . Scarcely one among the Monthly Magazines now devotes a single page to the subject; and the Quarterly Reviews consider it as not coming within the range of their legitimate duties."[23] He rued that "political contests and other engrossing events, so completely fill the columns of the newspapers, that the 'still small voice' of Art has no chance of being heard amid the tumult."[24] As he put it toward the end of his life, "I had to *create* a public for Art."[25] Moreover, Hall early on saw the intimate connection between public events and artistic consequences. Was there war on the horizon? Hall's first thought was whether that would affect the committee planning decorations for the new Houses of Parliament. Was there Chartist fever in the air? Hall was quick to boast: "We find our patrons not alone in the atelier of the Artist, in the library of the Connoisseur, and in the house of the Manufacturer; but, we rejoice to say, also in the work-room of the Artisan."[26]

The program Hall offered is worthy of praise. Though at first he advertised his *Art-Union* (as the magazine was called for the first ten years) as a service for artists "to provide such information as the more experienced and independent may require [and] to obtain early and accurate intelligence upon all matters connected with Art," he soon widened his scope to embrace the masses: "We shall endeavour, by rendering 'good Art cheap,' to place its meritorious examples in the hands of the 'the many'—so to become sources of pleasure and instruction."[27] Looking back over his career, Hall praised his own courage in attempting to be a "teacher of the many instead of instructor of the few"[28] and summed up his role in the art world succinctly: "In 1843 I commenced . . . to show 'the commercial value of the Fine Arts,' that 'beauty is cheaper than deformity.' "[29] Hall was certainly not the only writer to preach the doctrine of applied art as a form of beauty; but when the message appeared in the pages of *The Art-Journal* it was far more persuasive than when it subsequently appeared in *The Commonweal,* William Morris's journal of applied socialism. Only in the former did the doctrine coexist with long articles on morality and nationalism in art, some of them written by Hall himself. The artist, Hall preached in 1843, "must remember that, like the historian, he must narrate general truths"; paintings must accordingly be "lessons expressive of moral truth and national greatness."[30] Here, expressed over and over again, are the general didactic moralisms about the public role of art that one seeks in vain in Hamerton's *Portfolio* or deapairs of finding after the first few years of *The Graphic*. Whether or not one agrees with Hall's position, one must acknowledge the clarity and the vigor that his moral code lent to his discussions of individual works.

For example, Hall championed the work of his fellow Irishman, Daniel Maclise, R. A., despite Maclise's frequent "harshness" of color and mannered business of incident. Hall did so in large part because Maclise, unlike most academicians who used their official honors to gain lucrative private commissions, never shirked from his public responsibilities: He always sent a selection of his current works to the annual public exhibition, and he accepted a series of commissions for frescoes in the new Houses of Parliament. The task broke Maclise's health, and the results (exposed to gas fumes, heat, and pollutants) hardly seem worth Hall's praise; but for the sake of Maclise's "lesson . . . of moral truth and national greatness," Hall seized every opportunity to pressure the government to raise Maclise's fee and to urge the public to visit the works:

We are a maritime power, but ["The Death of Nelson"] is the only picture which we yet possess entirely worthy of our naval history. . . . The extreme tenderness with which the national vanity of our neighbors is dealt with [in a fresco of Waterloo] is a new and most generous trait in battle painting. . . . [In] Mr. Maclise's "Spirit of Justice" . . . we are made to ascend from much that is human to much that is divine.[31]

After more than a century, the criticism of *The Art-Journal* contains some of the most perceptive comments on Maclise.

But the question remains whether with a panegyric like the above, the didactic model of art journalism may ultimately reach a limit no less than the other models. If Thomas's pandering to public demands led to sentimentality and finally the banal, Hall's setting himself up as the guide to national prosperity in the arts led to an equivalent pompousness and a similar banality. The difference between them and between Hall and Hamerton finally comes down to a matter of taste. Taste is a subject that led to a confusion of response in all Victorian art editors. On one of the first occasions when Dilke wrote about art for *The Athenaeum,* he spoke of the need to educate the taste of England: "If art is ever again to equal its old renown, Englishmen . . . must become co-equal in knowledge of art with the old merchants and traders in the free states of Italy."[32] "Imitations of the ancient masters," Dilke felt, should be encouraged not merely to train artists but to train art's audience: "Let the opinion of the public change, and the practice of artists will follow it. But to change the taste of the public, is the province of the artist, and the artist only."[33] With this crucial distinction between fashion and taste Hall agreed completely, avowing that—though one could create a desire for certain kinds of art among the people—one could not create "a *taste* (that was the gradual result of persevering zeal)."[34] Hamerton's policy for *The Portfolio* has been well described as "the intention of informing public taste without startling it."[35] If one were to base one's judgments of these art editors on their verbal definitions of taste, one would anticipate little difference in theory but a vast difference in practice. And that is exactly what one finds. The true measure of these men's commitments to taste and to the education of the public can only be made through their policies on illustrations.

The editor's choice and placement of illustrations provide the perceptive reader of Victorian art periodicals with a positive index of each man's commitment, if any, to changing the taste of his readers. *The Graphic,* to its credit, is forever marked as the journal that dared to commission works such as "Houseless and Hungry" and that sent artists to Paris during the siege of 1870 to record the Prussian victory. As a result, the hundreds of other illustrations in each volume, which cumulatively affected the taste of its readers far more, have been skimmed over by modern critics. These other works fall into two basic groups: relatively objective recordings of splendid triumphs or terrible disasters, which include some effective engravings of artists such as Clarkson Stanfield and A. Boyd Houghton, and—especially after *The Graphic's* first two years—overtly sentimental genre scenes unmatched in their banality by any contemporary periodical except perhaps *Household Words.*

The artists hired by *The Graphic* to engrave works hung on the walls of the Royal Academy (Fig. 2) or to create illustrations of foreign seats of war from sketches sent back by free-lance correspondents made the pages of this periodical a source unmatched by its competitors for accurate reportage. It is to these illustrations that Thomas referred when he called his magazine "an artistic record of the times in which we live." Yet one cannot help suspecting that Thomas really saw his magazine as a vehicle for idealizing the records if one may judge by the growing proportion of sentimental images, which only purport to be factual. In the third number of *The Graphic,* for example, Matthew W. Ridley published the first of his many contributions to the magazine, an illustration to an article on emigration entitled "Leaving Old England" (Fig. 3). The triteness of anecdote in the scene is far more obvious than in its well-known model, H. N. O'Neil's "Eastward Ho!" of 1857; and it becomes even more marked when one compares it to Samuel C. Hall's approach to the subject of emigration a year later. Hall commented on the rise in emigration by publishing engravings of paintings dedicated to the subject, including Ford Madox Brown's magnificent evocation of the emigrant's mixed emotions, "The Last of England" (Fig. 4).

An inspection of *The Graphic's* coverage of the Franco-Prussian War indicates another possible cause for the wide unevenness of its illustrations: The editors seem to have accepted everything submitted to them without distinguishing between pictures that truly recorded their times and those that grossly distorted them. In one issue there might appear Hubert

Herkomer's sensitive portrayal of French women waiting for their husbands to return from battle or A. Boyd Houghton's moody piece of realism depicting soldiers of the Commune surrounded by dead comrades and the snows of winter (Fig. 5); in another issue the front cover might blazon a thoroughly sentimental picture of "Peasant Girls Tending the Wounded" (Fig. 6).

By the later 1870s *The Graphic* no longer boasted of being a periodical in which artists "see Nature . . . and translate it into mass imagery";[36] instead, it boasted of printing every illustration in its Christmas 1878 number in full color or of obtaining exclusive rights to reproduce the forgettable "My Love is like the Melody that's Sweetly Played in Tune" (Fig. 7). With no taste at the top, there was little chance for the Fildes and Herkomers to win out over the Ridleys and Lawsons. The problem was present from the start, inherent in the sheer inclusiveness of Thomas's vision and the innate preference for the sweet over the true. A single image sums up *The Graphic's* dominant tone: a portrait of the drowned Virginie from Saint-Pierre's famous novel (Fig. 8). The disarranged stocking reveals the girl's fate in the most indirect way; even the caption suggested that "the pale violets" of death have "imperceptibly merged" with the hues of alluring sleep.[37] When one so distorts the record that it becomes a tale of *virginis puerisque,* yet continues to maintain the fiction of authenticity, the record itself is in danger of being lost.

This is, of course, a danger inherent in all periodical illustration; the closer that illustration is asserted to be to reality, the easier it is for the image to supplant our recognition that reality is necessarily more various, more asymmetrical, even dirtier than the static, monumentalized scene before us. It is precisely because *The Graphic* asserted early on that "our art has not been tinctured by the old fashioned classicality which . . . shrunk from accuracy wherever a feature presented itself of a character that might be thought too homely or uncomely"[38] that each descent from that high standard is felt so keenly.

No periodical is immune to this temptation to sentimentalize. Hamerton was always eager to pander to his public through resort to favorite Victorian themes, and *The Portfolio* often ran series etchings such as "The Lion in Modern Art" or etchings of children or idealized portrayals of life after death (Fig. 9). Hall himself seldom refrained from paying homage to these Victorian idols of the tribe, but at least he had the taste to select works by Horace Vernet, Joseph Clark, and other fine academic painters; even in that didactic world, however, a bathetic image like "On the Way to School" (Fig. 10) occasionally appeared to spoil the lesson.

What makes Hall's journal stand out therefore is that elusive word introduced earlier, *taste*. Though in his championship of practical art he occasionally faltered and reproduced some of the worst excesses of Victorian design along with the best, by his insistence that the artwork reproduced in his journal be representative of the nation rather than simple aesthetic whim, Hall single-handedly created a paradigm of taste for his readers. He sought and obtained permission to reproduce several of the major collections in England: the Vernon collection, the Chantrey Bequest, and other components of what is now the National Gallery collection. A highlight was his series of more than twenty works after Turner in which as much care was taken with the engraving as with the selection; perhaps the best of the resulting group is a sensitive transformation of "Ulysses Deriding Polyphemus" into black and white (Fig. 11). *The Portfolio,* for all its emphasis on black and white art, never achieved the standard set by *The Art-Journal* in these *hommages* to national art; Hamerton's ability to choose the best illustrations of his subjects was somehow lacking. When he ran a series of articles on English painters of the present he never once managed to choose a work that posterity would

judge worthy; of all Millais's works, for example, he found only
the most sentimentalized of the *Parables of Our Lord,* "The Pearl
of Great Price" (Fig. 12).

Thus a fairly well-defined spectrum of taste is evident among
Victorian editors. Toward one end is the popular *Graphic,* with
its insistence on "telling a story that really interests . . . the man
of less educated taste."[39] Somewhere toward the middle would be
Hamerton, who yearned to live the life of the great art critic but
who still sought to maintain a broad-spectrum magazine; Dilke,
whose concern for "an educated public" never manifested itself in
direct control over the art writing in his magazine; and Quilter,
whose ringing affirmations of "beauty . . . intensity . . . and
essential truth of feeling or of fact" in art could not disguise his
total lack of sensitivity to placement or preserve his magazine
from swift deterioration. And at the far end would be Samuel
Carter Hall: untrained, erratic, yet possessed of a conviction that
great art could be a source of "pleasure and instruction . . . for-
warding the great cause of humanity."[40] When one can do that for
forty-one years, one may add a final item to the list of prere-
quisites for effective taste: The editor must serve art, not himself.
If one seeks the fullest expression of taste in the world of Victorian art periodicals, one must go to *The Art-Journal.*

NOTES

1. *The Athenaeum,* 14 May 1831: 315.
2. *The Athenaeum,* 1 December 1855: 407.
3. *The Athenaeum,* 8 May 1852: 516.
4. *The Athenaeum,* 4 December 1852: 1334.
5. *The Athenaeum,* 19 February 1828: 123.
6. *The Athenaeum,* 29 February 1828: 172.
7. *The Graphic,* vol. I (1869-70): 1.
8. *The Graphic,* 12 March 1870: 351.
9. *The Graphic,* vol. I, 1.
10. *The Portfolio: An Artistic Periodical,* vol. 21 (1890): 2.

11. Hamerton was one of the first art critics to rely on more than superficial evidence when making his attributions; in this he set the pattern for the great reattributors to come, such as Bernard Berenson.

12. *The Portfolio,* vol. 2 (1871): 146. One might compare this expression to that of Samuel C. Hall who inserted in the columns of the February 1871 issue of *The Art-Journal* his "earnest hope" that "the artists of Paris, . . . who are, in a sense, the property of the world," might be saved. He sent on to urge manufacturers to seek out and patronize the artisans who had fled France and were not able to use their talents productively (*The Art-Journal,* February 1871: 62).

13. *The Portfolio,* vol. 21 (1890): 231.

14. *The Portfolio,* vol. 21 (1890): 1.

15. *The Portfolio,* vol. 6 (1875): 12.

16. *The Portfolio,* vol. 21 (1890): 2.

17. "Art Historians and Art Critics—IX: P. G. Hamerton, Victorian Art Critic," *The Burlington Magazine* cxiv (January 1972): 28.

18. *The Portfolio,* vol. 21 (1890): 1.

19. *The Universal Review, no. 1 (May-August 1888): 60.*

20. *The Art-Union,* May 1839: 65.

21. "S. C. Hall and The Art Journal," *The Connoisseur,* March 1976: 208-209.

22. *The Art-Union,* September 1840: 139.

23. *The Art-Union,* February 1839: 1.

24. *The Art-Union,* February 1840: 22.

25. *The Art-Journal,* December 1880: 353.

26. *The Art-Journal,* December 1849: 357.

27. *The Art-Union,* February 1839: 1; *The Art-Journal,* January 1849: 1.

28. *The Art-Union,* February 1839: 1.

29. *The Art-Journal,* December 1880: 354.

30. *The Art-Union,* September 1843: 232; May 1842: 105.

31. *The Art-Journal,* October 1864: 302; January 1862: 12; January 1850: 16.

32. *The Athenaeum,* 14 May 1831: 315.

33. *The Athenaeum,* 29 February 1828: 172.

34. *The Art-Journal,* December 1880: 353.

35. "Art Historians and Art Critics," 28.

36. *The Graphic,* 12 March 1870: 351.

37. *The Graphic,* 2 July 1870: 9.

38. *The Graphic,* 18 February 1871.

39. *The Graphic,* 8 January 1870: 123.

40. *The Art-Union,* May 1839: 66.

List of Illustrations

1. Luke Fildes, "Houseless and Hungry." *The Graphic,* 4 December 1869, p. 9.
2. Clarkson Stanfield, "Moonlight." *The Graphic,* 12 March 1870, p. 349.
3. M. W. Ridley, "Leaving Old England." *The Graphic,* 18 December 1869, p. 60.
4. F. M. Brown, "The Last of England." *The Art-Journal,* August 1870, p. 237.
5. A. B. Houghton, "Buried Quick and Unburied Dead." *The Graphic,* 31 December 1870, p. 645.
6. F. W. Lawson, "Peasant Girls Tending the Wounded." *The Graphic,* 27 August 1870, p. 193.
7. J. Parker, "My Love is Like the Melody that's Sweetly Played in Tune." *The Graphic,* 7 September 1878, p. 248.
8. M. J. Bertrand, "Virginia Drowned." *The Graphic,* 2 July 1870, p. 9.
9. W. Cave Thomas, "Angels Regarding Men." *The Portfolio,* 1871, p. 149.
10. E. Davis, "On the Way to School." *The Art-Journal,* November 1870, p. 329.
11. J. M. W. Turner, "Ulysses Deriding Polyphemus." *The Art-Journal,* March 1863, p. 46.
12. J. E. Millais, "The Pearl of Great Price." *The Portfolio,* 1871, Frontispiece.

Sheila R. Herstein

The *English Woman's Journal* and the Langham Place Circle: A Feminist Forum and Its Women Editors

The *English Woman's Journal* has been described as a pressure group periodical that virtually brought the British feminist movement into existence in the 1860s.[1] Certainly it provided a forum for a national exchange of ideas and information, and its offices quickly became the London hub of feminist campaigns. The *Journal* first appeared in March 1858, its major purpose being the promotion of female employment. Its editors filled their magazine with articles on notable women in history, news items relating to women's legal status, letters from distressed gentlewomen in the provinces, and a variety of articles outlining alternatives for providing women with work. Priced at one shilling, the magazine had only a few hundred subscribers during its first year.[2] However, this small core of women from all parts of Britain used the *Journal* to create the country's first effective feminist network. Its pages carried more than inspiring prose. The editors advertised an Employment Register that won so overwhelming a response that it grew into the Society for the Promotion of the Employment of Women.[3] This was only one of a variety of feminist activities initiated at the *Journal's* offices and supported by letters and articles within its pages. The *Journal* and its women editors were instrumental in raising female consciousness and structuring the agencies active in the women's movement throughout the sixties.

The first organized feminist activities in Britain were the work of a small group of women from upper-middle-class social, economic, and religious backgrounds. The movement began to assume an organized shape during the 1850s. Feminist struggles were not isolated phenomena. The participants in the mid-Victorian women's movement were for the most part members of a select group of families responsible for a variety of reform efforts. These efforts were amateur in the best sense, reflecting the attitudes of a unified, culturally-concerned segment of society. Specialization in the modern sense had yet to develop, and a real professionalization of society was some distance in the future. The essentially amateur quality of Victorian reform efforts is demonstrated in many areas: in the magazines and reviews of the period, in the proliferation of local statistical societies, and in the committees and associations established for the study and the improvement of the human condition. The families that dominated the reform movements of the sixties and seventies made up an intellectual aristocracy identified and analyzed by Noel Annan.[4] The wives, daughters, and maiden aunts of this intellectual elite became the leaders of the women's movement. Evangelical, Quaker, and Unitarian families were drawn together by the humanitarian inspiration of the antislavery movement. Mingling, often intermarrying, in a world of culture and intellect, economically secure on the basis of manufacturing interests, Macaulays, Wedgwoods, Darwins, Gurneys, and Smiths worked for intellectual and religious freedom and the recognition of merit and talent. By 1853 their ideals were expressed in the Northcote-Trevelyan Report on civil service reform. In the sixties and seventies they were drawn together in campaigns for franchise reform, an end to university disabilities, and the improvement of female education. The women of this comfortable upper-middle-class world organized and activated the first real changes in the legal and social status of Victorian women of all classes.

In 1849 a wealthy Unitarian widow, Elizabeth Jesser Reid, established Bedford College for Women. Reid and her friends Mary Mohl, Anna Jameson, and Julia Smith formed an intimate circle revolving around Harriet Martineau. The group was instrumental in giving Bedford its character as a nondenominational institution in which women shared management responsibilities equally with men. It supported the feminist activities of Julia Smith's young niece Barbara Smith who attended classes with her friends at Bedford.

Barbara Smith (1827-1891) was the granddaughter of William Smith, a Unitarian member of Parliament who was a close friend of William Wilberforce, a leader in the antislavery campaign and a fervent advocate of civil and religious liberty. Her father, Benjamin Smith, was an active supporter of the repeal of the Corn Laws. It is not quite clear what decided Barbara Smith to begin a campaign in 1854 against the existing laws of property as they affected married women. She was single, wealthy, and took her independence and equality as a matter of course within her private circle. It seems likely that the marital problems of her Aunt Julia's friend, Anna Jameson, spurred her activity. An unhappy marriage and separation left Jameson dependent on friends and her pen to sustain herself and her family. Jameson, a great influence on Smith and her friends Bessie Parkes, Adelaide Proctor, and Anna Mary Howitt, became the patroness of many feminist projects and was prominent in the extraparliamentary activities in support of a Married Women's Property Bill in 1856 and 1857.

Parkes, Howitt, Proctor, and Smith had been friends since girlhood. Parkes and Smith shared a similar family background. Like the Smiths, the Parkes family was Unitarian, upholding a long tradition of radical politics. The Unitarian preacher and scientist Joseph Priestley, Parkes's great-grandfather, was an ardent supporter of the French Revolution. Her father, Joseph Parkes, was a leading Birmingham radical active in the parliamentary reform movement and the anti-Corn Law campaign. As teenagers Parkes and Smith formed the Portfolio Club where they exhibited sketches and read poetry. Anna Mary Howitt, Adelaide Proctor, and Christina Rossetti were members.

In 1854, with advice from a family friend, Matthew Davenport Hill, the Recorder of Birmingham, Barbara Smith wrote a concise pamphlet explaining the inequities in the marriage laws, *A Brief Summary in Plain Language of the Most Important Laws of England Concerning Women*. It sold for a few pence and created a sensation. Reaction was strong in the monthly periodicals. There were some demands for reform of the marriage laws, but many condemned Smith's supposed attack on the family, the foundation of Victorian stability.[5]

Discussions in pamphlets and periodicals could not change the law. Women were excluded from Parliament so that other means had to be found to effect legislation. Late in 1855 Smith and Anna Mary Howitt decided that petitioning Parliament might result in action. Howitt's parents, the noted authors William and Mary Howitt, gave enthusiastic approval, asserting that Smith had an excellent opportunity to organize an extraparliamentary reform organization.[6] The "grand scheme" involved setting up a committee of women to obtain signatures in support of a change in the property laws. In December 1855 Smith brought a small group of women together in her father's drawing room in Blandford Square to approve the text of her petition and coordinate its distribution and the signature campaign. This was the first committee of women in England to discuss the rights of their own sex, and it brought a new political force into existence. Unable to vote or speak in favor of legislative reform, the women members of the first Married Women's Property Committee constituted the first organized feminist group. Some years later Bessie Parkes noted that although the married women's property issue was important, it was the establishment of that first committee structure that signaled a real beginning for the women's movement. The committee initiated a communication network that linked women throughout the country and laid the foundation for organized feminist efforts of the future.[7] Previously women such as Mary Wollstonecraft and Caroline Norton had publicly condemned injustices against women. More reticent persons such as Florence Nightingale had written of them in private and struggled against personal frustration. But never before had a group of women met together in England to discuss and organize political action to change the status of the sex.

Despite the petition-gathering effort, Sir Erskine Perry had no success with his Married Women's Property Bill. The Divorce Act of 1857 drew attention from it by alleviating some of the worst hardships Perry's bill addressed. The married women's property campaign came to an abrupt end; the issue remained largely ignored for the next ten years. The women's committee that Smith had organized did not dissolve, however. The new force turned from its parliamentary defeat to the issues of women's occupational and educational alternatives. It formed the nucleus of the Langham Place Circle, that group of women, led by Barbara Smith and Bessie Parkes, who began the *English Woman's Journal* in 1858 and set up the employment registry and associated societies that coordinated feminist efforts during the next decade.

The idea of a journal originated during the married women's property campaign. In October 1856 Bessie Parkes was intrigued by an issue of the *Waverly Journal,* an obscure Scottish periodical that advertised that it was edited by women. She made inquiries and became convinced that if the magazine were altered to emphasize women's issues and moved from Edinburgh to London, it could provide a permanent forum for the budding feminist cause. The proprietor invited her to contribute articles, hoping to increase the circulation of his journal, which had until then consisted primarily of stories, poems, and occasional articles on charity efforts. Parkes and Isa Craig, a Scottish recruit to the feminist circle, submitted several pieces, and Barbara Smith, now married to Eugene Bodichon and living half the year in Algiers, contributed "Women and Work," an article largely ignored until its later republication in pamphlet form. In April 1857 Parkes, traveling in Rome, received an offer of full control of the periodical. She had until then had little to do with editorial policy, merely serving as a contributor. Anna Jameson urged her to accept the editorship, and by June 1857 Parkes had returned to England to undertake the project. Bodichon placed a large sum of money in the hands of solicitor George Hastings for the improvement and if it became desirable, the eventual purchase of the magazine.[8]. The magazine did not attract much public attention during this period. Its offices remained in Edinburgh.

George Eliot wrote encouraging notes of advice to Parkes. She applauded those articles that dealt with philanthropy and social progress but tried to discourage a tendency toward "second rate literature." She urged that female achievement be demonstrated by the content of the magazine, not by labeling it the product of exclusively feminine efforts.[9] Negotiations for the purchase of the *Waverly Journal* continued through 1857, but there were financial difficulties with the proprietor and Hastings advised Bodichon and Parkes that the property was not worth the money and effort already expended. They accepted his advice, ended their association with the magazine at the end of 1857, and in

March 1858 published in London the first issue of a new periodical, the *English Woman's Journal.* [10]

In February 1858 Bessie Parkes wrote to George Eliot concerning the limited liabililty company that had been set up to finance the *Journal:* "We are beginning with £1000 and a great social interest."[11] In actuality Bodichon provided most of the money since others in their feminist circle were unable to afford more than token contributions. The first issue of the magazine declared that the new monthly was interested in industrial employment for women, both intellectual and manual, the best methods for cautiously expanding the sphere of that employment, and the reform of the laws affecting the property and condition of the sexes.[12]

Bessie Parkes and Matilda M. Hays were the magazine's coeditors. Hays, a shadowy figure in the feminist circle, is known today only for her translations of the work of George Sand. She was primarily concerned with the *Journal's* literary content. In actuality Parkes and Bodichon determined editorial policy, while Hays remained in the background. Parkes assumed primary responsibility for the *Journal* because Bodichon spent at least half each year out of England.

The *Journal* reprinted speeches on women's issues and eagerly followed the reports of the law courts dealing with the working of the 1857 divorce law. The annual report of the Governesses Benevolent Institution was the basis of an article in the first issue describing the wretched situation of that ill-paid group of working women. In other issues campaigns were waged for improved physical education for girls and for the abolition of stays and the adoption of simpler feminine clothing.

Parkes asked George Eliot to contribute to the new periodical but beyond letters of advice got only a polite refusal. Eliot discussed the work of the magazine with Parkes and Bodichon but stated that she wished to devote her energies to her fiction.[13] Eliot described the *Journal* to a friend as "just middling." She confided: "Bessie has talent and real ardour for goodness, but I fear Miss Hays has been chosen on the charitable ground that she had nothing else to do in the world. There is something more piteous almost than soapless poverty in this application of feminine incapacity to literature."[14] The *Journal* depended for contributions on the nucleus of feminists who had made up the original Married Women's Property Committee. Bodichon sent articles from Algiers and directed *Journal* operations when she was in England. She shared Eliot's concerns regarding the literary quality of the *Journal*. Bodichon was pragmatic about its potential influence and was disturbed that Parkes overestimated its impact. She expected the magazine to serve the reform movement but worried that it might be destroyed by an insular self-righteousness and a lack of literary discipline. From Algiers she confided these concerns to Eliot, fearful of Parkes's ecstatic appraisals of the *Journal's* success.[15] They agreed after lengthy correspondence that Bodichon would have to offer some unpopular criticism on her next English visit.

Three features were common to every issue of the *Journal*. "Open Council" provided a forum for readers' opinions. "Passing Events" was devoted to news items about women and their individual achievements as well as legislative and court action affecting their legal status. "Notice of Books" concentrated on recently published books related to the women's movement but included more general literary items as well. Bodichon wished to be certain that the remainder of each issue included a small portion of well-written fiction or poetry but, more important, carefully argued nonfiction articles on women's issues that would not give already hostile antifeminists an excuse to ridicule the magazine. By December 1859 Eliot was more sanguine about the *Journal's* prospects and reassured Bodichon, back in Algiers for another winter, of her belief in the *Journal's* success: "The

English Woman's Journal must be doing good substantially – stimulating women to useful work and rousing people
generally to some consideration of women's needs."[16] The 1860
volume showed the balance Bodichon sought to achieve. It
included, in addition to the poem "A Lost Chord" by Adelaide
Proctor, an article by the respected educator W. B. Hodgson on
"The General Education of Women" and articles on "Medicine as
a Profession for Women" and "Employment of Women in Germany." Parkes always maintained that it had never been the intent
of the editors to compete with "the able monthlies" that boasted
the best writers of the day among their contributors. She asserted
that the search for popularity would have necessitated the aban-
donment of all dangerous subjects. Popularity was never the goal;
rather, the *Journal* was designed as a print platform for the infant
women's movement.[17]

Favorable press notices for the new magazine were patronizing
and stressed the special feminine qualities that merited praise.
Thus the *Daily News* noted its "perfect good taste" as well as a
tone of "high and deep humanity." The *Weekly Dispatch*
described it as "lofty in spirit, pure in sentiment and practical in
purpose," and the *Brighton Examiner* rejoiced "that the spirit and
intelligence of the softer sex are now becoming so effectually
aroused to the necessity of supplying deficiencies, and asserting
rights, in their proper sphere."[18] These praises pleased the *Journal's* editors who, despite their advocacy journalism, wished to
avoid the label of strong-mindedness. They proudly quoted
passages like these in their advertising pages. However, when
serious questions regarding expanding employment opportunities
for women were raised in the *Journal,* reactions were less
favorable. The *Saturday Review* was one of many journals to
echo the fear that the balance of an already overburdened and
limited labor market would be destroyed by the addition of
female workers.[19]

It was the issue of employment that spurred the *Journal's* editors to expand their activities. One of the most important columns in the magazine was "Open Council," which asked for readers' opinions on women's issues. Letters came from women in the provinces describing their own situations. Scores of unemployed governesses, needlewomen, widows, and orphans, suddenly thrown into the labor market impoverished and untrained, looked to the *Journal* for help. Confronted with the poignant reality, Parkes and Bodichon turned from writing articles to keeping an employment register. It was an inadequate beginning. On any given day twenty requests for employment might be received from women who only knew that they did not want to be governesses and asked for advice: "We had no sooner explained to the ladies who came on Thursday that the formation of model classes or businesses for a select number did not imply an ability on our part to find remunerative work for indiscriminate applicants, than the same task had to be gone over again on Friday."[20] The list of women seeking work grew, but few positions became available to them.

The difficulty of placement through the employment register was compounded by the fact that two distinct groups of women were applying for assistance and two problems existed. The first group consisted of "born and bred ladies" who were seeking professional employment. There was no question that class was a real distinction, and simple trades would not suffice for women of breeding.[21] The second group of women might be sustained through entry into semimechanical occupations such as printing, law copying, or telegraphy, but even that seemed an unattainable goal. Men went on strike when women entered their workshops.

In April 1859 Harriet Martineau brought the issue of "Female Industry" before the readers of the *Edinburgh Review.* Taking the themes of Bodichon's earlier contribution to the *Waverly Journal,* "Women and Work," for her own and echoing recent issues of the

English Woman's Journal, Martineau, assured of a wider
audience than those that other forums could attract, explored the
problem of female-employment alternatives. Her article focused
national attention on the issue.[22] Bessie Parkes took up the question at the October 1849 conference of the National Association
for the Promotion of Social Science. She read a paper on "The
Market for Educated Female Labour." To augment Parkes's
presentation, which dealt only with educated women, Jessie
Boucherett, a recent arrival among the London feminists,
delivered a paper on "The Industrial Employments of Women,"
describing work she had begun in Lincolnshire.

Boucherett (1825-1905), the youngest daughter of a Lincolnshire landowner, came to London inspired by Martineau's
"Female Industry."[23] She had read the *English Woman's Journal*
and arrived at its offices eager to join the staff. She wished to
found a society that might directly address the problems of
women seeking employment. The ebullient company at Cavendish Square welcomed Boucherett. The editors realized that their
employment register was inadequate, and by July 1859 a Society
for the Promotion of the Employment of Women had been
established.[24] Membership required a £5 donation. The honorary
secretaries were Jessie Boucherett and Adelaide Proctor.
Bodichon, Parkes, and Emily Faithfull served on an advisory
committee. In October 1859 the Society officially affiliated with
the Social Science Association at that organization's annual conference in Bradford. The *Journal* moved from Cavendish Square
to 19 Langham Place at the end of 1859, and the Society
established its headquarters there. Rooms were designated in that
building for a ladies' club, which included a dining room and a
library.[25]

No consideration of the *Journal* would be complete without an
analysis of the Society that grew out of it and shared its offices.
The women who edited and wrote the *Journal* built and operated

the Society, presented papers to the National Association for the Promotion of Social Science, and initiated practical experiments such as the Victoria Press to solve the problem of inadequate female employment opportunities. The work of the Society represented the first practical effort to prepare women of the lower middle classes for new occupations. After careful consideration the reformers chose to work first with lower-middle-class women. Parkes explained: "For highly educated women we could for a time do nothing; women of no education could do nothing for us, that is to say we could open no new channels for the labour of the former and our experiments would have failed owing to the inefficiency of the latter."[26]

Printing was the first trade considered. Despite the heavy work involved in presswork, it was determined that women could easily work as compositors. On March 25, 1860, the Victoria Press was opened by Emily Faithfull in Great Coram Street, Russell Square. It became the printer for the *Journal* and produced the yearly *Transactions* of the Social Science Association.[27]

Law copying was another area that could employ women. The Society opened a law stationer's office in Portugal Street, Lincoln's Inn, which began by employing and training female clerks.[28] In 1860 the Society opened a business school for young women, where they were taught to write letters, calculate without a slate, and keep accounts by single and double entry. Jessie Boucherett ran the school, which charged a shilling a week for instruction.[29] Since many women came from outside London and had no place to live while being trained, a Ladies' Institute was opened that accommodated fifty residents.

The initial projects of the Society made a small impact on the enormous pool of unemployed women. By 1862, when the controversy over what to do with redundant women was raging in the national press, many reformers concluded that female emigration was a major part of the solution.[30] By that time the Female

Middle Class Emigration Society had been established by Maria Rye as a subsidiary of the Society for the Promotion of the Employment of Women. Rye (1829-1903) had been a member of Bodichon's original Married Women's Property Committee and had organized the law-copying operation for the Society for the Promotion of the Employment of Women. Assisted by Jane Lewin, she organized immigration to Australia and New Zealand for numbers of lower-middle-class women.

The Society for the Promotion of the Employment of Women began to create a network of provincial chapters during its second year of operation. Emily Davies started a branch for the districts of Northumberland and Durham in Newcastle on October 24, 1860. Davies (1830-1921), the perennial secretary for almost every women's committee during the early days of organized feminism, was the daughter of a clergyman from Gateshead. In 1857, while on a trip to Algiers with an invalid brother, she met and became friendly with Barbara Bodichon's sisters. Davies's eldest brother, Llewelyn, had purchased a London home in Blandford Square in 1856, and Davies soon became a member of Bodichon's feminist circle. In January 1862 she moved with her widowed mother to a permanent London home. On July 18, 1862, Davies agreed to take on the editorship of the *English Woman's Journal* beginning with the September issue.[31] Bessie Parkes was restricting her active role in the feminist movement and wished to withdraw from the editorship. Throughout 1862 and 1863 Davies frequently corresponded with Bodichon about the troubled finances of the magazine. It was steadily losing money because quality contributors refused to write without payment and the circulation remained limited. In January 1863 Bodichon sent a check to cover rent and expenses, and it was agreed that serious consideration should be given to ending the publication when she arrived in England for the summer months.[32] Davies and Bodichon decided to end the failing periodical. Bickering among the Langham Place feminists in addition to financial problems made it impossible to continue. In 1864 the *Journal* ceased publication, and Davies became an editor of the new *Victoria Magazine,* which was published by Emily Faithfull at the Victoria Press. Parkes gave her support to the *Alexandra Magazine,* which attempted to supersede the *English Woman's Journal,* but Bodichon withdrew to concentrate on suffrage reform. Parkes retired from the project within a year when she contracted scarlet fever, and the *Alexandra* ended in little more than one year.[33]

The work of the Society for the Promotion of the Employment of Women progressed at Langham Place even after the cessation of the *Journal.* The feminist circle continued to function. Boucherett went on to become the first editor of the *Englishwoman's Review,* which began in 1866. As late as 1872 the Victoria Discussion Society, with Faithfull as chairman, held meetings on the question of female employment. Bodichon and Parkes contributed to the *Victoria Magazine,* the *Alexandra Magazine,* and the *Englishwoman's Review* but withdrew from all editorial responsibilities.

Special interests were beginning to divide feminists. Separate campaigns needed to be waged if progress toward improved education or increased political participation was to be achieved. Many reformers believed that only by opening these areas to women could employment opportunities be expanded. The Langhamites remained a loosely connected circle for decades, meeting one another in a variety of new feminist committees, each with roots in Bodichon's Married Women's Property Committee of 1856. Seventy-eight numbers of the *English Woman's Journal* were published during its six-year existence. Despite mediocre writing and steady financial losses, the *Journal's* pivotal role in the feminist movement is clear. The activities of the Langhamites coalesced around its offices. There they not only spoke and wrote about reform but also created the first concrete agencies to promote the change in women's legal and social status that took place during the second half of the nineteenth century. The *Journal* served the movement as a platform for ideas and linked feminists in the first women's network in Great Britain.

NOTES

1. Brian Harrison, "Press and Pressure Group in Modern Britain," in *The Victorian Periodical Press: Samplings and Soundings,* ed. Joanne Shattock and Michael Wolff (Toronto: University of Toronto Press, 1982), p. 282.

2. Bessie Rayner Parkes, "The Industrial Employment of Women." National Association for the Promotion of Social Science, *Transactions,* (1860) I:812.

3. Ibid.

4. Noel Gilroy Annan, "The Intellectual Aristocracy," in *Studies in Social History: A Tribute to G.M. Trevelyan,* ed. J. H. Plumb (London: Longmans, Green & Co., 1955), pp. 241-287.

5. See Margaret Oliphant, "Laws Concerning Women," *Blackwood's Edinburgh Magazine* 79 (April 1856): 379-380.

6. Mary Howitt, *Autobiography,* 2 vols. (Boston: Houghton Mifflin, 1889), II, p. 115.

7. Bessie Rayner Parkes, *Essays on Woman's Work,* 2d ed. (London: Alexander Strahan, 1866), p. 60.

8. Bessie Rayner Parkes, "A Review of the Last Six Years," *English Woman's Journal* 12 (October 1864): 364.

9. George Eliot to Bessie Parkes, 1 September 1857, *George Eliot Letters,* ed. Gordon Sherman Haight (New Haven, Connecticut: Yale University Press, 1954-1955) II, p. 379.

10. Parkes, "Review of the Last Six Years," p. 364.

11. *George Eliot Letters* II, p. 430.

12. *English Woman's Journal* I (March 1858): 75.

13. George Eliot to Bessie Parkes, 3 February 1858, *George Eliot Letters* II, p. 431.

14. George Eliot to Sara Hennell, 2 March 1858, *George Eliot Letters* II, p. 438.

15. Barbara Bodichon to George Eliot, 26 April 1859, *George Eliot Letters* III, p. 57.

16. George Eliot to Barbara Bodichon, 5 December 1859, *George Eliot Letters* III, pp. 225-226.

17. Parkes, "Review of the Last Six Years," p. 365.

18. *English Woman's Journal,* advertising page following p. 72 in 2 (September 1858).

19. "The *Saturday Review* and the *English Woman's Journal,*" *English Woman's Journal* 1 (May 1858): 202.

20. Parkes, "A Year's Experience in Women's Work," *English Woman's Journal* 6 (October 1860): 113-114.

21. Ibid., pp. 115-116.

22. Harriet Martineau, "Female Industry," *Edinburgh Review* (American Edition) 109 (April 1859): 151-173.

23. Jessie Boucherett, "The Industrial Movement," in *The Woman Question in Europe,* ed. Theodore Stanton (London: Sampson, Low, Marston, Searle & Rivington, 1884), p. 96.

24. National Association for the Promotion of Social Science, *Transactions,* 1860 (1861) I, p. xviii.

25. *English Woman's Journal* 6 (September 1860): 54-60.

26. *English Woman's Journal* 6 (November 1860): 147.

27. Emily Faithfull, "The Victoria Press," National Association for the Promotion of Social Science, *Transactions* (1860) 1, pp. 819-82.

28. Ibid., p. xix: "Annual Report of the Society for the Promotion of the Employment of Women."

29. "The Society for the Promotion of the Employment of Women," *English Woman's Journal* 5 (August 1860): 394.

30. See W. R. Greg, "Why Are Women Redundant?" *National Review* 14 (April 1862): 446.

31. Emily Davies, "Family Chronicle," p. 263a, Manuscript in Girton College Archives, Cambridge.

32. Two letters from Emily Davies to Barbara Bodichon, January 1863, Girton College Archives, Cambridge.

33. Davies, "Family Chronicle," pp. 288-291.

Barbara Quinn Schmidt

In the Shadow of Thackeray: Leslie Stephen as the Editor of the *Cornhill Magazine*

In 1859 George Murray Smith was unwilling to begin his proposed magazine unless William Makepeace Thackeray was involved because his writing was respected, popular, entertaining, and moral and would most likely attract the right audience. Several years later, Charles Dickens confirmed Smith's assessment when he wrote that the *Cornhill Magazine* had been accepted beforehand on the basis of Thackeray's name.[1] And when Anthony Trollope, who also wrote realistic novels of manners, was available to serve as the chief novelist, Thackeray became the editor.

As the editor, he insisted, "the magazine must bear my cachet."[2] He set a trend with the title, and the cover he chose helped create a sense of good fun. From the first issue of January 1860, Thackeray began a series of informal chats between the editor and the reader. Using the familiar essay mode that gave him free rein for his emotions, his *Roundabout Papers* helped immeasurably to establish the successful, sophisticated tone of the *Cornhill*. In order to soften the effect of the criticism inherent in those lay sermons, Thackeray provided a narrator, a man of the world who was able to merge wisdom with nostalgia and mellowness as he would at a dinner party, telling anecdotes, frankly admitting his prejudices, making moral and social pronouncements, and commenting sympathetically on the contradictions and the caprice of everyday life. Spencer Eddy stated:

All those descriptive words which critics have used to define the tone and character of these *Roundabout* essays — charm, warmth, sentimentality, nostalgia, natural discursiveness, compactness, gentle humor, authorial pronouncement, autobiographical confession, wit, sustained harmonic tone, topicality, felicity of detail and allusion — are present from the start.[3]

This series of essays was among Thackeray's greatest writing and certainly his best in the magazine. Leslie Stephen praised the *Roundabout Papers* as "models of the essay which without aiming for profundity, gave the charm of the graceful and tender conversation of a great writer."[4] The sporadic continuation of such essays remained a hallmark of the *Cornhill* even when written by Stephen, James Payn, and, in the next century, Anne Thackeray Ritchie.

Thackeray's buoyant enthusiasm and excitement at being the editor certainly brought smiles to the recipients of his letters during those early months. Consequently, he was able to cajole the literary elite, even Alfred Tennyson, into submission. Contributors were "to tell what they know, pretty briefly and good humouredly," not "in a manner too obviously didactic."[5] Thackeray expected "Good manners, good education and good English," with an awareness that "ladies and children are always present." When experienced writers who were not gentlemen contributed, Thackeray carefully reworked their offerings. "The ideal of the middle class gentleman was held up for imitation."[6] "A gentleman," Thackeray wrote in *The Book of Snobs*, "is to be honest, to be gentle, to be generous, to be brave, to be wise, and, possessing all these qualities, to exercise them in the most graceful outward manner."[7]

Thackeray and Trollope believed that the social stability of England depended on social change being controlled or managed by leaders who were gentlemen whose consciously moral behavior provided a way of living that was challenging and consoling. Both writers sought to enrich the human spirit rather than to improve the material environment or reform society by means of the application of principles of truth, justice, and kindness wisely administered. By writing about the humaneness, including the failures, of clergymen, Trollope eased the anxiety about rising religious doubt among the readers. The collapse of faith need not result in the disintegration of morality and society.

Desiring to make his readers feel good, Thackeray avoided anxiety-building moral controversy but not all controversy, for that would be dull. As long as there was a lightness of touch rather than an argumentative stance, he believed the audience would accept gentlemanly disagreement suitable to a "man of the world Magazine."[8] Some controversy was good for circulation. If people talked about ideas expressed in the *Cornhill,* they could not ignore its existence. But having just the right quantity of controversy was not easy to achieve. There was a fine line between a sophisticated debunking of commonplaces and an attacking of cherished social beliefs. Thus readers forced a premature end to Ruskin's *Unto This Last;* artistic stature was no protection from reader outrage.

In an attempt to broaden the general knowledge of the readers, Thackeray wanted experts to write informative essays about their professions. This tactic appealed to the middle-class pride in work and the desire for knowledge. Although he sought to stimulate readers intellectually, he feared that ideas that were expressed too stridently would alienate them by appearing vulgar.

Seeking a sophisticated, urbane tone, he unabashedly identified himself with the London point of view,[9] thereby denying that urban living could be a social problem. He celebrated its congenial aspects, making frequent reference to the *Cornhill* as a banquet at which the readers were guests.

The public responded enthusiastically, making the *Cornhill* fashionable, but fashion is fickle. The initial phenomenal circulation of 110,000 copies did not last. Fewer copies were sold each month because the conception of the magazine as a miscellany with fiction, literary essays, superb illustrations, and an attractive cover being both dramatically different and suitable for family enjoyment and education was too much to deliver regularly, especially once so many imitators were in the field and the number of skilled journalists did not grow proportionately. Unfortunately, guaranteeing that nothing would offend led to an inevitable blandness. Security replaced excitement, but even so, many readers were satisfied with the best that was available on safe themes, and the magazine continued to sell well.

Even without Thackeray and Trollope, it retained quality but lacked originality. With George Henry Lewes, Frederick Greenwood, and Dutton Cook as successive editors, Smith suceeded in keeping the *Cornhill's* reputation among the best but was unable to recapture the initial spark. Smith consistently selected a variety of novelists, often major ones, but none appeared regularly. In fact, most of the seventeen novels by major writers that appeared in the *Cornhill* did so under his direction. Yet circulation declined to 25,000, and so in 1871 Smith sought a new editor and something of a new direction.

Leslie Stephen, who first appeared in the *Cornhill* in 1866 with "American Humour," was a man of ability who sought the assistance of the right man at the right time. In order not to disappoint his father who had his heart set on one of his sons becoming a clergyman, Leslie, being the youngest and lacking career plans of his own, obliged and took Holy Orders. When he discovered his lack of belief and consequently left his post at Cambridge, he sought the help of his only surviving brother who found him employment as a journalist for the same periodicals that Fitz-james himself regularly wrote for, one of which was the *Cornhill*. In 1871 Leslie was offered the editorship of *Fraser's,* which, like the *Fortnightly,* published his more serious work. Yet he sought Smith's advice and was promptly offered the *Cornhill* with a salary of £500, one fourth of Thackeray's. Smith was often impulsive and did not like to lose valued workers, and so if Stephen wanted to be an editor, why not of the *Cornhill?* Stephen "accepted the more willingly from its connection with Thackeray,"[10] whose *Vanity Fair* was the first book Stephen had ever purchased and whose daughter was Stephen's wife. Thus Leslie Stephen, a man unsure of himself, relied on others' good judgment for his own success.

Smith's reasons for hiring Stephen as the editor of the *Cornhill* were based on the latter's connection with Thackeray, on his skill as an essayist, and on his good sense. Even before he was the editor, he "had much influence with the proprietor"[11] and therefore suggested that Meredith's *The Adventures of Harry Richmond* appear in the magazine. "At that time to be serialized in *The Cornhill* meant success for a novelist."[12] The series of a dozen sketches by "A Cynic," published from May 1869 to the beginning of his editorship, "were full of Stephen's genius of common sense, his quaint humour, his dislike for extravagance, his disgust for false sentiment and artificial gush."[13] These qualilties were not unlike those of Thackeray; thus Smith may have hoped that, at long last, he had found an editor of equal merit in persuading the public to buy.

Unlike Thackeray's editorship, Stephen's was not noted for its quantity of good serial fiction at least partially because large sums of money were no longer available to pay novelists. Smith carefully trimmed costs to match sales. In addition to continuing serial novels, Stephen added more short fiction, much of it excellent, and a variety of articles on noncontroversial subjects, especially concerning travels to exotic places. He wrote to James Russell Lowell: "I hope I shall make some of my articles more intrinsically valuable."[14] He did succeed in establishing the quality literary essay as paramount.

Fearing that the religious doubts of middle-class urban Victorians might weaken the moral fiber of society, he was cautious rather than supportive or adventuresome. He protected the audience from controversy in the *Cornhill* because he did not appreciate the value of controversy. He realized the importance of applying a light touch to his essays and made frequent use of irony. But Stephen did not understand that the audience would far prefer to be mildly shocked, so they could have an interesting topic of conversation at dinner parties, than to be always treated with great care as one would treat a maiden aunt. Although they knew they could count on the *Cornhill's* consistent good taste, on a deeper level they found such regularity uninteresting. To appeal to casual readers, Stephen offered romance fiction and noncontroversial essays whose titles did not promise exciting new information.

The product of a vigorously Christian home—his father gave up smoking because he enjoyed it—Stephen had little empathy for those just passing the time. Recreation was to have a purpose. For him climbing the Alps was a spiritually and a physically refreshing experience. Like Thackeray, he was sensitive and emotional, but he masked his feelings to the detriment of his writing and his health. The heartiness of Thackeray's good cheer and the poignancy of his nostalgia for the past were not present to Stephen, whose muted feelings, at first glance, may have appeared bland and somewhat dull or ironic and distant.

The magazine's initial success had come partially because it encouraged readers to hope. Through reading Trollope's novels, especially *Framley Parsonage,* and Thackeray's *Roundabout Papers,* readers gained insight into human behavior while they were encouraged to strive for higher personal moral standards. However, Stephen did not offer a possibility for happier living. He saw such programs as they appeared in novels to be humbug, full of sentimentality and preaching or pamphleteering.

> . . . a novel with a purpose means a book setting forth that a villain is hanged and a good man presented with a thousand pounds—that is silly and really immoral; for, in the first place, the imaginary event is no guarantee for the real event; secondly, a particular case does not prove a rule; thirdly, it is not true that virtue is always rewarded and vice punished; and fourthly, virtue should not be inculcated with a simple view to money or the gallows.[15]

He did not condemn all writers' moralizing, only moralizing that was poorly handled.

> Instead of leaving their readers to be affected by the morality which permeated the whole structure and substance of their poetry, they chose to extract little nuggets of moral platitudes, and so far failed.[16]

Ultimately art was not amoral:

> Art is the means by which the men who feel most strongly and think most powerfully appeal to the passions of their weaker brethren. To say that they produce no moral effect is to say that they produce no effect at all, and the proposition is about as absurd as to say that example has never any influence upon practice.[17]

For Stephen a writer was obligated to provide ethical direction in his work. Oscar Maurer maintains that "the *Cornhill* under Stephen made no concessions to the nascent 'Aesthetic Movement.' "[18] Thus his essays written about the relationship between art and morality are among his most vehement and the closest he came to controversy in the *Cornhill.* Although an agnostic, he was a firm believer in morality and its importance to the fabric of society. Like Thackeray before him, he was a frequent preacher of lay sermons.

The mid-1870s for Stephen was a time for careful analysis and facing the truth, but that meant reading the controversial, thought-provoking articles in *Fraser's* and the *Fortnightly* and writing some of his own. But neither of these magazines was directed to the family. And Stephen considered the *Cornhill's* policy to be sacrosanct: "What can one make," he moaned, "of a magazine which excludes the only subjects in which reasonable men take any interest: politics and religion?"[19] Therefore it should not have been surprising to him that he was not successful in pleasing; after all he did not seem to believe that as the editor he had the right to alter the editorial policy established by Thackeray. How could such timidity be popular?

In deprecating Stephen, Noel Annan argued,

A good editor should have a flair for sensing changes in public taste and Stephen, preoccupied with his own writing, was too content to run in the old grooves. The *Cornhill* public were tired of the serialized novel, and wanted less solid reading, a more ephemeral magazine for half-hour snatches between the games, amusements and new pastimes which the late Victorian age was discovering.[20]

As an alternative, Stephen contributed to a Queen Anne revival in essays and verse in the magazine because he believed the eighteenth century was one "of sound common sense and growing toleration, and of steady social and industrial development."[21] Studying the past by providing an understanding of society's evolution and a guarded optimism for its continued progress helped one face the present or the future. Stephen's clear analysis of this process appears to advantage in *English Literature and Society in the Eighteenth Century,* the last five pages of which name the specific changes in thinking by Scott, Burns, Wordsworth, and Coleridge that separated them from their predecessors. However, this approach did not have general appeal.

Writers' attitudes pervaded their books and had a lasting effect on readers, according to Stephen. "Biography and the novel show life in motion, but they help us to appreciate its significance."[22] Stephen claimed that the novelist was "the true historian of the time. He tries to show us, as clearly as his powers allow, the real moving forces in the great tragi-comedy of human life."[23] Unfortunately, he lamented, no great novelists were writing during his years as the magazine's editor. Yet from 1860 through the end of the century, the *Cornhill* published all the major novelists except Dickens and George Moore and provided a more representative sample of Victorian fiction than any other magazine. And Stephen himself published Thomas Hardy and Henry James.

Stephen believed it to be his duty to provide analyses of contemporary and earlier novelists that pointed out their contributions to social evolution. Through depicting social history a novelist could strive to show the unchanging aspects of mankind, providing a kind of historical security. If things have always been in flux even though people do not realize it, then life has the potential to continue indefinitely, albeit evolving slowly. Muddling through somehow, the human species will show itself fit to survive. Stephen insisted on the necessity of preserving a firmly based science of ethics in which the mode of conduct adapted itself to a changing environment. Caution was essential since he believed that great harm could come from undermining the religious beliefs and consequently the moral behavior of most people. Although Stephen believed that old doctrines were being abandoned, "What is to be the religion of the future? I have not the slightest idea."[24] "It exists only in germ."[25] And

for the present a man who would abandon the old doctrines is compelled to stand alone. He must find sufficient comfort in the consciousness that he is dealing honestly with his intellect; he must be able to dispense with the old consolations of heaven and hell. . . . Undoubtedly, this is to accept a position from which many people will shrink.[26]

Regardless, people need to be "true to themselves and gentle to their neighbors."[27]

I would not conceal my own views, but neither could I feel anxious to thrust them upon others; and that for the very simple reason that conversion appears to me to be an absurdity. You cannot change a man's thoughts about things as you can change the books in his library. The mind is not a box which can have opinions inserted and extracted at pleasure. No belief is good for anything which is not part of an organic growth and the natural product of a man's mental development under the various conditions in which he is placed. To promote his intellectual activity, to encourage him to think, and to put him in the way of thinking rightly, is a plain duty; but to try to insert ready-made opinions into his mind by dint of authority is to contradict the fundamental principles of free inquiry.[28]

Stephen expressed the dilemma of preserving a delicate balance: One should not attack established religion unless offering something in its place, but one should not ignore it and make the mistake of thinking it harmless. As a writer he found it easy enough to express ideas such as those in magazines directed toward an intelligent audience and to write urbane, witty literary essays to entertain and educate the *Cornhill's* less thoughtful readers. But it was harder for him to be at ease as an editor avoiding conundrums unsuitable to the magazine's audience. To call him a hypocrite is too facile because he was too much of an earnest seeker of the truth and enough of a poet to see the ambiguities in any belief.

Oscar Maurer, in contrast, maintains that Stephen did not feel "reluctance to unsettle people's beliefs,"[29] explaining instead that it was more a matter of a proper medium. However, I believe that he envisioned two audiences: thoughtful readers used to controversy and thoughtless readers who could be confused and distressed by the loss of their outworn creed without a meaningful replacement. Thackeray and Trollope had emphasized that change required moral, gentlemanly leaders and a cohesive community. By Stephen's time the question of leading to *what* became paramount. And the manner was important to both periods.

Writers were especially to avoid morbidity and disease, diligently seeking and preserving healthy minds and bodies.[30]

Noel Annan takes a different perspective in criticizing Stephen: Because Stephen's taste often coincided with that of his public, "he had to be careful, since his religious views and his politics were not those of a gentleman writing for gentlemen."[31] In contrast, Maurer excuses the discrepancy he sees between practice and belief as Stephen's loyalty to his publisher, his deference to his readers' feelings, and his consequent fear of following his own lights.[32] Whatever the reasons, in practice Stephen exercised caution rather than innovative leadership.

Although he maintained that an author's ethics were revealed in his work, Stephen strenuously sought to compartmentalize his own thought, and as an additional safeguard, he was quite reticent about being known as the editor; his name was not mentioned in advertisements or on the title page. Although recruited and groomed by Stephen, W. E. Norris, one of the more talented short story writers and frequent contributors, discovered after writing for the magazine for over a year "the identify of my editorial patron."[33] Norris remembered,

as an editor, he was not indulgent. He himself was at infinite trouble over the discharge of his duties, and he did not mind calling upon his contributors to be equally painstaking. More than once he made me re-write whole chapters, and often I was required—a little against the grain I must confess—to strike out passages or incidents which he thought likely to jar upon the susceptibilities of his readers. One's tidyness used to come back scrawled all over with alternatives and emendations in his diminutive script, which was not always over-legible . . . it was difficult for him to keep his hands off anybody's manuscript.[34]

Stephen complained to Norris that "he was conscious of an inability to discern the shifting currents of public taste."[35] Yet he was alert to their desire for more short fiction.

The areas he was most sensitive about were those that also proved difficult for Thackeray: sexual morality and religion. In general, the fiction was uncritical of religion and even reflected a bias toward the Church of England.[36] But he had to cut short Arnold's *Literature and Dogma* series because of its religious content. To encourage readers to learn from the past and from nonagnostic writers, Stephen examined other authors' views in his literary criticisms. Thackeray had used his *Roundabout Papers* as a forum for expressing his own opinions about life directly.

Like Thackeray, Stephen was very fearful of offending young ladies. Sir Edward Cook remembered: "Thou shalt not shock a young lady: this Leslie Stephen used to say was the first editorial commandment; nor shock accepted creeds either."[37] Thus he changed words as well as chapters and ideas in manuscripts. His work with Thomas Hardy is an excellent example of his procedure and of his unresolved conflict between allowing artistic integrity and fearing an adverse effect on public morality.

Stephen sought work from Hardy for the *Cornhill* but cautioned, "it is necessary to catch the attention of readers by some distinct and well-arranged plot."[38] Shortly after the appearance of the first installment of Hardy's *Far from the Madding Crowd* in January 1874, Stephen, who was extremely sensitive to criticism, felt compelled to write Hardy,

that an unexpected Grundian cloud, though no bigger than a man's hand as yet, had appeared on our serene horizon. Three respectable ladies and subscribers, representing he knew not how many more, had written to upbraid him for an improper passage in a page of the story which had already been published.[39]

Hardy responded to the criticism with dismay and inquired why Stephen had not altered the text before publishing. " 'I suppose I ought to have foreseen these gentry, and have omitted it,' he murmured."[40] His specific alterations of what he knew was an excellent novel ("I am sorry that the 'Madding Crowd' has come to an end"[41]) irritated his own critical sense, but he did offer valuable assistance as well. Having looked at the editorial corrections in the manuscript, James Purdy has called Stephen the finest critic that Hardy encountered in his career as a novelist.[42]

To what extent Smith insisted on the *Cornhill's* slavishly following the Grundian path is unknown. Maurer explains that

When Stephen became editor, Smith apparently relaxed his direct control over the magazine; and yet it was Smith who turned down Meredith's *Beauchamp's Career,* in 1874, as not "good for the market." On the whole, however, Stephen was given a free hand.[43]

Stephen was definitely satisfied with his working relationship. He wrote to Charles Eliot Norton in 1876:

One of the best pieces of luck that I have had is in finding an employer like G. S., who is also a warm friend and a thorough gentleman. I might have been in bondage to the Xs or 'Y and Z'! The Lord be praised for my escape![44]

Yet after Smith's death, Stephen reflected on their relationship and mused:

our great advantage of the *Cornhill* was that George Smith, already a valued friend, was the most considerate of proprietors and treated me with, if anything, an excess of confidence. Otherwise, perhaps, I might have been less content to stick in old ruts. The brilliant youth of the periodical was over; it had rivals, and we kept pretty much to our traditions; we did not dazzle the world by any new sensations.[45]

Stephen regretted Smith's not telling him sooner of the continued decline in sales and may have wished he had more awareness of the handling of the business affairs. But what might be have done differently?

Stephen exercised editorial power easily enough in accepting or rejecting manuscripts upon first reading, alert to the effect a work might have on his readers. Thus instead of the truth being explicitly stated about Fanny's illegitimate baby in *Far from the*

Madding Crowd, it was merely whispered by one character into another's ear. As Maurer has noted,

And no direct mention is made, in the serial version, of the fact that on opening the coffin Bathsheba finds not only the unfortunate Fanny but also the illegitimate child. In revising for publication in book form, Hardy clarified this episode; he also made numerous verbal changes, mainly in the dialogue of the rustics, which show the restraint imposed in the serial. For example, "gross," "wicked," and "sinful," in the *Cornhill,* became "lewd," "loose," and "bawdy," in the book.[46]

Not wishing to appear hypocritical, Stephen explained his position to Hardy:

I have ventured to leave out a line or two in the last batch of proofs . . . from an excessive prudery of which I am ashamed; but one is forced to be absurdly particular. May I suggest that Troy's seduction of the young woman will require to be treated in a gingerly fashion when, as I suppose must be the case, he comes to be exposed to his wife? I mean that the thing must be stated, but that the words must be careful. Excuse this wretched shred of concession to popular stupidity; but I am a slave.[47]

It must have been far easier to hide behind prudery than to suggest to an author that he might damage the morals of young women!

The effects of his censorship on behalf of public morals cannot be fully established, but most of the novels that appeared in the *Cornhill* were bland or sardonic in their attitude toward particular events and happenings within the framework of the story. Whether he, on the whole, accepted only the tamer stories or whether he toned them down is not known; nor is it known at what point novelists fully realized, if ever, the limitations on content expected by the editor of the *Cornhill.* As the rate of pay declined because of the circulation, the best paid novelists were Margaret Oliphant and Anne Thackeray, both frequent contributors. Stephen also introduced to the *Cornhill* W. E. Norris, Richard D. Blackmore, Eliza Lynn Linton, William Black, and

Grant Allen, all of the second rank, and his Cambridge friend Robert E. Francillon, Margaret Veley, and other third-rate writers, continuing the pattern of variety begun in the early years. And somewhat surprisingly, Stephen wrote in the preface to the posthumous collection of Margaret Veley's poetry that her novel *For Percival,* which had appeared in the *Cornhill,* showed "true literary distinction, a graceful, clear, and pointed style, a strong sense of humour, and a keen perception of character approached by few of her contemporaries."[48] Truly, in writing such an essay he had to pay compliments, but are these simply kind words? They seem to suggest that Stephen had different standards for judging popular fiction.

Certain patterns emerged in the *Cornhill* fiction that were typical of popular middle-class magazines: The heroes were preponderantly gentlemen, and the stories were based on the life and expectations of either the landed gentry or the professional middle class. Money and the ways of acquiring it continued as important themes. No female characters had much education, and few male characters worked with their muscles.

Samuel Jones Tindall has suggested that Anne Thackeray's *Old Kensington,* the only novel to appear several months without a rival serial running concurrently, met Stephen's editorial standards.

Its quietness must have been, to this man of cultivated tastes, a welcome relief from the sensationalism of many of the other stories. The nostalgia for the time some two decades past and for the old suburb of Kensington, now spoiled by the stream of progress, is genuine and moving; the descriptions of the quiet old neighborhood are evocative; and the setting is perfectly suited to the subdued action of the story, in which the toss of a handful of snow is a major incident. Thus, Stephen's regard for a strong feeling of time and place in a novel must have been well satisfied by Old Kensington.[49]

It also appealed to his need for tranquility. He sought quiet repose at the shore or in his beloved Alps as often as possible, but such works soothed him when he was unable to take a vacation. Smith also admired the book so much that he named a sailing ship after it.

Henry James was the only other first-rate novelist to appear in the *Cornhill* under Stephen, and James, who became famous following the appearance of *Daisy Miller* in the magazine in 1878, was acutely conscious of an audience. Leon Edel believes that James feared

there had been, perhaps, a little too much laughter at Daisy Miller's expense in England, and Henry did not want to appear in the invidious role of a satirist to the English world of Americans abroad. His suspicions were borne out by a review of "An International Episode" (after it had appeared in the *Cornhill*).[50]

There was no such problem concerning *Washington Square,* which required no judicious editing, and Tindall believes that it

is probably the ideal *Cornhill* novel: original and strong in character portrayal, humanly significant in action, and devoid of any questions of decorum, it must have seemed to Stephen the work he had been waiting for as editor of a popular literary magazine. Unfortunately . . . it is doubtful that James' excellent little novel increased the sales of the *Cornhill*.[51]

The magazine's audience enjoyed James's criticism of America but not his criticism of England and found *Washington Square* lacking in event.

The third major writer to appear during Stephen's editorship, Robert Louis Stevenson, proved to be the most popular, contributing primarily essays and a few stories regularly for over seven years. On balance, few major works of fiction appeared during Stephen's time; excellent essays provided the basis for the *Cornhill's* continued high stature, and he himself wrote approximately one fourth of them. In fact, Stephen's work can be said, according to Tindall,

to provide the nucleus of the magazine: around it he built, from the contributions of other critics, a periodical unsurpassed at the time in quality of literary criticism. Stephen himself sets the standard. His own work consistently meets the rigorous criteria he has established, and of his contributors he demanded work of comparable quality—for, if he was to maintain the excellence of the *Cornhill* primarily by means of its critical offerings, he had to insure first-rate quality in every essay, both his own and other writers.[52]

Maurer insists that Stephen ranked "next to Arnold, the most useful of Victorian critics" because of his logical good sense and clear simple style.[53] Stephen also introduced Edmund Gosse, Sidney Colvin, Andrew Lang, Kegan Paul, and J. T. Fields to the *Cornhill* audience. Their talents were recognizable to readers because Stephen established the practice of initialed and, later, signed articles in the magazine. Stephen actually may have been more comfortable working with essayists because the readers of essays were not likely to be young ladies; therefore writers could be freer, although Stephen carefully pruned inappropriate words and phrases that were restored when the essays were collected. Readers of essay collections were likely to be thoughtful readers able to handle such material. Stephen may have selected essays for the thoughtful readers and novels for the casual ones and avoided the vulgar readers at all costs. Stephen regretted that

I have never clearly discovered what it is that attracts the average reader. Many popular authors would suffer considerably, and at least one obscure writer would gain, if everybody took my view of their merits . . . . Books succeed, I hold, because they ought to succceed. A critic has no business to assume that taste is bad because he does not share it. His business is to accept the fact and try to discover the qualities to which it is due.[54]

As he admitted, his talent lay in interpreting taste and popularity after the fact. His two multivolume collections, *Hours in a Library* and *Studies of a Biographer,* attest to this.

The high caliber literary criticism and biographies he wrote and chose for the *Cornhill* did not provide the basis for the popularity of a family magazine. Such an audience sought entertainment and trend-setting ideas. Because he could not please enough of the Victorian public to keep up circulation, the latter dipped to 12,000. Stephen believed that the *Cornhill* could not appeal to a divided audience. Instead of seeking new marketing techniques, he sought identity for the magazine in its contents: It must either become serious and emphasize the essay, including such topics as politics and religion, or become popular. Stephen expressed his preference for making it a serious magazine like the *Fortnightly,* but that, he was aware, would "frighten away all our old readers."[55]

At Stephen's suggestion, Smith replaced him in 1882 with James Payn and directly appealed to the popular audience; instead of trying to enlighten as well as entertain, the *Cornhill* would simply entertain at a cheaper price with fewer pieces and, as a result, fewer contributors to pay. The plotted story, light and entertaining, became a standard feature, but it alienated Stephen's audience and did not attract a large new one.

Thus in contrast to Thackeray who promoted his ideal of the gentleman as successfully incorporating the essence of social stability, Stephen saw himself as a moral gentleman who was obliged to be a cautious watchdog of mores and an earnest guardian of scholarship. He was determined to live and die a gentleman, doing no harm to the moral fiber of society; his policy at the *Cornhill* was, on the whole, too conservative and cautious, although he did bring the literary essay to a higher art and increased the amount of short fiction to appeal to the popular demand for shorter pieces. But he was responding rather than leading.

NOTES

1. Charles Dickens, "In Memoriam. Thackeray," *Cornhill Magazine* IX (1864): 130.

2. J. W. Robertson Scott, *The Story of the Pall Mall Gazette* (London: Oxford University Press, 1950), p. 65.

3. Spencer Eddy, *The Founding of the Cornhill Magazine* (Muncie, Ind.: Ball State University Press, 1970), p. 44

4. Scott, p. 79.

5. Ibid., p. 67. Thackeray's comment on good manners is from this source.

6. Gordon Ray, *Thackeray: The Age of Wisdom, 1847-1863* (New York: McGraw-Hill Book Company, 1958), p. 301.

7. As quoted by Joseph E. Baker, "The Adventures of Philip," in *Thackeray: A Collection of Critical Essays,* ed. Alexander Welsh (Englewood Cliffs, N.J.: Prentice-Hall, 1968), p. 164

8. Scott, p. 65.

9. Ray, p. 337.

10. Frederic William Maitland, *The Life and Letters of Leslie Stephen* (New York: G. P. Putnam's Sons, 1906), p. 257.

11. Siegfried Sassoon, *Meredith* (New York: The Viking Press, 1948), p. 106.

12. Ibid., p. 106.

13. Frederic Harrison, "Sir Leslie Stephen In Memoriam," *Cornhill Magazine,* n.s., XVI (1904): 442.

14. "To J. R. Lowell," 20 February 1871, in Maitland, p. 225.

15. Leslie Stephen, "Art and Morality," *Cornhill Magazine* XXXII (1875): 101.

16. Ibid., p. 96.

17. Ibid., p. 91.

18. Oscar Maurer, "Leslie Stephen and *The Cornhill Magazine,* 1871-82," Univ. of Texas *Studies in English* XXXII (1953): 77.

19. Maitland, pp. 257-58.

20. Noel G. Annan, *Leslie Stephen: His Thought and Character in Relation to His Time* (London: MacGibbon & Kee, 1951), p. 76.

21. Harrison, p. 444.

22. Annan, p. 223.

23. Leslie Stephen, "The Moral Element of Literature," *Cornhill Magazine* XLIV (1881): 37.

24. Leslie Stephen, "The Religion of All Sensible Men," in *An Agnostic's Apology and Other Essays* (London: Smith, Elder & Co., 1903), p. 355.

25. Ibid., p. 364.

26. Ibid., pp. 364-65.

27. Ibid., p. 365.

28. Ibid., p. 363.

29. Maurer, p. 85.

30. Bruce Haley, *The Healthy Body and Victorian Culture* (Cambridge, Mass.: Harvard University Press, 1978), pp. 50-68, passim.

31. Annan, p. 52.

32. Maurer takes a kinder view of the disparity between Stephen's beliefs and his actions as the magazine's editor. See Maurer, p. 67, where he explains Stephen's "loyalty to his publisher" and "deference to the feelings (moral or theological) of his readers."

33. W. E. Norris, "Leslie Stephen, Editor," *Cornhill Magazine*, n.s., XXVIII (1910): 47.

34. Norris, pp. 48-49.

35. As quoted in Norris, p. 49.

36. R. W. Hyde, "The Short Story in the *Cornhill Magazine*, 1860-1900: A Study in Form and Content," Diss. George Peabody College for Teachers, 1966, p. 52.

37. Sir Edward Cook, "Fifty Years of a Literary Magazine," in *Literary Recreations* (London: Macmillan & Co., 1919), p. 89.

38. "To Thomas Hardy," December 1872, in Maitland, p. 271.

39. Ibid., p. 275.

40. Ibid.

41. Ibid.

42. As quoted by Arthur Frederick Minerof, "Thomas Hardy's Novels: A Study in Critical Reception and Author Response, 1871-1903," Diss. New York University, 1963, p. 76.

43. Maurer, p. 69.

44. "To Charles Eliot Norton," 3 December 1876, in Maitland, p. 295.

45. Leslie Stephen, *Some Early Impressions* (London: The Hogarth Press, 1924), p. 143.

46. Maurer, p. 86.

47. Maitland, pp. 274-75.

48. Leslie Stephen, "Preface," *A Marriage of Shadows and Other Poems* by Margaret Veley (London: Smith, Elder & Co., 1888), p. x.

49. Samuel Jones Tindall, "Leslie Stephen as Editor of the *Cornhill Magazine*," Diss. University of S. Carolina, 1969, p. 177.

50. Leon Edel, *Henry James: 1870-81. The Conquest of London* (Philadelphia: J. B. Lippincott Co., 1962), p. 316.

51. Tindall, p. 183.

52. Ibid., p. 28.

53. Maurer, p. 78.

54. Stephen, *Some Early Impressions*, p. 146.

55. Maitland, p. 354.

Part Two

THE CONTEXT OF EDITING

Christopher Kent

The Editor and the Law

The editor, both in title and function, is essentially a nineteenth-century creation. Walter Bagehot claimed that the "trade of editorship" was virtually invented by Francis Jeffrey of the *Edinburgh Review:* "before him an editor was a bookseller's drudge."[1] Indeed, the word itself was new: The earliest use in its modern sense cited in the *OED* is 1802. Yet it was not long before Carlyle declared that "the true Church of England at this moment lies in the editors of its newspapers," and even Mr. Pott, the editor of the *Eatanswill Gazette,* solemnly assured Mr. Pickwick that "I trust, Sir, . . . that I have never abused the enormous power I wield."[2] So quickly did the editor become a central feature of the literary landscape that it was hard to imagine his absence, and as Leslie Stephen noted, even the historically sensitive Thackeray introduced an editor into the eighteenth-century world of *Henry Esmond,* quite unaware that he was making a considerable anachronism.[3] Yet any Victorian editor, intoxicated by

Carlyle's definition or Trollope's "Tom Towers" of the *Jupiter,* would have been quickly sobered by a consideration of what the law had to say about himself: it said virtually nothing. Certainly it gave him no fixed legal status.

This eloquent silence was not a calculated legal affront as much as a corollary of the attitude of the law toward the periodical press in general. The press was no fourth estate of the realm but a branch of commerce, though one with unusual potential for political mischief. Rather than ringing statements about freedom of the press such as one finds, for instance, in the United States Constitution, British law offers the cooling dictum of Lord Chief Justice Mansfield: "To be free is to live under government by law. The liberty of the press consists in printing without any previous licence, subject to the consequences of the law."[4] "Previous licence" refers to official censorship, a practice that had been abandoned in England at the end of the seventeenth century. From that time on most of the attention the press received from the law on matters of content came via the laws of libel.

Libel, broadly the offense of publishing defamatory statements in permanent form, is an offense punishable under either the civil or the criminal law.[5] In the former case it is the subject of private action by the libeled seeking damages from the libeler for injury to his good name. In the latter it is treated as a public crime, a provocation of the libeled to commit a breach of the peace to defend or vindicate his good name by violence. Here the punishment may be a fine or imprisonment. Yet another category of criminal libel virtually moribund today but once very important is the "disorderly libel," the publication of sentiments injurious not to any particular person but to the state itself because it is likely to provoke disorder or to outrage public feeling. The three disorderly libels are seditious, blasphemous, and obscene. These, particularly the first two, constituted the main grounds of legal pressure on journalism until about the end of the nineteenth century.

Since prosecutions for libel required the identification of specific individuals legally responsible for them, they brought out sharply the question of the authority structure of journalism. From the practical standpoint of enforcement it was most convenient to take the commercial view of the matter and see the proprietor and the printer as the most responsible persons in the publication process since they seemed the most easily identified and the most vulnerable in terms of having property at risk. The actual author of the libel was the least easily identifiable person under the well-entrenched convention of anonymity. The editor was often regarded as merely someone hired by the proprietor and thus his servant: He might easily be a straw man or a sacrificial figure. It has been suggested that the editor originated in the late eighteenth century as a convenient front man for the real authority, the printer, absorbing or deflecting complaints and abuse.[6] The publisher seems to have been the most shadowy figure of all, legally and practically. The law never offered any clear definition of this position, though it imposed certain legal responsibilities on him and required that his name and address, along with the printer's, be printed on each issue of a newspaper. It is evident that the publisher so named was quite often a nominal position, a person of no authority, though here it was perhaps less a matter of willful deception than of the fact that for many periodicals the position was practically meaningless. As for the proprietor, even his identity could be fairly easily concealed in the absence of fully effective registration procedures.[7] The printer then was a prime target, and particularly in the nervous late eighteenth and early nineteenth centuries, considerable legislation was devoted to identifying and monitoring his activities. Finally by an act of 1836 any defendent in a civil libel suit could be ordered to disclose the proprietors, printers, and publishers of the journal in question.[8] Significantly this act did not pertain to the editor, thus conferring on him some slight protection. In principle, however, responsibility for a libel lies with any and all involved in its publication, this being taken in its widest sense to include wholesalers and retailers.

In the heroic age of the radical press journalists such as William Cobbett, Richard Carlile, and William Hone were harried by criminal libel prosecutions. In such cases the distinctions among proprietor, publisher, editor, author, and printer were often extremely hazy, one man being frequently all of them. And Carlile referred to himself as the editor-printer of his paper *The Republican* (although he was not the printer) in order to protect the actual printer.[9] His prosecutors, in their desperation to find someone they could apprehend in the physical act of publication, took to prosecuting shop people and street vendors. These prosecutions became less common, however, as their frequent counterproductivity became evident. They afforded massive publicity for the accused, and there was a considerable risk of acquittal since under Fox's libel act of 1792 it was the jury that decided not only the fact of publication but whether the words complained of were indeed libelous.[10] What was in the case of a disorderly libel an essentially political judgment was thus left for the jury, not the judge, and the two did not always agree, even when the former was a special jury handpicked by the crown.[11]

Apart from the content controls of libel law, there was a panoply of economic controls by means of which the government tried to restrict the circulation of the press among the dangerous classes by keeping its costs artificially high through advertising, stamp, and paper duties.[12] Beginning in the late 1830s, however, governments were in retreat from interventionist policies toward the press. Direct subsidies from the secret service fund, favoritism in allocating government advertising, postal rate relief, and exclusive information—all these methods of encouraging and rewarding a friendly press were more or less abandoned by 1850.[13] The newspapers they had supported were often otherwise unviable, and the government came to terms with a journalistic marketplace in which the strong flourished without official assistance and the weak discredited themselves by accepting it. The doctrines of free trade also doomed the economic controls—the press duties so tellingly stigmatized by their opponents as "taxes on knowledge." By the early 1860s they had succumbed to a well-organized radical campaign.[14] The millennia of free trade and a free press arrived hand in hand.

All these developments contributed in different ways to the growth of editorial status and authority. The decline of press venality was a great boost to the self-respect of editors: While John Delane of *The Times,* sought out by ministers and shaking ministries, was *sui generis,* lesser editors drew on his example to enhance their own self-esteem. The tacit admission by government that official opinion was not public opinion supported the growing pretensions of editors to represent or articulate the latter as somehow the worthier of the two. The reduction in publication costs brought about a great proliferation of periodicals and hence of editorships. The growing commercialization of periodicals may also have been advantageous to editors in other ways. The great profitability of, for example, *The Times, Punch, Athenaeum,* and *Illustrated London News* inspired sober businessmen to pay respect to the periodical press as a business, a field for investment. Such proprietors were less likely to take an interventionist approach and were more likely to regard their journals as products and to respect their editors as specialists with a functional sphere of expertise and authority requiring considerable autonomy. Thus in the more commercially viable sort of periodical, one suspects that a fairly clear contractual definition of the editorial sphere usually existed, though it differed from one journal to the next. We know of proprietors intervening in the editorial sphere—that, for instance, it was George Smith, the proprietor of the *Cornhill Magazine,* not Thackeray or Leslie Stephen, the respective editors, who required the abrupt termination of Ruskin's *Unto This Last* and Matthew Arnold's *Literature and Dogma*. It is evident that the proprietor had very extensive rights that he could exercise and that the editor's chief recourse was resignation.

The law was very clear on this point at least—that the editor, being "simply the agent of the proprietor, it follows that he can have no power, as against the proprietor."[15] Moreover, according to the same authority, when a contract did exist between the editor and the proprietor, the courts would not enforce it. The few recorded cases in this area include one between the printing firm of Bradbury and Evans and Charles Dickens, who, with some others, were joint owners of *Household Words* and had expressly agreed that no partner could sell his share without giving his copartners a chance to buy it. Under this same agreement Charles Dickens was the editor "with absolute control over the literary department and over all agreements, rates of payment and orders for payment." When Dickens withdrew to start a new journal after a personal dispute with Bradbury and Evans, he announced the discontinuation of *Household Words*. They applied for a restraining order. Dickens ingeniously argued that the real title of the journal was "*Household Words*, conducted by Mr. Charles Dickens," and since he had withdrawn as the editor, the journal had to be discontinued. He lost the case.[16] In a comparable case, W. Crookes applied for an injunction against the owner of the *Photographic News* for withdrawing the words "Edited by W. Crookes FCS" from the front page and taking the paper out of his hands contrary to an agreement that he was to be the editor for a fixed number of years. The court refused the application, leaving Crookes to sue for damages in breach of contract.[17] It is plain that property rights were paramount here over all other considerations in the eyes of the law. The main protection of the editor against the proprietor was from arbitrary dismissal. Here, express contract apart, the court gave consideration to the size and the importance of the publication and the degree of editorial responsibility. When the experienced editor H. R. Fox Bourne was dismissed from the *Weekly Dispatch* with six months notice, he went to court claiming twelve as the practice. Before the lord chief justice and a jury he failed to establish his claim.[18]

One important consequence of the legal relationship between the editor and the proprietor was the liability of the proprietor for illegal matter inserted in a periodical by the editor. This point was clearly demonstrated when Henry Colburn, publisher of the *Court Journal,* having been convicted of libel for matter published without his knowledge or authority by his editor, P. G. Patmore, sued the latter for damages and lost, the judges declaring in effect that no criminal can recover compensation against his partner in crime.[19] The problem of the owner's liability, particularly in criminal law, for an action by his editor became an increasingly troubling one as the distinction between the two roles sharpened and the assumption that the owner was actively responsible for the contents of his journal became less realistic. It seemed plainly unjust, especially to proprietors who simply regarded their journals as commercial property, that they should be placed in the unusual position of being held responsible for the criminal actions of another person. Some relief from this anomalous situation was afforded by the libel act of 1843, which allowed a proprietor to plead not guilty on the grounds that libelous matter appeared without his authority and knowledge and "from no want of due care or caution on his part."[20] However, the interpretation of "due care or caution" still left the proprietors vulnerable, and the defense was confined solely to criminal libels. Yet the act is significant in that it shows that the statute law was beginning to articulate a new attitude toward the press. Hitherto almost without exception statutes directly concerning the press had been in some way restrictive. Here at last was a law that recognized and to some degree met the special and changing needs of the press.

Nonetheless, John Stuart Mill felt justified in declaring in *On Liberty* (1859) that "the law on the subject of the press is as servile to this day as it was in the times of the Tudors," though he recognized that there was "little danger of its being put in force against political discussion except during some temporary panic."[21] Mill's remark calls attention to the fact that the liberalization of the law regarding the press was mainly a matter of relaxation and nonenforcement of laws that nevertheless remained available for use, notably, the laws of disorderly libel. For example, the law still required substantial bonds to be posted with the government by newspaper proprietors as security against adverse legal judgments, though this law was largely ignored. Yet in the area of case law very notable developments about which the statute book was virtually mute had long been germinating. These had the effect of conferring legal privileges on the press, which diminished its vulnerability to the libel law in certain important respects. The result was to strengthen the claims of the press as the organ of public opinion and of the editor as its personification. Here one must confront the important but still little studied phenomenon of the extension of what constituted the "public sphere" in Victorian England—that area of consensual common interest about which it was not only legitimate but even mandatory to inform oneself and pass judgment, an area that was largely defined by the periodical press and by the editor in particular.

No one familiar with the Victorian press will have failed to wonder at the tremendous appetite of its readers for extensive verbatim reporting of parliamentary, judicial, and other forms of public proceedings. Beyond the long transcripts of parliamentary debates, those formidably long and solid blocks of type, unrelieved by subheads, often contained fascinating, even appalling, reading. Their visual sobriety belied the fact that they may have contained extensive details about sensational court cases—

murders, indecent assaults, breaches of promise, "criminal conversations," bankruptcies, or libels. Not unreasonably it has been suggested that although the crime story is a preeminently English creation, it is more particularly the creation of the English editor and journalist.[22] To read these stories, particularly in respectable journals such as *The Times*, is to get a sense that some sort of double standard was at work. The society that was so prudish, as Thackeray and others maintained, about what was proper to the novel could read the fullest accounts of the coarser aspects of life every morning and especially on Sundays. This was so because such accounts had a peculiar privilege in the eyes of the law, being largely exempt from the sole legally enforceable form of censorship—libel proceedings.

The struggle of the press for freedom of parliamentary reporting is fairly familiar. Although it was in 1771 that the House of Commons made its last major attempt to enforce the complete prohibition of publication of its proceedings on grounds of parliamentary privileges, it was not until 1875 that it ceased to be possible for any MP to demand that the gallery be cleared of reporters.[23] It was not until 1840 that those employed by parliament to publish its debates and reports were extended that privilege (technically *absolute privilege*) from civil or criminal proceedings for libel in respect of their contents, which MPs had long enjoyed in parliamentary utterances. This protection, though in a qualified form ("qualified privilege"), was also extended to newspaper reports since publication in the newspaper press of libelous parliamentary material was deemed defensible only if done "in good faith and without malice."[24]

Less familiar is the winning by the press of freedom of legal reporting, in many respects a more remarkable victory since what went on in the courts was not so manifestly a matter of public concern, most cases being dealt with there being of a private nature. Here the advances of the press were ratified through a series of landmark judicial decisions beginning in 1796 when the owner of *The Times* was found not guilty of libel for a report of legal proceedings in which the plaintiff claimed his good name had been damaged. In summing up, the judge declared that "being a true account of what took place in a court of justice which is open to all the world, the publication of it was not unlawful."[25] Two years later this decision was reinforced in a similar case, the judge observing that "though the publication of such proceedings may be to the disadvantage of the particular person concerned, yet it is of vast importance to the public that the proceedings of Courts of Justice should be   universally known."[26]

Despite occasional legal checks and reversals, the press pushed its way during the nineteenth century into not only the higher courts but the police and magistrates' courts as well, reporting not only trials but magistrates' examinations and committals. Here were to be found the extraordinary doings of ordinary people, the stuff of the true mass press. Numerous newspapers—the *Police Gazette, Lloyd's,* and many other popular papers now defunct, as well as two now respectable journals that have escaped their raffish origins, the *Sunday Times* and *Observer*—devoted themselves almost entirely to this. Appearing on Sunday, the one holiday of the common man, they lived very largely off the police blotter (and ironically owed their survival to illegality in more ways than one since Sabbatarian laws dating to the seventeenth century, unrepealed but largely unenforced, prohibited the Sunday sale of everything except milk and mackerel).[27] Freedom to report the proceedings of magistrates' courts was not simply a matter of publication, but in many cases one of actual physical access since magistrates' proceedings, especially in rural areas, could be very irregular in every sense. Unpaid amateur judges with extensive summary jurisdiction over a wide variety of lesser offenses could be minor despots in their localities, and relationships between them and the prying, zealous press were not always cordial, especially since the press did not abstain from criticizing them directly on occasion. Some tried to exclude the press by holding court in private houses and other inaccessible places at unpublicized times. Since they were still not required to keep a record of even their summary proceedings, the press in many cases took the task upon itself.[28]

Yet the press could be seen even by magistrates as an aid to justice. At a time when England was still ineffectively policed, as it was throughout most of the nineteenth century, the purpose of punishing those unfortunate enough to be caught was often clearly exemplary. For exemplary punishment to work it needs, of course, to be publicized. Hence the press was an important means of conveying the message—a frightening one, it was hoped, to wrongdoers, a reassuring one to honest citizens who often needed reassurance. A series of important acts of the late 1840s and 1850s regularizing the proceedings of magistrates' courts made it clear that they were in fact open courts and therefore accessible to the press. This was particularly welcome to the rapidly expanding provincial press that was thereby secured a prime source of copy. Yet court reports were not always a deterrent, some feared, or edifying, or even in the public interest. In 1859 Queen Victoria wrote in dismay to the lord chancellor about the reporting of the divorce courts established by an act of 1857. Its cases "fill almost daily a large portion of the newspapers and are of so scandalous a character that it makes it almost impossible for a paper to be trusted in the hand of a young lady or boy." She continued, "none of the worst French novels . . . can be so bad." Lord Campbell (once a parliamentary reporter for the *Morning Chronicle)* replied sympathetically but declared that "he was helpless to prevent the evil,"[29] so firmly established by this time was the principle that publicity was essential to justice of every kind.

The legal extension and redefinition of the public sphere culminated in the libel acts of 1881 and 1888, which gave formal definition to the public meeting and conferred qualified privilege on all newspaper reports of such meetings as long as the reports were free of malice and not unfairly or inaccurately reported. There occurred in the Victorian era such a proliferation of public occasions—meetings of school boards and other burgeoning agencies of local government, charitable groups, creditors, electors, religious and professional bodies, and pressure groups of various kinds—that definition was needed. This was, according to the libel act of 1888, "any meeting bona fide and lawfully held for a lawful purpose and for the furtherance or discussion of any matter of public concern, whether the admission thereto be general or restricted." Privilege was extended only to newspapers defined as "containing public news and appearing at intervals of not more than twenty-six days"; moreover, privilege applied only when reports were indeed "news"—that is, "published contemporaneously" with the meeting concerned.[30]

Behind these laws lay certain powerful and widely held assumptions about the press and journalism that, taken together, amounted virtually to an ideology based on the ideal of the neutral reporter and editor—an ideology of transparency based on the assumption that reality was substantially translatable into words, and that a newspaper report was a sort of colorless medium. Central to this was the invention of shorthand, particularly the Pitman system, which from its appearance in the late 1830s swept aside earlier and less satisfactory systems to become the necessary qualification of Victorian newspaper journalists, most of whom started out reporting law courts and public meetings in the manner of Charles Dickens.[31] It is interesting, in passing, to contemplate the significance of shorthand for the Victorian novel and the whole social construct of reality with which the novel was so intimately connected. It was in fact shorthand that made possible those dense verbatim transcripts with which Victorian newspapers bristled and which reflected a certain faith in the superior virtue, truth—reality, in short—of *in extenso* reporting. It was, after all, a society brought up on such transcripts that consumed three-decker novels so unflinchingly. This faith can be glimpsed, for instance, in testimony given to an 1879 parliamentary select committee on libel law in which, among other things, was discussed the question of whether reporters should be held liable for the reporting of slanderous utterances made in public meetings. Arguing that they should not, one newspaper editor said that "a reporter should go to a meeting of the kind as a mere machine," his task being "to sit there to photograph the meeting to the public."[32]

Tightly bound to this ideology of transparency was the idea of anonymity, a powerful convention that comprehended the whole journalistic enterprise in one way or another. The convention of authorial and reportorial anonymity certainly contributed to editorial authority. The law was clear on this point: "In the case of anonymous contributions the editor's right to alter may be regarded as practically unlimited. The author suffers no wrong by such alteration."[33] The same authority noted that the case was clearly different for signed contributions since the author's reputation and character were at stake, "but there is very little judicial authority to guide us here." The extension of signed journalism in the late nineteenth century was confined chiefly to periodicals of "opinion" rather than of "fact."

Certainly the newspaper press adhered almost totally to anonymity. It was, among other things, the warrant of authority, of neutrality, of depersonalization. It also ensured greater frankness by protecting against personal reprisals—so ran the standard defense—though, of course, such arguments cut both ways.[34] Interestingly, anonymity extended to the editor as well. A few flaunted their names on their mastheads—Dickens of

Household Words, Edmund Yates of the *World*—others, such as Thackeray of the *Cornhill,* were widely publicized for their reputations; but most were content to remain unknown to the general public. Indeed, Richard Cobden created a sensation when in 1863 he publicly addressed the editor of *The Times* by name in the culmination of a long-standing quarrel with John Delane.[35] Cobden was critical of the irresponsible "wegotism" of editorial anonymity that fabricated an artificial and inaccessible identity claiming peculiar public authority. But to publicize the editor's name was to create a public assumption that the journal's identity was subordinate to the editor's, which would greatly lessen the authority of proprietors over editors and impair the journal's value as a commercial property. (It is significant that both Yates and Dickens were proprietor—editors.)

Not that owners were particularly eager to publicize their identity either. One, testifying to the parliamentary committee on libel law, argued that owners should be able to keep editors' names secret—as he cautiously put it: "it may impair the usefulness of a man as editor for his name to be known." He was also against the requirement of printing the proprietor's name because it would deter respectable men from the business.[36] In fact the status of the newspaper proprietor was not what many felt it should be. They protested the government policy of not appointing owners as justices of the peace—a mark of social recognition from which other successful businessmen were not excluded. The official explanation that conflict of interest was at issue is, however, understandable in the light of what has been said about relations between the press and the magistracy.[37] Although the government did bring in effective ownership registration procedures with the 1881 libel act, it did not require the publication of ownership. And of editorial and authorial anonymity the law remainded fully supportive.[38]

Yet there was an inescapable contradiction between the convention of anonymity and the gentlemanly code that abhorred concealment—not for nothing did the standard hero of Victorian fiction have a "frank, open face." The gentleman spoke his mind and bore the consequences of doing so. Part of the original gentlemanly code was dueling, which the government had been trying to suppress since Tudor times. In fact the facilitation of libel actions was originally done deliberately to provide an appropriate legal alternative to dueling as means of defending one's reputation.[39] Still the practice persisted into the nineteenth century, and some of its most ardent practitioners were editors such as John Black of the *Morning Chronicle* and James Stuart of the London *Courier.* The Scott-Christie duel involving the editors of the *London Magazine* and *Blackwood's* and the Maginn-Berkeley duel between the editor of *Fraser's* and an enraged reviewee both turned on the practice of anonymity. Dueling was one means by which socially insecure editors could claim gentlemanly status. Unfortunately, their opponents did not always design to confer such status on them, and the resort to the horsewhip was not unknown even into Victoria's reign. As late as 1869 Grenville Murray, the editor of the *Queen's Messenger,* was publicly horesewhipped by a peer whose father's reputation he had attacked. It was Henry Labouchere who most effectively discredited the practice of physically assaulting editors by turning it into farce, as when he reduced one would-be assailant to appealing to bystanders in the street for a horsewhip he could borrow.[40]

By the midnineteenth century libel proceedings had become the accepted means of individual recourse against offending editors. The personal libel action had replaced the disorderly libel as the main legal threat faced by editors. But such actions could be either civil or criminal according to the wishes of the injured party. The criminal law carried the threat of imprisonment as well as fine; the civil action involved only damages. Moreover, in criminal proceedings it was not a sufficient defense to prove the truth of the words in question (the plea of justification); it also had to be shown that their publication was in the public interest. In civil law, by contrast, truth is a complete defense, though the burden of proof is on the defendant in both civil and criminal cases. Criminal proceedings were more likely to be instituted by someone of social prominence and wealth who would be concerned less with recovering damages than with inflicting punishment. Such a person would have little trouble finding a magistrate who shared his view of the seriousness of the matter.

But libel law was not a complete substitute for the duel, for whereas dueling was a purely private settlement, a libel case makes even more public the matter at issue. This was, of course, the main safeguard of the press against libel actions – the subjects would often not welcome the additional publicity of a trial. Moreover, as we have seen, the law of libel developed in such a way as to expand that public sphere in which it had been inoperative. The notion of the "public figure" diminished personal protection under the libel law for those who fell within its expanding definition. In the words of the jurist Fitzjames Stephen, "Every person who takes a public part in public affairs submits his conduct therein to criticism."[41] Yet an expanding press, well aware of the circulation-building appeal of "personalities" in journalism (as long as they were not the journalists'), pushed aggressively outwards the frontiers of the public sphere and in so doing clashed increasingly with the well-developed English notion of privacy.

It has been asserted that Victorian England reached the "apex of the privacy graph," though in legislation pertaining to the press and libel the private sphere was not explicitly defined, as it was, for instance, in continental law. The absence of any clear legal definition of privacy in a sense argued for a general consensus that it could be taken for granted. Thus a good deal of prejudice existed among the sort of people who were potential jurors in libel actions toward a press that was perceived as trading in personal privacy. Certain journals did so quite blatantly. In the early Victorian period certain scandal sheets, notably, the *Age, Satirist,* and *John Bull,* practised a variety of extortion by offering not to print certain personal items in return for payment by those concerned. Their demise was assisted by Lord Campbell's act that specifically prohibited this practice as well as by the pressure of libel actions. But in the 1860s and 1870s there arose a generation of papers, the so-called society journals, of which *Truth,* the *World,* and *Vanity Fair* were the better examples and the *Englishman, Social Notes,* and *Figaro* the worst. In all cases their editors emphasized personalities, and some notable libel cases resulted, bringing prison sentences to at least four editors. An editor who successfully avoided prison was Henry Labouchere, who specialized in attacking fraudulent businessmen, a less dangerous quarry than gentlemen.

The threat of criminal libel proceedings and the arbitrary way in which they could be commenced weighed heavily on the minds of respectable editors and proprietors. Their representations to Parliament were effective to the extent of altering the law: Under the libel acts of 1881 and 1888 an order from the director of public prosecutions and the consent of a judge in chambers were required before a criminal prosecution for libel could be instituted against the press.[42] The report of the parliamentary committee reveals strong opposition to the call made by some newspaper interests for the complete abolition of such criminal charges. A prime reason for this opposition was the fact that the most irresponsible society papers were financially precarious and their conductors could easily dodge the damages and the costs of civil action by closing down and reopening under another name. The more respectable and prosperous journals saw the other side of the coin, regarding themselves as all too frequently the victims of libel law. Civil suits could be launched against them by non-entities who either hoped to win substantial damages on minor matters or at least frighten them into settling out of court to avoid the high costs of litigation. According to the solicitor for *The Times,* obviously a prime target for such vexatious actions, his paper faced between 1872 and 1879 twenty-one libel actions, of which fourteen were abandoned by the plaintiff without settlement; of the remaining seven that went to trial, *The Times* won four. The legal costs to the newspaper of dealing with the cases was approximately £3,500; it recovered virtually nothing in costs even when awarded them.[43]

The last decades of the nineteenth century constituted a veritable golden age of the libel case—golden especially for the high priced barristers who won great reputations for themselves in this particularly theatrical kind of litigation. Many of the most celebrated cases involved newspaper editors, some of whom were themselves not particularly averse to the publicity it won them; in any case, the publicity was generally advantageous to their journals whether they won or lost. Ruskin was in a sense the editor as well as the chief contributor and the owner of *Fors Clavigera,* the peculiar journal in which he published his celebrated libel against Whistler. The forgotten Mrs. Georgina Weldon became a national figure through her bizarre libel actions in the 1880s taking on a number of editors (though one herself). Interestingly, she was in this area the first beneficiary of the Married Women's Property Act of 1882, which finally enabled a married woman to proceed independently in a civil action, without having to act through her husband.[44] By an appropriate symbiosis, the newspaper-generated libel action was one of the best sources of newspaper copy—an editor's dream. Even the libel itself could effectively be republished, under privilege, in newspaper reports. Henry Labouchere, dubbed by his solicitor the "Napoleon of litigation," was the star of numerous libel cases (civil and criminal), frequently conducting his own defense with great skill. Labouchere was eager to claim complete personal responsibility for the contents of *Truth,* of which he was the sole owner, even to the point of admitting authorship.[45] This policy served to lighten the legal onus on his printer and publisher (the latter once admitting in court that he was entirely nominal and "in fact knew nothing about the paper").[46] Labouchere strikingly expressed the ambiguity of an editor's position. For twenty-five years he called himself the editor of *Truth,* though for most of this period he had little to do with the day-to-day operation of the paper, this being left to Horace Voules, his trusted lieutenant. When Voules finally conveyed to him his chagrin at being long denied the title he thought he deserved, Labouchere apparently expressed surprise and told Voules he was welcome to the title, which he regarded as meaningless. He later remarked, "I have now been connected with newspapers over thirty years and I have never yet discovered what an editor is."[47] Neither did the law.

NOTES

1. "The First Edinburgh Reviewers," *Collected Works* (London, 1965), I, p. 332.
2. Cited in Alfred Baker, *The Newspaper World* (London, 1890), p. 49.
3. "The Evolution of Editors," *Studies of a Biographer* (London, 1889), I, p. 38.
4. Cited in Donald Thomas, *A Long Time Burning* (London, 1969), p. 33.
5. A good guide with a useful hisitorical introduction to libel law is P. F. Carter-Ruck, *Libel and Slander* (London, 1972), especially pp. 19-48. See also James Fitzjames Stephen, *A History of the Criminal Law of England* (London, 1883), II, pp. 298-395. There are a number of legal commentaries and guides to the law of the press in nineteenth-century England, of which perhaps the most useful is J. R. Fisher and J. A. Strachan, *The Law of the Press,* 2d ed. (London 1898).
6. Anthony Smith, "The Long Road to Objectivity and Back Again,. . ." in *Newspaper History,* ed. George Boyce et al. (London, 1978), p. 165.
7. A. Aspinall, *Politics and the Press* (London, 1949), p. 38 n. 2.
8. 6 & 7 Will. 4, c. 76.

9. I owe this point to Joel Wiener.

10. 32 Geo. 3, c. 60.

11. For an example, see George Spater, *William Cobbett: The Poor Man's Friend* (Cambridge, 1982), I, pp. 476-81.

12. On these matters, see Joel H. Wiener, *The War of the Unstamped* (Ithaca, 1969), esp. pp. 1-15; Patricia Hollis, *The Pauper Press* (London, 1970), pp. 3-92.

13. Aspinall, pp. 369-384. This is not to say that governments ceased to cultivate the press on a partisan basis by less official means, as is plainly shown in Stephen Koss, *The Rise and Fall of the Political Press in Britain: The Nineteenth Century* (London, 1981).

14. C. D. Collet, *History of the Taxes on Knowledge, Their Origin and Repeal*, 2 volumes (London, 1899).

15. Fisher and Strachan, p. 53.

16. Ibid., p. 56.

17. Ibid., pp. 53-56.

18. Ibid., p. 66.

19. Ibid., pp. 56-54.

20. Frequently referred to as "Lord Campbell's Act," 6 & 7 Vict., c. 96.

21. Ch. 2, para. 1.

22. Marjorie Jones, *Justice and Journalism* (Chichester, 1974), p. 19.

23. Thomas, p. 104; Aspinall, p. 36.

24. 3 & 4 Vict., c. 9.

25. Jones, p. 11.

26. Ibid., p. 13.

27. Aspinall, p. 13. See also V. Berridge, "Popular Sunday Papers and Mid-Victorian Society," in Boyce, pp. 256, 384 n. 44.

28. Jones, pp. 22-23.

29. Cited in ibid., pp. 68-69. The English press had free run of the divorce courts until 1926, when they were restricted not so much on grounds of privacy as public decency.

30. 51 & 52, Vict., c. 64.

31. Smith, pp. 161-63.

32. *Report from the Select Committee on the Law of Libel . . . ,* Sessional Papers 1878-9, vol. XL, Questions 692, 696.

33. Fisher and Strachan, p. 59.

34. On anonymity, see Christopher Kent, "Higher Journalism and the Mid-Victorian Clerisy," *Victorian Studies* XIII (1969): 181-198; Oscar Maurer Jr., "Anonymity vs. Signature in Victorian Reviewing," *University of Texas Studies in Literature* XXVI (1948): 1-27.

35. John Morley, *Life of Richard Cobden* (London, 1906), pp. 889 ff.

36. *Select Committee Report,* Questions 1078-80.

37. Jones, p. 43.

38. Some interest in regulating anonymity by law was created in the 1850s by the famous French *Loi Tinguy* of 1850, which made signature compulsory in every *article de discussion* in the press. A prominent English politician expressed some doubts about anonymity in 1858, but nothing came of it (Koss, p. 132). Continental law generally required she "personification" of a journal, the naming of a person, *gérant* in France, *Redacteur* in Germany, who was legally responsible for the paper before the law (Fisher and Strachan, p. 306).

39. Sir William Holdsworth, *A History of English Law* (London, 1937), pp. 353, 364.

40. Hesketh Pearson, *Labby: The Life and Character of Henry Labouchere* (London, 1936), p. 115.

41. James Fitzjames Stephen, *Digest of Criminal Law* (London, 1877), Art. 354.

42. C. H. Rolph, *Books in the Dock* (London, 1969), p. 140.

43. *Select Committee Report,* Questions 1480-82.

44. Edward Grierson, *Storm Bird: The Strange Life of Georgina Weldon* (London, 1959), pp. 202-03.

45. *The Times,* 28 May 1879, p. 12.

46. Ibid., 12 June 1879, p. 6.

47. Algar Thorold, *The Life of Henry Labouchere (London, 1913), pp. 460-61.*

Derek Fraser

The Editor as Activist: Editors and Urban Politics in Early Victorian England

I

During the middle decades of the nineteenth century the provincial press came of age. Before the nationalization of the British press and the coming of the ubiquitous national daily, the provincial weekly and later daily newspapers reigned supreme in their own fiefdoms. Indeed, a Victorian press historian predicted in 1872 that "the mighty power over the public mind" that the provincial papers exercised locally would soon be "even mightier than that which is exercised by the Metropolitan Press."[1] The supposed influence so impersonally wielded by a newspaper was in practice derived from its editor, who thereby occupied a pivotal position in local affairs. Notwithstanding the press historian's *crie de coeur* over anonymity (which is broken only with the greatest ingenuity and industry), the provincial newspapers of Victorian England provided editors with one great political asset—visibility. As Alan Lee remarked, "editors and journalists of provincial papers were likely to be well known to their readers"; similarly, Stanley Harrison noted that the editors of the Chartist press "were also the movement's charismatic leaders and orators, frequently known to the people far and wide by their first names."[2]

Two developments tended to enhance the editor's potential for political activism. First was the increased readership of newspapers that marked the midnineteenth century. Newspaper circulation is notoriously difficult to ascertain, and the figures frequently cited by the papers themselves were usually pieces of Boosterism and thereby unreliable. The contemporary bugbear, the hated newspaper stamp, does provide some guide to newspaper circulation in particular towns.[3] It may be tentatively concluded that the number of newspapers circulating in provincial towns doubled during the early Victorian period. For example, the weekly average of all Nottingham papers rose from around 3,000 in 1833 to 6,500 in 1852; that for Leicester for the same period from 2,600 to 4,600; in Cambridge the weekly average was 2,650 in 1835 and 5,140 in 1849. Similar trends can be identified for individual titles; both the *Glasgow Herald* and the *Newcastle Courant* doubled their circulation between 1836 and 1854, and the *Manchester Guardian* doubled its sale within the first decade of Victoria's reign. There was a further spectacular growth in circulation with the appearance of the provincial dailies in the wake of the abolition of newspaper stamps, which ushered in "the Modern Revolution" of 1855-1861.[4] Hence the editorial pearls of wisdom reached a larger audience, and the editor's visibility and potential importance were augmented.

This larger circulation existed within a context in which newspapers were increasingly viewed as a vehicle of propaganda. This is the second factor conducive to an active political role for an editor since his professional identity was bound up with the pursuit of political objectives. Though a modern scholar has decried the political importance of the provincial press by asserting that "their political pretensions were as often exaggerated as disparaged,"[5] contemporaries undoubtedly viewed the press as a means of representing certain interests and advancing certain causes. It is clear from the research on individual newspapers and regions that the most common reason for establishing a provincial newspaper was the perceived lack of journalistic support for a political or a religious viewpoint.[6] In this, as in the creation of provincial dailies, the Liberals led the way perhaps because radicals and dissenters had a longer list of grievances to state and the multiplication of Liberal papers was justified by the distinctive political identity each new paper wished to adopt. Thus the fragmentation of the Liberal party in Leicester in the 1830s explained the need for a second Liberal paper there when the radical *Leicestershire Mercury* was launched in 1836 as a rival of the more cautious *Leicester Chronicle*. Similarly, in 1857 radical Liberals founded the *Leeds Express* to voice a brand of reform politics no longer represented by the venerable *Leeds Mercury*. On the right too the press was recognized as a political asset, and in the midst of Peel's Corn Law crisis a new paper was launched in Nottingham specifically because pro-Corn Law opinions had been deserted by the Conservative *Nottingham Journal*. When the *Journal* converted to Peelite free trade, local protectionists established the *Nottinghamshire Guardian* in 1846. So pronounced were the views of the *Guardian* that its politics were not adequately conveyed by the designation conservative: Even in the 1870s its "decided Toryism" was manifest.[7] Perhaps the most successful Conservative provincial paper was the *Yorkshire Post,* launched in 1866 as "a foe to democracy and revolution but the firm friend of all constitutional reform."[8] It soon outsold its regional rivals, the luminaries of northern Liberalism, the *Manchester Guardian* and the *Leeds Mercury*.

Three kinds of newspaper shunned an overtly political complexion. First, there were specialist business journals that supplied commercial news and information to a particular economic
interest, such as the grain trade and the metal interest. The *Liverpool Mercantile Gazette,* for instance, had no politics, and it provided marine and commercial intelligence to the Mersey shipping
trade. Second were the advertising sheets distributed gratis or at
low cost, which contained perhaps 75 percent advertisements and
relied on a large circulation to attract custom and revenue. In
1836 in Birmingham the *Midland Counties Herald* was launched,
and in 1842 *Payne's Leicester and Midland Counties Advertiser*
was born, aiming to exclude all acrimonious feelings and political
controversy."[9] Both were pilloried for their neutral political
stance, but both achieved high circulation. Third were a small
number of traditional, well-established papers that swam against
the tide of editorial commitment and preferred to eschew political
bias. Such was the well-known print begun in the eighteenth century, *Aris's Birmingham Gazette.* Though occasionally drawn into
a mild conservatism, it would have welcomed the subsequent
description, "not much of the character of a political journal."[10]
These were very much the exception, for the provincial press in
Victorian England was both politically committed and politically
divided. Every town, as in Eatanswill, had its "Blue *Gazette*" and
its "Buff *Independent.*"

The platform thus established for the advancement of decided
political principles gave to a Victorian editor a natural entrée into
provincial politics. And it was his identity qua editor that provided a potential political role. Whereas it was common for a nationally known periodical to enhance its reputation by attracting a
writer of elite status, the relative social positions of the provincial
newspaper and its editor were almost always the reverse. The
newspaper gave to the editor a social reputation that his own independent means could not have supplied. The occupation of

journalist was not highly regarded, and it was the political muscle that the editor could draw on through his paper that counteracted his otherwise lowly social status. For a small but influential group of newspaper editors, the management and editorial direction of a provincial newspaper created a ladder of opportunity that permitted that self-helping upward mobility so beloved of Samuel Smiles (himself an editor in the 1840s). This was particularly true of the families that created a modest newspaper dynasty, such as the Suttons (Charles, Richard, John F.) who ran the radical *Nottingham Review* for three generations and the Thompsons (Thomas and James) who guided the Liberal *Leicester Chronicle* for over half a century.

One of the most famous of these newspaper families, the so-called Bainesocracy of Leeds, sent to Parliament three of its members in a period of forty years. Yet its origins were of the humblest. Depending on the political perspective, it was a matter of ridicule or of pride that Edward Baines Senior had walked from Preston to Leeds in search of work as a printer. Richard Oastler continually referred to this humiliating origin in order to pour scorn on "the Mercury hack penny-a-liner." His version was that "the beggar tramped on foot with all his sins and all his 'wardrobe' on him," embroidering the tale with the accusation that Baines had left it to the parish to support the pregnant girl he had deserted.[11] The filial biography by Baines Junior invests the same journey with moral, even biblical, significance. To have "crossed the hills into Yorkshire with no companion but his staff, and all his worldly wealth in his pocket" and still have established a notable career was a tribute to the great moral worth of the individual and the virtues of the English social system.[12] Such a virtuous life did not obscure from Macaulay that Baines as a member of Parliament would not have "quite so much polish or literature as the persons among whom he will now be thrown"; similarly, Earl Fitzwilliam in the late 1840s sneered at the younger Baines as part of "the 2nd rate aristocracy of leeds."[13] Yet the family that elite Whigs might look down on wielded a critical influence in Yorkshire Liberal politics, and, as Cobden found to his cost, no decisive move could be made in the West Riding without them. He bemoaned of Baines Junior, "literally speaking he and he alone is the obstacle. By hereditary prestige rather than any native qualities . . . he occupies a position from which he cannot be deposed . . . Baines is destined to be a standing obstacle."[14] The "hereditary prestige" was not that of wealth or social status but that derived from the editorial control of the *Leeds Mercury.*

A Victorian provincial editor was thus uniquely placed, in the words of one cleric, "to work by tongue and pen for the social political mental moral and religious *advancement* of the people."[15] In Yorkshire a network of prominent Liberal editors, Baines in Leeds, William Byles in Bradford, and Robert Leader in Sheffield, as "newspaper patriarchs and pioneers," formed "an undesigned alliance of colour and purpose whose influence on the thought and feeling of the West Riding has been very deep."[16] As political activists, these men had been able, like Feargus O'Connor, to place the power of the press in the service of the platform.[17] That these and many other editors achieved a local political prominence was largely due to their connections with a newspaper press that had grown out of its derivative newsheet origins. As a southern paper expressed it in 1849:

The newspaper is something of a far higher order than a mere chronicler of events. It is both a mirror and a monitor of what is passing around us; and as such it is a vehicle of moral instruction. . . . Expressing, and in many cases guiding, public opinion, it is rapidly assuming a comparative sovereignty over civilized nations[18]

It was this "sovereignty" of the press that permitted Victorian editors to assume so prominent a political role in local affairs.

II

If there was one area more than any other in which the editor could play an active role, it was in the politics of local administration. In this area an editor could exploit his visibility to direct public attention toward pressing local issues. In particular, the editor was equipped to determine the nature and the contents of the local political agenda. By promoting some issues and deflecting others the editor might set the stage of local politics and almost choose the players on it. This aspect of political activism will be illustrated by four main examples taken from the 1840s. The case studies involve James Thompson of the *Leicester Chronicle,* John F. Sutton of the *Nottingham Review,* John Jaffray of the *Birmingham Journal,* and William Byles of the *Bradford Observer.*

In Leicester undoubtedly the key political question in the early nineteenth century was municipal reform. Leicester Corporation was one of the worst examples of a self-elected, corrupt, exclusively Tory, closed corporation, and its wrongdoing achieved even parliamentary notoriety. J. F. Winks, a radical reformer who secured his own visibility by running the short-lived *Leicester Corporation and Parochial Reformer,* expressed it rather well when he wrote that the Corporation's "foul and filthy corruptions have stunk in the nostrils of the whole nation."[19] In the campaign against the Corporation the *Leicester Chronicle,* as the only spokesman of local Whig opinion, had played a major role. Begun in 1810 to counteract the bile of the Tory *Leicester Journal,* the paper came into the exclusive ownership of Thomas Thompson in 1814. Thompson, like Baines, a native of Preston, ran the paper himself until in the late 1830s his son James became involved as a reporter. In 1841 they became joint proprietors, and James became the editor.

For two decades the *Chronicle* had lashed the Corporation, but the benefits of municipal reform were slow in coming, for the new Liberal Council was bowed down by the burden of municipal debt bequeathed by its predecessor. When James Thompson began to involve himself in the paper, he pushed the *Chronicle* toward one of his own special causes, the improvement of sanitation in the town. As early as 1839 James began writing in his characteristic way in the language of priorities: "first utility absolute utility — next comfort — and lastly matters of taste and luxury."[20] As the question of improvements developed in Leicester during the 1840s, the issue of priorities assumed central importance.

By the early 1840s the problem of the borough debt eased, and James Thompson began to campaign for the improvement of sanitation, a question he judged second only to municipal reform itself. He urged the Council to demonstrate the superiority of the new system of local government over the old by replacing "selfishness, sensuality and ignorance" by "philanthropy, public spirit and enlightenment," and, he pronounced, "something more than mere counting house merit is required in municipal matters."[21] Through 1843 Thompson regularly hammered away at the problem, urging an inquiry into this long-standing local condition. He particularly developed the argument that a working class already sapped by poverty was "additionally cursed by fever," and he gave great publicity to a statistical survey that showed that of twenty-seven towns only three had a higher death rate than Leicester.[22] In 1844 he returned to the idea of priorities and spelled out his belief that drainage was the most pressing need: A new town hall was last in his list of six improvements.

An editor who might by persistence thrust an issue on to the local political agenda nevertheless lacked the political authority to deal with it. That authority lay with the Council, and when in 1845 it was moved to action by the promptings of the *Chronicle*, it proposed a method of proceeding that Thompson found himself obliged to oppose. A radical activist, William Biggs, a sort of embryonic Joseph Chamberlain, dreamed of leaving his mark on Leicester by emulating Caesar, "who found Rome built of brick and left it built of marble." Biggs, unlike Thompson, placed the highest priority on beautifying the town by embellishments such as a fine "Brummagen Town Hall," a new market, and a rebuilt post office. The questions of sanitation pertaining to town drainage and a cemetery, he believed, could be left to a joint stock company. Thompson unequivocally backed Joseph Whetstone, also a Liberal councillor, who wished the Council itself to address Leicester's serious problem of sanitation. The issue of priorities was joined with that of money, for Biggs's supporters were dubbed the extravagant party and the Whetstone school the economists. A bitter political battle ensued that split the Liberal party on the Council, a fragmentation publicized and perhaps exacerbated by the polarization in the press, the *Chronicle* for Whetstone and the *Mercury* for Biggs.

Unfortunately for Thompson, there was a majority on the Council in favor of the Biggs Improvement Bill, and so there was some point in the *Mercury* line, which denounced the *Chronicle* as "the mere tool and organ of a factious coterie" and argued that Leicester should not be governed by a minority.[23] Thompson, no doubt frustrated by his own lack of success, increasingly personalized the dispute by casting doubt on the motives of William Biggs who, he asserted, "did not care to meddle with the 'dirty work' of Town Drainage. There was no glory to be gained in 'washing sewers with cold water,' laurels were only to be won by the builder of Town Halls."[24] In any event, neither faction was successful, and the improvement scheme collapsed. Not until Leicester adopted a public health act in 1849 and established a local board of health did the potential exist for real improvement in sanitation. Thompson noted wistfully in 1849 that the Council had accumulated a further debt of £46,000 without a penny having been spent on the problem that the *Chronicle* and the Whetstone party had claimed was preeminent–"the Drainage and Sewerage of the Town."[25]

In Nottingham also an editor was able to sensitize local opinion to the public health question, as always with a peculiar local variant. The Suttons of Nottingham had even more impressive journalistic credentials in local radical politics than the Thompsons of Leicester. Charles Sutton, a Methodist printer, began the *Nottingham Review* in 1808. It immediately adopted a strong radical position, supporting peace and parliamentary reform. Sutton was closely watched by the Home Office and was belatedly prosecuted for publishing a letter in October 1814 signed by General Ludd. Sutton's son, Richard, believed that the prosecution was instigated by local political opponents. Charles Sutton paid for his radicalism by spending a year in jail, a sojourn that did nothing to dampen his ardor for reform; on his release he promised to make the *Review* a "still more earnest advocate of the Peoples' Cause."[26] In 1828, just a year before his death, Charles surrendered control of the paper to his son Richard who continued the tradition of radicalism, even earning Feargus O'Connor's gratitude for his support of chartism. In the 1840s the next generation was drawn in, when one of Richard's seven sons, John, took over the writing of editorials. It was J. F. Sutton who made public health reform the editorial plank of the *Review*.

The peculiar variant in Nottingham's public health problem was the town's physical straitjacket. Nottingham was one of the most insanitary Victorian towns largely because it was cramped. The town was hemmed in by aristocratic landowners, such as the notorious Duke of Newcastle (whose property was burned in the Reform Bill riots of 1831), who were reluctant to sell land for overspill. The town also suffered because of the doubtful boon of nearly 1,500 acres of common land owned by the Corporation and burgesses, which gave rights of recreation and pasture to the freemen. The result was to make building land scarce, to concentrate the working population in dense courtyards, and to push death rates to epidemic proportions. A strange alliance of slum landlords and the so-called cowocracy of the poor freemen prevented an enclosure of common land for over half a century. In 1835 the Royal Commission on Municipal Corporations cited the lack of enclosure of this *lebensraum* as the main cause of the town's housing and economic problems. The old Corporation was, unusually, an exclusive Whig body, and this may have toned down the Commission's critique and accounted for the *Review's* general approval of the Corporation's record.[27]

The new Council was no more enthusiastic than the unreformed Corporation when it came to the question of enclosure, and it is highly likely that many councillors owned slum property and feared for their rents if new building land were released. The freemen could always be persuaded by extolling the virtues of green fields and fresh air and by pleas to protect the birthright of the poor vested in the common land. A modest 55 acres was enclosed in 1839: What was needed was a general enclosure act to which the Council was opposed.

John F. Sutton sought to break down this inertia by employing shock tactics. He wanted to undermine the complacency that had sabotaged all proposals for the reform of sanitation. The local water engineer, Thomas Hawkesley, presented evidence to the Health of Town's Commission in 1844, which denied the often stated theory that the common land around the city was healthful. This was the evidence Sutton needed, and he began a year long campaign to obtain

an immediate, total and equitable enclosure of the restricted lands by which the enlargement and improvement of the town have been so long prevented, and under the baneful operation of which, the prosperity of the town has declined, the demand for labour has diminished, wages have sunk, destitution has increased, and the population have become pent up in dwellings unfit for human habitations, the prey of disease—the victims of death.[28]

Throughout the latter part of 1844 and into 1845, Sutton kept up the momentum of his campaign, printing lurid descriptions of working-class housing, advocating daily inspections of actual sanitary conditions for those opposed to enclosure, and publicizing the remarkable variations in death rates between the wards of the town.

J. F. Sutton received only lukewarm support from the other Nottingham papers. The Tory *Journal* was concerned about the implications for local taxation of an improvement scheme and was not wholly convinced that great benefits would accrue from enclosure, while acknowledging that enclosure was long overdue to reduce overcrowding.[29] The reaction of the Whig *Mercury* was more complex. The precise details are unclear, but Nottingham's leading Whig alderman, Thomas Wakefield, owned all or the major part of the *Mercury* and though he never edited the paper, it was undoubtedly his mouthpiece on the enclosure question. Wakefield was a major property owner in the built-up area, and there are grounds for suspecting that his high-flown defense of freemen rights of common was less than altruistic. He announced in the Council chamber that he "had been a steady opponent of every attempt to enclose the common lands . . . and he could look with satisfaction on that opposition."[30] The *Mercury* followed suit, proudly defending the freemen's right of pasture and bitterly regretting the loss of the meadows when a scheme was finally agreed in 1845.[31] Sutton's counterblast was to repeat the argument that enclosure would improve housing conditions and remove some of the causes of the town's high mortality. J. F. Sutton was more successful than James Thompson, for in 1845 a scheme was approved for a general enclosure, and in the following year a sanitary committee was appointed. Sutton was rightly proud of his part in forcing the enclosure question into the public eye and hailed the final victory as "a glorious termination to a glorious struggle for the emancipation of the poor man."[32] If his prediction that Nottingham would "rise phoenix-like from its ashes" was decidedly optimistic, the day of local improvement was at hand. This was a worthy outcome of a piece of editorial propaganda.

Yet another variant in the early Victorian urban health issue was to be found in Birmingham. There too there was a certain complacency that the natural advantages of site and water protected the town from the worst evils of high death rates. Even when public awareness of the health question grew in the 1840s, there was a peculiar local barrier to effective action in Birmingham—the structure of local government. Birmingham had been one of the three test cases for the legality of incorporation under the 1835 act. Its infant Council had suffered the double blow of local opposition and national disgrace: Local political opponents simply acted as though the Council did not exist, and it was pilloried nationally for its failure in policing during the Chartist riots. Only in 1842 was the charter of incorporation legally confirmed, and even then there remained a serious defect. Because Birmingham had been an unincorporated town (thus, unlike Leicester or Nottingham, having no corporation), there had developed a complex network of township bodies that remained entirely untouched by municipal reform. The authority of Birmingham Town Council was severely impaired by the rival jurisdiction of no less than eight local institutions, and so, in the words of the city's first civic historian, "the Corporation was deprived of its natural and necessary powers and . . . was obliged to content itself with a merely fragmentary jurisdiction."[33]

A prerequisite for any effective assault on the public health question was clearly an amalgamation of the powers of all the minor institutions in the Town Council. There had to be unitary borough government. This was the political objective of John Jaffray who became the editor of the *Birmingham Journal* in 1844.

The *Journal* had achieved considerable publicity on the coattails of Thomas Attwood. Begun in 1825 as a Tory paper, the *Journal* became the mouthpiece of Attwood's Birmingham Political Union during the Reform Bill crisis and of his revived B.P.U. in the early years of Chartism. Once the leadership of the Attwood school had been rejected by Chartism, something of the sparkle went out of the paper and R. K. Douglas (author of the National Petition) was forced to sell it in April 1844. The new proprietor, John Frederick Feeney, brought in Jaffray, then a young writer, as the editor. Feeney and Jaffray later achieved journalistic prominence as the founders of the *Birmingham Daily Post* in 1857.

As soon as he became the editor, Jaffray made amalgamation his top priority and through his campaign launched his own political career. He attacked the "Babel of confusion" in local administration, stressing particularly the sanitary consequences of fragmented town government. He wanted to shake people out of their acceptance of environmental decay, knowing full well the local predeliction based on familiarity: "We are essentially a congregation of manufacturers; we love the dirt and dinginess of our walls and chimnies for they are natural to us."[34] Jaffray believed that if Birmingham used its natural advantages properly, it would have the power to become "a model for the sanitary government of other towns." When one of the minor township bodies sought a new act of Parliament to strengthen its autonomy, Jaffray roared his disapproval:

The town is sick of a mob of municipal governors. We pay too dear for their amusements. The ratepayers of Birmingham now claim one municipal government for the entire borough. . . . We are a bye-word in the country for our senseless and self-destructive local factions, and so we shall continue to be till our municipal government is consolidated. . . . It is the constant impolicy of Birmingham to present itself before the kingdom as an arena of disgraceful local contentions — as a populous town without self-government . . . as a community of rank party spirit and jarring elements of social contention.[35]

Jaffray's cry had its effect, for town meetings rejected further powers for the minor bodies and voted for amalgamation. This did not, however, lead to the accomplishment of Jaffray's objective, which was not to be achieved until 1851. The Birmingham municipal scene was riven by dissension, political and social. Conservatives were hostile to increasing the powers of a body that was so obviously Liberal dominated; extreme radicals actually favored decentralized local government and the veto of localized public meetings; elitist politicians had previously been drawn to the Birmingham Street Commission, an eighteenth-century foundation, whose social status was superior to that of the Council. Hence Jaffray's long campaign bore no immediate fruit, and there was a labyrinthine municipal history before the consolidation of local government occurred. The complex details are not relevant here[36] but throughout the late 1840s, as various possibilities emerged, Jaffray maintained his position that great sanitary benefits would accompany amalgamation. He remained a persistent critic of the local bodies, particularly the Street Commission, through the long, drawn-out negotiations, which were full of pitfalls and false hopes, that finally led to the Birmingham Improvement Act of 1851. Again, although the power to remedy the evil lay in hands other than those of an editor, a vigorous editorial campaign could create the climate for change and provide the editor with status and prominence. In the tortuous municipal history of Birmingham between 1844 and 1851 and its crucial issue of amalgamation, Jaffray had a significant and visible place. As the civic historian confirmed, from 1844 "public opinion was being slowly matured by a series of appeals made in the *Journal*, by Mr. Jaffray, who insisted strongly upon the sanitary aspects of the questions and these appeals and efforts were continued, almost without intermission, in the same columns and by the same writer, with most beneficial effect until the object was finally accomplished."[37] From the obscurity of township government Jaffray was propelled into the magistracy in 1865 and the baronetcy in 1892.[38]

Bradford was yet one more stage behind Birmingham in its civic development, for in the 1840s it was still unincorporated and was under the tutelage of outmoded parochial and township government. "Worstedopolis," as the center of the British worsted industry was nicknamed, was the fastest growing city in the country, and the pace of its growth generated acute social problems. Two worries concentrated the minds of contemporaries.[39] First was the ever-present problem of law and order, for the swarming undisciplined crowds were prone to disturb the public peace. In the late 1830s and early 1840s Bradford was on several occasions the scene of riotous behavior, and public order was only reestablished by the military. Scared magistrates, lacking an effective police force, resorted to a permanent military presence. Second, Bradford had appalling health problems, the combined result of industrial effluence, insanitary housing, and inadequate building controls. As statistical evidence emerged in the 1840s, Bradford's reputation as one of the most insanitary British cities was fully confirmed. Fundamental to a resolution of both the public order and the public health questions was the establishment of an effective system of local government. The incorporation of the borough of Bradford was the prime objective of William Byles of the *Bradford Observer* during the 1840s.

Like so many other newspapers in provincial England, the *Bradford Observer* was established in order to advance the case of Liberal dissenters. Launched in a manner similar to the *Leeds Mercury* and the *Manchester Guardian,* the *Observer* began publication in 1834 as the mouthpiece for its long list of manufacturing, nonconformist shareholders. Byles received the invitation to move from London to Bradford via the nonconformist network. During its early years the *Observer* steadily lost money, and Byles sometimes contemplated giving up. His patience was rewarded in 1842, when two of the original shareholders, Robert Milligan and Henry Forbes, who were also among the richest and the most powerful of the Bradford mercantile elite, became his financial backers, securing the paper's future and Byles's own control.[40]

By 1842 Byles had established himself through the *Observer* as an important member of that commercial and industrial connection of Liberal nonconformists who sought social, economic, and political preeminence in the town. This was the new elite struggling to wrest control from the established, traditional elite of gentlemen and merchants: The two were fundamentally opposed in both religion and politics.[41] Byles was well placed to promote the incorporation campaign. He was the secretary of the local anticorn law association and of the United Reform Club, the key political association in Bradford: Moreover, in 1843 he was appointed an improvement commissioner, an ideal platform for local government reform. In November 1843 the commissioners called a town meeting to discuss an application for incorporation, a proposal supported by Byles with powerful articles in the *Observer*. Byles stressed the need for effective policing, for improvement in sanitation, and for democratic self-government.[42] As in other towns, the editorial wish was not necessarily the public's command, and the Liberals were defeated by a Tory-radical alliance. Byles pointedly commented on this setback. "All persons who are interested in housebreaking, all admirers of dirt and smoke will be quite content that Bradford should remain as it is — exposed to the burglar, covered with dirt and wrapt in pestilential diseases."[43]

The logic that suggested that incorporation was both a natural and a necessary consequence of Bradford's current predicament escaped many groups in the town. Traditional governors simply resented and resisted the spurious claims of the newcomers; parochial and township loyalties were often stronger than identification with the new borough; extreme radicals believed the municipal franchise to be highly undemocratic; working-class Chartists feared the imposition of a harsh police regime; and municipal economists rejected the increased local taxation that would follow from a public cleanup of the manufacturers' wasteland. The alliance of these contradictory forces was strong enough to embarrass Byles and the incorporation party by presenting counterpetitions against incorporation. When in 1845, with much trumpeting in the *Observer,* an incorporation petition was presented to the Privy Council, it was rejected, for the anticorporationists had been able to muster more signatures. As Elliott has shown, this was largely a party political battle, more about who should control the town than about how it should be governed.[44] Byles seemed genuinely demoralized by this defeat, but two factors favored the Liberals in Bradford. The fall of Peel's government in 1846 inaugurated a Whig-Liberal administration sympathetic to incorporation. Despite the political controversy, there was a widespread local feeling that things could not be allowed to continue unchecked. When the campaign was renewed with better planning than before, success was assured and in 1847 Bradford received its charter. At the first meeting of the new Town Council, when Robert Milligan was elected mayor and Henry Forbes alderman, the symbolic presence of William Byles at the very heart of Bradford Liberal politics was confirmed.

III

The achievement of a charter of incorporation was one sign of Byles's influence, and in the same year his importance was further confirmed in the general election, when his mediation was crucial in holding his party together. Elsewhere in the West Riding the Whig-Liberal alliance dissolved because of the controversy over state education. In perhaps the best example of an editor as political activist, Edward Baines Junior roused the dissenters of the north to seek vengeance on the Whigs in the name of voluntaryism. It is inconceivable to think of Baines achieving what he did without the *Leeds Mercury* under his control. Here Baines was able to assume regional, even national visibility: Many felt that he turned his great political asset to destructive use by splitting his party and sacrificing many safe seats at the 1847 election.[45] It was indeed in the realm of electoral and agitational politics that an editor might launch himself beyond the parish pump and find fame or notoriety. Baines Junior was merely emulating his father, though with less success. In 1830 Baines Senior pulled off a spectacular coup by imposing the Whig Henry Brougham upon an unwilling Yorkshire constituency. The promotion of Brougham through the pages of the *Mercury* was the critical factor. A year later Baines staged a repeat performance by doing the thinking for Leeds Liberals and nominating Thomas Babington Macaulay as parliamentary candidate. The Liberals were satirized for accepting such dictation, and as one squib put it, "all those timid birds who can only flutter and crow on his dunghill will prick up their ears, as if some new light has just broken in on them; and everyone will coquet and find some fresh recommendation in favour of the Honourable *Intended*."[46] Macaulay had never even visited Leeds, yet Baines managed to pull it off, a tribute to the influence of a powerful local newspaper.

In another well-known example, R. K. Douglas placed himself at the very vanguard of Chartism by committing the *Birmingham Journal* at a critical moment. For a brief period, notwithstanding the *Northern Star,* the *Journal* became the tactical brains of Chartism, for it was Douglas who wrote the National Petition and the Birmingham men who launched the campaign for it in 1838. Birmingham leadership was soon thrown over as much because of the local social and economic structure as of the attack from O'Connor.[47] Yet Douglas's name did not disappear from national affairs, for he surfaced even within the walls of Westminster. He and a veteran radical journalist George Edmonds (who had run a series of short-lived papers around 1820) were both given posts in the new Council established in 1838, no doubt as political spoils. When the Bull Ring riots occurred, Peel vilified the Council and cited these two wholly unsuitable appointments as compelling evidence why the city could not be trusted to run its own police affairs.

No doubt in Victorian England there were many editors who shunned publicity and whose identity now foxes us. There were also many, like Douglas, Baines, and the rest, who stepped boldly onto the political stage and left some personal mark on the historical record. Their newspapers and their positions as editors were the vital stepping-stones to such political prominence. The few examples discussed in this paper are but part of a growing catalogue of editors as political activists, which modern research is gradually revealing.

NOTES

1. James Grant, *History of the Newspaper Press,* III, *The Metropolitan Weekly and Provincial Press* (London, 1872), p. 205.

2. Alan J. Lee, *The Origins of the Popular Press, 1855-1914* (London, 1976), p. 107; Stanley Harrison, *Poor Men's Guardians* (London, 1974), p. 104.

3. A useful introduction to the stamp return is provided by Joel H. Wiener, "Circulation and the Stamp Tax," *Victorian Periodicals: A Guide to Research,* ed. J. Don Vann and Rosemary T. VanArsdale (New York, 1978), pp. 149-173.

4. So called in the classic work on the English press, H. R. Fox Bourne, *English Newspapers: Chapters in the History of Journalism* (London, 1887), II, p. 232.

5. Stephen Koss, *The Rise and Fall of the Political Press in Britain: The Nineteenth Century* (London, 1981), p. 61.

6. See, by way of example, the cases mentioned in Ivon Asquith's essay, "The Structure, Ownership and Control of the Press, 1780-1855," *Newspaper History: From the Seventeenth Century to the Present Day,* ed. George Boyce, James Curran, and Pauline Wingate (London, 1978), pp. 98-116.

7. Grant, p. 333; D. Fraser, "The Nottingham Press, 1800-1850," *Trans. Thoroton Society* LXVII (1963): 53.

8. *Yorkshire Post,* 2 July 1866; see M. Gibb and F. Beckwith, *The Yorkshire Post* (Leeds, 1954).

9. *Payne's Leicester and Midland Counties Advertiser,* 1 January 1842; both in fact occasionally deviated from a strictly neutral editorial policy — see D. Fraser, "Newspapers and Opinion in Three Midland Cities, 1800-1850," University of Leeds M.A. Thesis, 1962.

10. Grant, p. 312.

11. R. Oastler, *A Letter to a Runaway MP* (Huddersfield, 1836), p. 3. A variation on the same theme, also used by Oastler, was that Baines was driven out of Lancashire because his "playful tricks" threatened to overpopulate his parish.

12. E. Baines, *The Life of Edward Baines* (London, 1851), p. 21.

13. T. Pinney, ed., *The Letters of Thomas Babington Macaulay,* II (Cambridge, 1974), p. 361; Earl Fitzwilliam to Sir C. Eardley, 25 November 1848, Wentworth Woodhouse Mss., G7(d), Sheffield City Library.

14. R. Cobden to J. Bright, 22 December 1848, B. M. Add. Mss., 43,649, f. 107. For further details, see D. Fraser, "Voluntaryism and West Riding Politics in the Mid-Nineteenth Century," *Northern History* XIII (1977): 199-231.

15. Rev. Samuel Clarkson to E. Baines, 30 July 1851, Baines Papers 23/4, Leeds City Archives.

16. *Sheffield Independent,* 1891, quoted by D. James, "William Byles and the *Bradford Observer,*" in *Victorian Bradford,* ed. D. G. Wright and J. A. Jowitt (Bradford, 1982), p. 124.

17. For O'Connor's views and tactics on this, see James Epstein, *The Lion of Freedom: Feargus O'Connor and the Chartist Movement, 1832-1842* (London, 1982), Chap. 2.

18. *Kentish Gazette,* 2 January 1849.

19. *Leicester Corporation and Parochial Reformer,* 18 September 1835; for the history of the corporation and its reform, see R. W. Greaves, *The Corporation of Leicester* (Oxford, 1939), and A. Temple Patterson, *Radical Leicester* (Leicester, 1954).

20. *Leicester Chronicle,* 28 December 1839.

21. Ibid., 21 September 1844.

22. Ibid., 21 January, 19 August, 2 September, 18 November, 16 December 1843.

23. *Leicestershire Mercury,* 27 December 1843, 10 January 1846.

24. *Leicester Chronicle,* 17 October 1846.

25. Ibid., 3 November 1849.

26. Arthur Aspinall, *Politics and the Press, c.1780-1850* (London, 1949), p. 35; Ms. fragment "Commentary on the Legality of the Trial of Charles Sutton," Nottingham Reference Library, Archives M1001; *Nottingham Review,* 1 September 1815, 9, 16 February 1816, 14 February 1817.

142 Derek Fraser

27. For the Nottingham Corporation, see J. D. Chambers, *Modern Nottingham in the Making* (Nottingham, 1945); R. A. Church, *Economic and Social Change in a Provincial Town: Victorian Nottingham, 1815-1914* (London, 1966); Malcolm I. Thomis, *Politics and Society in Nottingham, 1785-1835* (Oxford, 1969).

28. *Nottingham Review*, 20 September 1844.

29. *Nottingham Journal*, 15 November, 20 December 1844, 28 February 1845.

30. D. Gray and V. Walker, eds., *Records of the Borough of Nottingham*, IX, *1836-1900* (Nottingham, 1956), p. 44.

31. *Nottingham Mercury*, 28 February, 7, 14 March, 6 June 1845.

32. *Nottingham Review*, 7 March 1845.

33. J. T. Bunce, *History of the Corporation of Birmingham* (Birmingham, 1878 I), pp. 290-291.

34. *Birmingham Journal*, 26 October 1844.

35. Ibid., 3 May 1845.

36. For these details, see D. Fraser, *Power and Authority in the Victorian City* (Oxford, 1979), Chap. 4.

37. Bunce, p. 296.

38. Lee, pp. 103, 205.

39. The best introduction to the history of Bradford in this period is now Jack Reynolds, *The Great Paternalist: Titus Salt and the Growth of Nineteenth-Century Bradford* (London, 1983).

40. See James, "William Byles," and H. N. Byles, *William Byles by His Youngest Son* (Weymouth, 1932).

41. See A. Elliott, "The Establishment of Municipal Government in Bradford, 1837-57," University of Bradford, Ph.D. thesis, 1976; "The Incorporation of Bradford," *Northern History* XV (1979).

42. *Bradford Observer*, 23, 30 November 1843.

43. Ibid., 7 December 1843.

44. A. Elliott, "Municipal Government in Bradford in the Mid-nineteenth Century," in *Municipal Reform and the Industrial City*, ed. D. Fraser (Leicester, 1982).

45. Fraser, "Voluntaryism and West Riding Politics"; J. A. Jowitt, "Dissenters, Voluntaryism and Liberal Unity: The 1847 Election," in *Nineteenth Century Bradford Elections*, ed. J. A. Jowitt and R.K.S. Taylor (Bradford, 1979), pp. 7-23.

46. *Principles and Not Men, A Dialogue Between Tom and Jerry* (Leeds, 1831), handbill Leeds Reference Library.

47. For an account that challenges the traditional picture, see C. Behagg, "An Alliance with the Middle Class: The Birmingham Political Union and Early Chartism," in *The Chartist Experience*, ed. J. Epstein and D. Thompson (London, 1982), pp. 59-86.

Josef L. Altholz

The Redaction of Catholic Periodicals

We speak of "the Victorian editor"; but in fact the editorship of most developed Victorian periodicals involved a complex of individuals of varying status, titles, and functions. There was the editor himself who was at the center of things but not necessarily supreme. He might be assisted by a subeditor or more than one assistant editor or some departmental editors. There might be an editorial committee or "cabinet" or a person without official title whom a leading Catholic editor, Richard Simpson, called "Cabinet minister without portfolio" or "exceptionally privileged contributor."[1] The editor might be under the direction of some powerful personage, a bishop perhaps, or a committee of directors with control but no official responsibility or, among Catholics, a "theological censor" with veto power. Then, of course, there was the proprietor or proprietors who frequently had something to do with the editorial direction. There was the publisher, properly an agent for the sale and the distribution of the periodical but often impinging on the proprietorship or the editorship. Finally there was the printer, also in principle an agent but frequently involved in editorial business if only because proofreading was often done in his shop. This is a long list of quasi-editorial personages, though frequently two or more of these characters might be combined in one person, such as a publisher-printer or a proprietor-editor, and in the more primitive stages of the development of periodicals one person might even perform all these functions. There really is no adequate term in English to describe this *mélange* as a totality: *conductors* or *management* is too vague, *team* is too American, and *staff* implies subordination. Another Catholic editor, Sir John (later Lord) Acton, felt a need to borrow a term from the French: *rédaction*.[2] I think we can naturalize the word *redaction* into the English language to serve as a technical term for the totality of the persons involved in the editorial process. Nearly every combination or permutation of redaction could be found somewhere in the Roman Catholic press, which may serve as a model for studies of redaction.

The earliest Catholic periodicals were the products of men who combined the functions of printer, publisher, proprietor, and editor; their primary occupation was that of bookseller.[3] These booksellers-publishers started magazines both to advance Catholic interests and to add to the sales of their firms; if they had literary pretensions, they edited the periodicals as well. The most notable of these publishers-editors was William Eusebius Andrews, originally a printer from Norwich, who started approximately ten series between his arrival in London in 1813 and his death in 1837, including three series of a monthly, the *Orthodox Journal*,[4] two weekly newspapers, and weekly miscellanies with titles such as *Weekly Orthodox Journal of Entertaining Christian Knowledge* and *London and Dublin Orthodox Journal of Useful Knowledge*.[5] Andrews had a rival, both journalistically and ideologically, in the established firm of Keating and Brown, one of whose members, George Keating, published and edited three journals between 1815 and 1826.[6] Obviously, the redaction of all these journals was a simple and harmonious affair.

The booksellers-publishers might also be responsible for periodicals for which they employed others as editors. In addition to the journals that George Keating edited, three generations of Keatings started journals, in 1801, 1828, and 1839, employing editors. It may be significant that the editors of the last two, both professional journalists, resigned after a year either because they were discouraged by the lack of support or because they went on to other journalistic ventures.[7] There was another established firm of Catholic booksellers, the house of Booker, which had abstained for two generations from publishing journals; but it was taken over between 1838 and 1840 by a relative, Charles Dolman, who had large ambitions for Catholic publishing. He was the second publisher of the *Dublin Review* from 1838 to 1844, and in 1838 he also took over an existing monthly, the *Catholic Magazine,* employing its former proprietor as the editor.[8] After a brief hiatus, he resumed this in 1845 as *Dolman's Magazine,* edited first by Miles Gerard Keon and after December 1846 by the Rev. Edward Price. In 1849 Dolman terminated his magazine in order to concentrate on publishing high-class Catholic books, an enterprise that eventually resulted in his bankruptcy. He gave his sanction to his cousin Thomas Booker to publish a journal claiming to be the successor of *Dolman's,* the *Weekly Register;* Booker continued Price as the editor of this, which ended in 1850 when Price resigned.[9]

These journals derived from the initiative of the publishers, even when editors were employed. There is another class of periodical that results from the initiative of a literary gentleman, a proprietor who usually serves as his own editor, with the publisher as a mere agent. In 1818 Charles Butler of an eminent old Catholic family started a *Catholic Gentleman's Magazine,* edited by himself (alias "Sylvester Palmer, Gent.") which lasted for a year.[10] More difficult to classify is the role of Ambrose Cudden, who started a monthly, the *Catholic Miscellany,* in 1822, purporting to be not only the proprietor and the editor but the publisher and the printer. For a while it appears that Andrews controlled the magazine; and after Cudden regained control he fell into financial trouble and had to sell out to a publisher, for whom, however, he continued to edit it. The publisher failed in 1828, and the magazine was bought by the Rev. T. M. McDonnell of Birmingham who revived it under his own editorship, employing a London publisher, until it failed in 1830.[11]

McDonnell is the link to a more important monthly, the *Catholic Magazine,* founded in 1831 as the organ of the "Cisalpines," the representatives of the English Catholic Enlightenment about to be swept away by the Ultramontane revival. The *Catholic Magazine* was owned by a number of clergy in the Midland District, five of whom served as an "editorial committee," with McDonnell in Birmingham as "acting editor"; among the contributors was the eminent historian John Lingard. The *Catholic Magazine* was perhaps the best of the early Catholic periodicals; but eventually its conductors seem to have discovered that the Enlightenment was over. They withdrew at the end of 1835, and the magazine appeared irregularly in 1836 as the *Catholicon* before fading away.[12]

In that year of 1836 the spokesman of the rising Ultramontanes, Nicholas Wiseman, founded the *Dublin Review,* the first Catholic quarterly. Wiseman shared the proprietorship with Daniel O'Connell, but "the Liberator" gave to the *Dublin* only his name and an annual contribution of £25.[13] Wiseman was in full control, but he was in Rome until 1840 and a bishop thereafter, and so a working editor was needed. The first was Michael J. Quin, an Irish lawyer in London, who had first proposed the review to Wiseman; but Quin resigned after two numbers.[14] After two interim editors, a permanent editor was found in H. R. Bagshawe, a barrister, who served from 1837 to 1863. Bagshawe's editorial role is hard to define: He functioned as an executive editor, doing the donkey work, but he never was in full command. Wiseman, after his return to England, took an active if irregular part in the direction and was regarded by many as the real editor.[15] There was also the Rev. Charles W. Russell, a professor at Maynooth College, who was a major and a privileged contributor, organized other Irish contributors and served as the editor for them, spoke of taking a role in the editorship, and in fact was at least an associate editor throughout this period.[16] Wiseman was not disturbed by this apparent disorganization—he ran his archdiocese much the same way—but as he became absorbed in his role as cardinal archbishop after 1850 and later came to be in ill health, more responsibility fell on Bagshawe who was not equal to it. Bagshawe offered to resign in 1858, but Wiseman persuaded him to stay on; he finally had to resign after being appointed to a county court judgeship in 1861. In the confusion, the *Dublin* missed deadlines and even issues just when a clear voice of othodoxy was wanted to counteract the liberal Catholicism of the *Rambler,* later the *Home and Foreign Review.*[17]

To rescue the *Dublin* Wiseman turned to the Ultramontane converts, giving the proprietorship in 1862 to his protégé and eventual successor, Henry Edward Manning,[18] who appointed as editor in 1863 the ablest lay Ultramontane, William George Ward. The *Dublin* thereupon began a vigorous polemical career; "you will find me," Ward told a subeditor, "narrow and strong—*very* narrow and *very* strong."[19] Lest he be too strong, he was placed under a theological censorship,[20] and Manning himself exercised strict control. Ward's interests were confined to theology and philosophy on which he wrote most of the articles himself. Because of this narrowness of interest, he left virtual freedom in the departments of politics, literature, and history—about half the review—to a subeditor, at first his fellow-convert E. Healy Thompson and beginning in 1865 an able Irishman, J. Cashel Hoey.[21]

Ward retired in 1878, and about that time Manning presented the *Dublin* to his own protégé and future successor, Herbert Vaughan, then bishop of Salford. Vaughan appointed as the editor a Benedictine monk, Cuthbert Hedley, who moderated the tome and widened the scope of the *Dublin*. But Hedley himself became a bishop in 1881, and in 1884 he resigned as the editor. Vaughan himself, at least nominally, then became the editor; but in fact the acting editorship was held by the subeditor whom he had inherited from Hedley, W.E. Driffield.[22] When Vaughan became archbishop of Westminster in 1892, he appointed as the editor Canon James Moyes, who was succeeded in 1906 by W.G. Ward's son Wilfrid. Thereafter the role of the editor was the conventional one of leadership, complicated only by the position of the review as an official organ of the archdiocese.[23]

The leading journals founded in the 1840s were the creations of proprietors who were their own editors. The first was the *Tablet,* a weekly founded in 1840 by a recent convert from Quakerism, Frederick Lucas. Lucas obtained financial aid from the brothers Keasley, leather merchants; but the Keasleys failed in 1841, and they were replaced in partnership by the printer, a Protestant named Cox.[24] Lucas had wide support among Catholics, but he also offended many by his too vigorous advocacy of Catholic claims and his warm support for the Irish. Cox entered into a cabal against Lucas, and the result was a rupture in February 1842. Lucas restarted the journal under his own control, calling it the *True Tablet* to avoid a lawsuit, while Cox employed Quin, the first editor of the *Dublin,* as the editor of the nominally continuous *Tablet.* For several months the two *Tablets* fought each other, on one occasion physically.[25] But Lucas kept the all-important subscriber list and won the support both of the Irish and of many English Catholics. By July 1842 Cox and Quin gave up and the *True Tablet* was left in possession of the field,[26] resuming in 1843 the name of the *Tablet.* But Lucas became increasingly devoted to Irish nationalism, especially after the Famine, and he lost much of his English support.[27] Eventually Lucas moved himself and his *Tablet* to Dublin late in 1849, and he entered Irish politics. The Irish phase of the *Tablet* continued until his death in 1855.

The next year the *Tablet* was purchased by an English barrister, John Wallis, who brought it back to London where he edited it himself. He also changed its politics, making it a Tory organ. His Toryism was palatable to Cardinal Wiseman but caused conflict with Wiseman's successor, Manning. In 1868 Wallis sold out to Manning's protégé Herbert Vaughan, who wanted an organ for the high Ultramontane position on the eve of the First Vatican Council. Vaughan edited the *Tablet* until 1872, when he became a bishop. His subeditor, G. E. Ranken, was then promoted to be editor. Ranken was succeeded in 1884 by Vaughan's relative and future biographer, J. G. Snead-Cox, who remained editor until 1920 and consolidated the position of the *Tablet* as a solid, temperate, and politically conservative journal.[28] Because of Vaughan's episcopal preoccupations, the *Tablet* had been transformed from a proprietor-edited periodical into a conventional journal managed by a professional editor.

The 1840s saw the first wave of Oxford converts, and it was inevitable that some of these educated men, especially ex-parsons forced back into lay status because they were married, would seek an outlet in periodicals. One such was John Moore Capes who founded the *Rambler* as a weekly magazine in January 1848. After two months he converted it to a weekly newspaper; but this demanded too much of a proprietor-editor who wrote most of the journal with some assistance from a few other converts, notably, his brother Frederick (who chose the art department) and James Spencer Northcote who was "Our Own Correspondent" in Rome in that year of revolution. In September Capes converted the *Rambler* into a monthly. Some of the Oratorian Fathers contributed, and Newman served as the "theological censor" (meaning adviser) unntil 1852.[29] In that year Capes, in ill health, gave the editorship to Northcote. When Northcote's wife died, liberating him to become a priest, he returned the editorship in 1854 to Capes who had been dissatisfied with his "cautiousness."[30] Capes sought a subeditor in a younger convert, Richard Simpson, who at first only agreed to become a contributor. In 1856 Simpson became the subeditor, and his contributions brought the *Rambler* into conflict with the hierarchy because of his liberalism.[31] It was not this conflict but continued ill health and the exhaustion of his financial resources that brought Capes to resign as the editor late in 1857 and to sell the magazine. One share each went to Simpson and to Frederick Capes, and two shares were taken by the German educated Liberal Catholic, Sir John Acton. An elaborate scheme for a Council was projected but did not materialize; in fact, beginning in 1858 the *Rambler* was run jointly by Simpson and Acton,[32] Simpson being the editor.

The new management proved too controversial for the taste of the hierarchy, and early in 1859 Wiseman and two bishops demanded Simpson's removal from the editorship. To save the magazine the proprietors prevailed upon Newman to become the editor. Newman made the *Rambler* a bimonthly, indicating increasing literary aspirations, and he edited it for two issues; but he too got in trouble for his writings, and upon a hint from his bishop he resigned.[33] Acton, deemed less controversial then Simpson, now took the editorship; but as a politician and a socialite, he was unable to devote full time to it, and he needed a subeditor. Newman found him one in a recent convert, Thomas

F. Wetherell, a clerk in the War Office. Wetherell was difficult to deal with: He had the curious notion that he was the coeditor rather than the subeditor;[34] he was frequently disabled by illness or overwork;[35] and he acted as Newman's agent to moderate the tone of the *Rambler;* but the suave Acton learned to handle him. In 1861 the hierarchy made another attempt to bring the *Rambler* to heel, using the publisher, James Burns, hitherto a mere business agent. Burns refused to publish the next number unless the management was turned over to an Ultramontane committee. The proprietors defeated the attempted *coup* by switching to a Protestant publisher, Williams and Norgate.[36] But a censure by the bishops, if not by Rome, was becoming likely. Partly to avoid this but mostly to enable their venture to grow to its full potential, Acton and Simpson decided in 1862 to transform the *Rambler* into a quarterly review with a new title. The *Home and Foreign Review* thus became the rival of the *Dublin Review,* itself in the process of restructuring.[37]

The *Home and Foreign* achieved distinction despite an uncertain redaction. Acton remained the editor, with Wetherell as the subeditor but thinking that he was the coeditor. Acton and Simpson were coproprietors, Frederick Capes having dropped out. Wetherell soon urged that Simpson also withdraw from the proprietorship because his reputation as a "terrible infant" hurt the review.[38] Simpson nominally withdrew, with the right of resuming his proprietorship; but he remained an "exceptionally privileged contributor" and an effective member of the redaction, leading to further conflicts with Wetherell.[39] In 1863 the redaction was expanded by an additional subeditor, the learned Orientalist Peter le Page Renouf;[40] and a young Anglican, D.C. Lathbury, joined the staff as a reviser of articles.[41] The end of the *Home and Foreign* came in 1864 not because of editorial difficulties but as a result of a Papal rescript condemning the principle for which the review stood, the independence of scholarship from ecclesiastical authority. Acton decided to "sacrifice the existence of the *Review* to the defense of its principles,"[42] a decision in which the others concurred.

The Acton-Simpson-Wetherell team made two further ventures into journalism, but they could not do so as professedly Catholic journalists. In 1867 they started a weekly newspaper, the *Chronicle,* underwritten by the Irish baronet Sir Rowland Blennerhasset, with Wetherell as the full editor, Lathbury as the subeditor, and Acton as correspondent in Rome; but the *Chronicle* was professedly an organ of Gladstonian liberalism.[43] It failed to pay its costs and expired after a year. In 1869 the same team took over the *North British Review,* previously the organ of the Scottish Free Kirk, and tried to make it an undenominational version of the *Home and Foreign.*[44] But Wetherell's health broke down in 1871, and Acton and Simpson were by now discouraged; and so the *North British* was allowed to expire.

At the end of the 1840s two weeklies, Thomas Booker's short-lived *Weekly Register* and a newspaper, the *Catholic Standard,* were founded. The founder of the latter (perhaps with some associates) was a Frenchman, E. Robillard, who was financially ruined by 1852, when Cardinal Wiseman sought to raise funds to rescue him.[45] Late in 1854 the *Catholic Standard* came under the control of Henry Wilberforce, son of "the Liberator" and brother of "Soapy Sam." In 1855 the *Catholic Standard* was merged with the defunct *Weekly Register* and was thereafter known by the latter name. The purpose of this maneuver was apparently to establish an English rival to the Irishness of Lucas's *Tablet;* but Lucas's death soon made this pointless.[46] The *Weekly Register* was nonetheless a rival of the *Tablet,* Wilberforce being a Liberal and Wallis a Conservative; their rivalry was a feebler counterpart to that of the *Rambler* and the *Dublin Review.* Despite (or perhaps because of) the employment of one or more subeditors, Wilberforce became weary of the burden of bringing out a weekly.[47] In

1863 or 1864 he sold out to another convert, Robert Walker.[48] Little is known of the subsequent management of the *Weekly Register* until 1881, when it was acquired by Cardinal Manning "to save it from extinction."[49] Manning gave it to Wilfrid Meynell, who edited it with the assistance of his wife, Alice, for nineteen years. Meynell did not give the *Weekly Register* his full attention, however, for he was busy with a more important venture of his own, the monthly *Merry England,* founded in 1883 with Lord Ripon and Charles Russell as sleeping partners. *Merry England* boasted a distinguished list of contributors in the dozen years of its existence.[50] The *Weekly Register* lingered on, passing in 1899 into the editorship of a recent convert, Robert Dell, who rashly embroiled it in the Modernist controversy, and in 1900 to Frank Rooke Ley. It was transformed in 1902 into the *Monthly Register,* which died the same year, removing the only liberal Catholic periodical.[51]

The 1850s saw the beginnings of Catholic popular periodicals. The most notable of these was the *Lamp,* "devoted to the Religious, Moral, Physical and Domestic Improvement of the Industrious Classes,"[52] founded as a weekly by T.H. Bradley at York in 1850. The *Lamp* went through a bewildering variety of changes of publisher, place of publication, proprietor, and editor until 1862, when it was purchased and edited by Mrs. Fanny Margaret Taylor, later the founder of the *Month.* She had the assistance of several Jesuit Fathers in her work. She sold the *Lamp* in 1871 to the convert Mrs. Lockhart, who initially kept Mrs. Taylor (now Mother Magdalen Taylor) as the editor, with Wilfrid Meynell as the subeditor, of what was now a monthly. Subsequent editors were James Coen, a barrister, and his sister Nora, until the magazine passed in 1890 to Charles Gilbert Ellis and after his early death in 1892 to George Cooke. The *Lamp* finally fell into the hands of Charles Diamond of the *Catholic Herald* and was put out in 1905.[53]

The first of the great popular newspapers was the *Universe,* begun in 1860 under the inspiration of Cardinal Wiseman and the management of members of a lay fraternity, the Society of St. Vincent de Paul. The committee that managed it was led by George J. Wigley, London correspondent of the French Ultramontane journal *L'Univers;* the printer was a London Irishman, Denis Lane, and the first of a series of unpaid editors was Archibald Dunn. At first the *Universe* avoided politics, and when politics had to be included to boost the circulation, the original staff resigned, and the printer, Lane, became the proprietor and ran the *Universe* with a firm hand (employing editors) until his death in 1906.[54]

The next important Catholic periodical to appear was the *Month,* founded in 1864 by Mrs. Taylor of the *Lamp* for a higher class audience. Mrs. Taylor's chief support came from the Jesuit Fathers. When she found the *Month* burdensome and unprofitable, she sold out in 1865 to the Jesuits who thereafter ran it corporately from the Farm Street community. Inevitably the Jesuits transformed it into a more serious monthly review. The redaction of the *Month* was of a more collective character than that of any other periodical. The editors served for long terms: Henry Coleridge, grandnephew of the poet and brother of a chief justice, 1865-82, Richard F. Clarke, 1882-94, John Gerard, 1894-97 and 1901-12, Sydney Smith, 1897-1901; they contributed to the magazine before and after their editorships; their personalities were not of particular significance, as the *Month* maintained an even level throughout, closely supervised by Jesuit provincials from Peter Gallwey, who had helped start the *Month,* to Gerard himself.[55] Farm Street was known as the "scriptorium,"[56] with priests assigned to it for the primary purpose of writing for the *Month* and other Jesuit publications. One such was the Modernist George Tyrrell, whose writings caused a deal of trouble at the turn of the century; but the *Month* survived.

Two other weekly newspapers for the general public remain to be noticed. One began in 1867 as *Catholic Opinion,* founded by Mrs. Lockhart and edited by her son, Fr. William Lockhart. It was purchased in 1873 by that great acquirer of periodicals, Bishop Vaughan, who used it as an educational supplement to the *Tablet.* Vaughan in turn sold it in 1876 to Fr. James Nugent, the "Apostle of Liverpool," who amalgamated it with a struggling local paper, the *Northern Press,* which had been founded in 1860. The resulting journal was called the *Catholic Times* and edited by an Irishman, John Denvir, who made it for a while the Home Rule organ in England. It was then owned by other priests and edited by lay editors until, after 1926, it became the organ of the Catholic Missionary Society.[57]

The other major newspaper was established in 1884 under the inspiration of Cardinal Manning as the avowed organ of "Catholic Industrial Democracy." This was the *Catholic Herald,* owned and edited by Charles Diamond for the next fifty years. Diamond's controversial writing got him into trouble, and the *Catholic Herald* did not win a mass audience until it came into other, quite different hands after 1934.[58].

With the establishment of the *Catholic Herald,* the national Catholic press had completed its development, although local and diocesan journals were the products of the next two decades. The Catholic press was not much different in kind from that of other denominations, except perhaps for the tendency of its journals to become the organs of parties within the church: "We are notoriously the most disputatious community in the kingdom," J. M. Capes had observed.[59] It is a curious fact that this most disciplined and hierarchical of churches left the foundation of periodicals entirely to individual (usually lay) initiative. This individuality of initiative may account for the distinctive feature of Catholic journalism, which has been the concern of this paper, the variety of redactional structures from the single-handed management of the earliest periodicals to the split personalities of the *Home and Foreign Review* to the corporate staff of the *Month,* for whom the editorial "we" was no fiction. But this was more characteristic of the first two thirds of the century than of the last third, when the acquisition of periodicals by Manning and Vaughan and the general triumph of Ultramontanism throughout the church restricted the diversity of editorial viewpoints. A similar narrowing took place in the structure of redactions. Booksellers, publishers, and printers receded into the background; management became a matter between proprietors and editors. There was a gain in professionalism (or at least consistency), but it was at the price of uniformity. The age of adventure was over.

NOTES

1. Simpson to Acton, 14 December 1863 and 2 March 1864, *The Correspondence of Lord Acton and Richard Simpson,* ed. Josef L. Altholz, Damian McElrath, and James C. Holland, 3 vols (Cambridge, 1971-75), 3: pp. 147-148, 175-176.

2. Acton to Simpson, 17 August 1863, ibid., p. 124.

3. Keating is listed as "bookseller" and Booker (Dolman's predecessor) as "bookseller and stationer" in *Johnstone's London Commercial Guide and Street Directory* (London, 1817), pp. 53, 172.

4. The series were numbered continuously despite long gaps in publication, leading some directories to treat them as one periodical. The first had the patronage of Bishop Milner, an extreme Ultramontane. See Francis E. Mineka, *The Dissidence of Dissent* (Chapel Hill, 1944), p. 77.

5. For these publications, see John R. Fletcher, "Early Catholic Periodicals in England," *Dublin Review* 198 (April 1936): 284-310.

6. Keating supported the Catholic Association, representing the "Cismontane," or national party, among the English Catholics.

7. Fletcher, "Early Catholic Periodicals," 293-94, 297-98, citing contradictory evidence from his two sources, F.C. H[usenbeth], "Catholic Periodicals," *Notes and Queries,* 3d s. 2 (5 January 1867), pp. 2-4, (12 January), pp. 29-31, and Joseph Gillow, *A Literary and Biographical History, or Bibliographical Dictionary of the English Catholics* (London, 1885-1903), 5 vols. Gillow also published a series of articles and letters on "Early Catholic Periodicals" in the *Tablet* between 22 January and 5 March 1881.

8. This was James Smith, a convert, who had founded it as the *Edinburgh Catholic Magazine* in 1832-33 and again (in London) in 1837. Smith briefly reappeared as the third editor of the *Dublin Review* in 1837. See Fletcher, "Early Catholic Periodicals," 295, 297.

9. The Dolman-Booker connection spawned a series of periodicals that succeeded each other, merged or putatively merged in so intricate a fashion that it is best represented by a genealogical chart: See Fletcher, "Early Catholic Periodicals," 305.

10. Fletcher says that it was "well got up," 291.

11. Ibid., 291-92.

12. The best account of the *Catholic Magazine* is Joseph P. Chinnici, O.F.M., *The English Catholic Enlightenment* (Shepherdstown, W. Va., 1980), pp. 136-48. Lingard, perhaps feeling that he had outlived his age, became disgusted with the magazine: See p. 142. Fletcher, "Early Catholic Periodicals," 294-95, gives the editorial structure and speaks of "the secession of its clerical proprietors."

13 *The Wellesley Index to Victorian Periodicals, 1824-1900,* ed. Walter E. Houghton, 3 vols. (Toronto, 1966, 1972, 1979), 2: p. 19 n. 50. After O'Connell's death in 1847 (or perhaps earlier), Wiseman treated the *Dublin* as his sole property.

14. He feared that the *Dublin* would be a financial failure and went to work for the *Morning Herald.*

15. Fletcher, "Early Catholic Periodicals," 297. When the young Acton submitted an article to the *Dublin,* he wrote directly to Wiseman: Acton to Wiseman, 17 February 1857, Archives of the Archdiocese of Westminster.

16. *Wellesley Index,* 2: pp. 12-13, is the best account of this situation. There really is no adequate term to describe Russell's status. *Wellesley Index,* 2: p. 19, also gives Frederick Lucas as "Co-Editor," 1839-42, overlapping his early years with the *Tablet* but perhaps irregularly.

17. See Josef L. Altholz, *The Liberal Catholic Movement in England* (London, 1962), pp. 34-39, 72-73, 182-84.

18. This is questioned by L. C. Casartelli, "Our Diamond Jubilee," *Dublin Review* 118 (April 1896): 251, 263, 270, saying that Ward was the owner during his editorship; so it is as well to give the text. "I give you full powers to deal with the 'Dublin Review' in every respect, as if your own property; and I shall be ready to ratify all your acts, concerning it; retaining no responsibility, or necessity of further reference to me in the transactions with publishers or editors etc." Wiseman to Manning, 9 September 1862, Manning Papers. This peculiar wording of a property transfer is in response to Manning to Wiseman, 8 September 1862: "May I ask your Eminence to write me a note stating that you transfer the Dublin Review to me. It will enable me more firmly to take the necessary steps." E. S. Purcell, *Life of Cardinal Manning, Archbishop of*

Westminster, 2 vols. (London, 1896), 2, p. 385. Purcell was the editor of the *Westminster Gazette,* 1869-79.

19. Quoted by Wilfrid Ward, *William George Ward and the Catholic Revival* (London, 1912), p. 223.

20. J. J. Dwyer, "The Catholic Press, 1850-1950," in *The English Catholics, 1850-1950,* ed. G. A. Beck (London, 1950), p. 477.

21. *Wellesley Index,* 2, pp. 14, 16.

22. Ibid., p. 19 n. 49.

23. Dwyer, "The Catholic Press," alludes to Ward's difficulties during the Modernist crisis, when his position was in danger and he in effect censored himself to avoid harm to the reputation of Newman, of which he had constituted himself the guardian.

24. I follow the account of Fletcher, "Early Catholic Periodicals," 299, though it is possible that Lucas was not an original coproprietor until Cox gave him a share to retain him as the editor.

25. For an account of this conflict, see Josef L. Altholz, "The *Tablet,* the *True Tablet,* and Nothing but the *Tablet,*" *Victorian Periodicals Newsletter* 9 (June 1976): 68-72.

26. Cox tried once more with a weekly called the *Catholic,* edited by D. D. Keane, 30 July-19 November 1842. Lucas himself started a second journal, *Lucas' Penny Library,* late in 1842, but he was unable to capitalize on the vogue for penny magazines. Fletcher, "Early Catholic Periodicals," 300-301.

27. Lucas thought that the *Rambler* was started against him in 1848: privately printed circular, Archives of the Archdiocese of Westminster. The *Catholic Standard,* founded in 1849, did in fact become the *Tablet's* opposition as the *Weekly Register.* Lucas has a biography, Edward Lucas, *The Life of Frederick Lucas, M. P.* (London, 1886).

28. Snead-Cox employed a subeditor. When Vaughan became the archbishop of Westminster in 1892, he transferred the proprietorship of the *Tablet* to the archdiocese, which retained it until 1936. For its later history, see Dwyer, "The Catholic Press," pp. 484-89.

29. In June 1851 it was thought necessary to publish a disclaimer that the *Rambler* was an Oratorian organ. *Wellesley Index,* 2, p. 734 n. 13.

30. Cited in Altholz, *Liberal Catholic Movement,* p. 23.

31. See ibid., ch. 2.

32. The Council was to be "suggestive, persuasive, and discussive, not dictatorial." The "draft constitution" is in a memorandum by Simpson among the Gasquet papers at Downside Abbey.

33. Newman's article "On Consulting the Faithful in Matters of Doctrine" (July 1859) caused him to be "under a cloud" at Rome. For the Newman episode, see Altholz, *Liberal Catholic Movement,* pp. 91-112, and *The Letters and Diaries of John Henry Newman,* ed. C. S. Dessain (London, 1961ff.), vol. 19.

34. Wetherell insisted to his last days that he never was anything less than "co-Editor with a full equal share of authority, responsibility and management": memorandum at Downside Abbey, probably intended for Abbot Gasquet, who was preparing *Lord Acton and his Circle* (London, 1906). Yet Wetherell wrote to Newman, 9 August 1860, after a brief resignation, that he had "again taken the Subeditorship": Altholz, *Liberal Catholic Movement*, p. 127 n. 49. He also told Gasquet that he had refused remuneration for his work on the *Rambler*. If this was true, it was not with the *Home and Foreign Review* beginning in 1862.

35. Simpson acted unofficially as the subeditor during these intervals.

36. For this episode, see *Correspondence of Acton and Simpson*, 2, pp. 163-177.

37. For the negotiations with the *Dublin* at this time, see Altholz, *Liberal Catholic Movement*, pp. 181-84.

38. Wetherell to Simpson, 27 October 1862, Downside Abbey, cited in ibid., p. 201.

39. Acton spoke of "an understanding preserving your present position really intact, sacrificing only the name of proprietor." Acton to Simpson, 21 December 1862, *Correspondence of Acton and Simpson*, 3, p. 68. Since there were no profits, the sole benefit of proprietorship was the right to refuse payment for articles, which Simpson stipulated. (There is a subtle element of "gentlemen v. players" in the Simpson-Wetherell relationship.) For further conflicts, see ibid., 3, pp. 147-51, 175-78.

40. Renouf, then professor of ancient history at the Catholic University of Dublin, became an inspector of Catholic schools later in 1863. His work for the *Home and Foreign* was kept secret and was limited by his new duties.

41. Lathbury's apprenticeship on liberal Catholic periodicals was the basis of a later career as the joint editor of the *Economist*, 1878-81, the editor of the *Guardian*, 1883-99, and the editor of his own journal, the *Pilot*, 1900-04. The *Pilot*, although Anglican, served as an occasional outlet for Roman Catholic Modernists denied an organ of their own.

42. Acton, "Conflicts with Rome," *Home and Foreign Review* 4 (April 1864): 667-90. See *Correspondence of Acton and Simpson*, 3, pp. 185-87. See also the sketch of the *Home and Foreign* in *Wellesley Index*, 1, pp. 547-49.

43. Blennerhasset, like Acton, had studied under Döllinger in Munich. The essentially political character of the *Chronicle* was stated by Wetherell to Gladstone, 4 February 1868, British Library Add. MS. 44414 ff. 73-76. See also Guy Ryan, "The Acton Circle and the 'Chronicle' ", *Victorian Periodicals Newsletter* 7 (June 1974): 10-24.

44. For the Liberal Catholic phase of the *North British*, see *Wellesley Index*, 1, p. 664.

45. Mary Griset Holland, "The British Catholic Press and the Educational Controversy, 1847-1865," Ph.D. Diss. (Catholic University of America, 1975), pp. 103-04.

160   Josef L. Altholz

46. Fletcher, "Early Catholic Periodicals," 304.

47. See *Correspondence of Acton and Simpson*, 2: 75, 153, 159, 189; 3: 123-26. A subeditor named Hodges seems to have caused financial loss, but this was not the main reason for selling. See also David Newsome, *The Parting of Friends* (London, 1966), p. 405.

48. The date is conventionally given as 1863, when the *Weekly Register* was offered for sale. Professor James C. Holland informs me that the first indication of actual transfer is the issue of 2 April 1864, when Walker replaced Wilberforce as the person to whom subscriptions should be sent. Wilberforce may have continued on the editorial staff even longer: See *Letters and Diaries of Newman*, 21, pp. 133, 209.

49. Dwyer, "Catholic Press," p. 405.

50. Ibid. Among the contributors was Meynell's discovery, Francis Thompson.

51. David G. Schultenover, S. J., *George Tyrrell: In Search of Catholicism* (Shepherdstown, W. Va., 1981), pp. 152. 382 n. 183, 385 n. 25.

52. Fletcher, "Early Catholic Periodicals," 305.

53. Ibid., 305-06, and Dwyer, "Catholic Press," pp. 503-04.

54. Dwyer, "Catholic Press,' pp. 506-07.

55. See Josef L. Altholz, "The *Month*, 1864-1900," *Victorian Periodicals Review* 14 (Summer 1981): 70-72.

56. Schultenover, *George Tyrrell*, p. 470.

57. Dwyer, "Catholic Press," pp. 506-07, and Fletcher, "Early Catholic Periodicals," 307-08.

58. Dwyer, "Catholic Press," pp. 508-09, and Fletcher, "Early Catholic Periodicals," 309-10.

59. Cited in Altholz, *Liberal Catholic Movement*, p. 13.

Joanne Shattock

Showman, Lion Hunter, or Hack: The Quarterly Editor at Midcentury

According to Walter Bagehot, Francis Jeffrey invented the trade of editorship. "Before him," he wrote in 1855, "an editor was a bookseller's drudge: he is now a distinguished functionary." In retrospect at least, Jeffrey does seem to have fathered a branch of the literary profession. Following on from him is a line of flamboyant, even magisterial figures who occupied editorial chairs of one kind or another—Mark Lemon of *Punch,* William Maginn of *Fraser's,* William and John Blackwood, John Forster of the *Examiner,* J. D. Cook of the *Saturday Review,* Leslie Stephen of the *Cornhill,* John Morley of the *Fortnightly,* Henry Alford of the *Contemporary,* Richard Holt Hutton of the *Spectator,* and James Knowles of the *Nineteenth Century,* about whom Sir Frederick Pollock made the comment embedded in my title, that he was "not an editor at all, but a literary showman, a lion-hunter."[1]

Significantly none of these was the editor of a quarterly. A closer look at Jeffrey's contemporaries and successors as quarterly editors produces no household names. William Gifford, the first editor of the *Quarterly,* is a little-known figure. Henry Southern and John Bowring, the joint first editors of the *Westminster,* are scarcely distinguishable from associates such as the Mills, T. P. Thompson, and others who were closely involved with the establishment of the review. One possible explanation is that the quarterlies were often the productions of conglomerates, the group of Benthamite radicals who sponsored the *Westminster* being a good example, or the group, with Scott and John Murray at its head, that founded the *Quarterly.*

A fair amount is now known about the early years of the major triumvirate of quarterlies (the *Edinburgh,* the *Quarterly,* and the *Westminster)* but very little about their middle years in the thirties, forties, and fifties and even less about their editors at that time. Why? It is not enough, I think, merely to repeat the standard rationale that the quarterlies at that period were beginning to be regarded as expensive and dull, with articles that were too long and unrelieved by the poetry and fiction that the more glamourous shilling monthlies offered, or that they were outmaneuvered on the political front by the snappy, pungent articles of weeklies such as the *Economist,* the *Spectator,* and the *Saturday Review.* As early as the forties people had begun to predict the death of the quarterlies, and yet they went on being founded, many in the forties and on through to the sixties. And they continued to be influential—the *Edinburgh* as the organ of the Whigs, the *Quarterly* with its hereditary links to the Tories, the *Westminster,* despite its proprietary vicissitudes, continuing to offer a home to "advanced" opinion. The quarterlies also continued to be influential in spheres other than the political: in literary criticism, science, art, and social questions. Here some of the new generation stole the thunder from the original three.

In this paper I shall examine the role and the status of the editor of the quarterlies in these middle decades. I shall concentrate on two quarterlies—the *Edinburgh* under Macvey Napier, George

Cornewall Lewis, and Henry Reeve and the *Quarterly* under Lockhart and his succesor, Whitwell Elwin, and, by way of contrast, conclude with a brief look at the most outstanding of the new generation of midcentury quarterlies, the *National* under Walter Bagehot and Richard Holt Hutton.

As one might expect, any discussion of the role and the status of editors of quarterlies is tied up with broader issues, such as the social status of journalists, the role of anonymity versus signature as it affected the editor, and the involvement of periodicals or rather "higher journalism" in politics and the world of affairs generally. It is also important to consider the "mechanics" of editorial work in the period, the duties and responsibilities of editors. How much control did an editor have over material that came under his scrutiny? Did he commission reviews or willingly accept what came his way? Was he eager to alter and amend? How conscious was he of the editorial "we," of the "voice" of his particular quarterly?

It has seemed to me in the course of my reading that just as a major quarterly established from the outset an image, a style of reviewing, a tone, or a voice, so too did it establish and maintain throughout its history a style of editing. Let me begin with Jeffrey. Just as the *Edinburgh* was the first of the new style of reviews and became a model for its successors, Jeffrey too became a legend within his lifetime, and it was a legend of a certain kind of editor. He denied any suggestion that he had magisterial powers or that he was an autocrat, describing himself on two occasions as "but a Feudal monarch who really had but slender control over his barons," although on another occasion, continuing the metaphor, he did say that he "would give a great deal for a few chieftains of a milder and more disciplined character." In the early years, with Francis Horner, Sydney Smith, and Henry Brougham, this was probably a fair analogy. But at the same time Cockburn, Jeffrey's biographer, said it was toward Jeffrey that the group gravitated; he became their "natural center." He "directed and controlled the elements he presided over with a master's judgment," Cockburn tells us. "There was not one of his associates who could have even held these elements together for a single year." His "value as an Editor was incalculable," he goes on. "He had not only to revise and arrange each number after its parts were brought together, but before he got this length he, like any other person in that situation, had much difficult and delicate work to perform. He had to discover, and to train authors; to discern what truth and the public mind required; to suggest subjects; to reject, and more offensive still, to improve, contributions; to keep down absurdities; to infuse spirit; to excite the timid; to repress violence; to soothe jealousies; to quell mutinies; to watch times; and all this in the morning of the reviewing day, before experience had taught editors conciliatory firmness and contributors reasonable submission."[2]

He was, apparently, a skilled hand at rewriting the contributions of others. Cockburn describes how he "without altering the general tone or character of the composition, had great skill in leaving out defective ideas or words, and in so aiding the original by lively or graceful touches, that *reasonable* authors were surprised and charmed on seeing how much better they looked than they thought they would."[3] (Note the word *reasonable*.) This talent was obviously well known at an early stage, for Sir Walter Scott, advising a somewhat apprehensive William Gifford of an editor's duties, cited Jeffrey's genius in accepting contributions from "persons of inferior powers of writing" provided they understood the books they were reviewing. The articles, Scott claimed, were of "stupifying mediocrity," which Jeffrey then "rendered palatable" by "throwing in a handful of spice," namely, any lively paragraph or entertaininng illustration that occurred to him in reading them over.[4] Even Thomas Carlyle later complained to Napier, Jeffrey's successor, of the almost "painful editorial hacking and hewing to right and left" to which his well-considered compositions were subjected.[5]

At the same time that he was doing all this with work he commissioned, Jeffrey was himself reviewing at an enormous pace—seventy-nine articles in twenty-six numbers at one point, or an average of one a month—a practice that he continued even when his legal career made more pressing claims on his time. He reviewed over a wide range of subjects besides the famous literary criticism. Biology, metaphysics, politics, and morals also attracted him, and he considered himself equally competent to tackle them.

Jeffrey and his colleagues epitomized the concept of gentlemanly amateurism. Cockburn again points out that none of them considered that either politics or letters would be his main career. The original intention was that they should be "all gentlemen and no pay" until Constable persuaded them to accept his fees. Indeed, the *Life* reflects a mild schizophrenia in Jeffrey between his devotion and indeed pride in the *Review* and its Whiggish principles, on the one hand, and his continuing fears, expressed over the years, that his connections with the *Edinburgh* would impede his advancement in the legal profession. Sometimes these worries were based on his fear that the *Review's* political stance would work against him, but increasingly it was the fact, as he expressed it to Horner, of "being considered as fairly articled to a trade that is not perhaps the most respectable" that might disadvantage him. "I have been anxious to keep clear of any tradesman-like concern in the Review, and to confine myself pretty strictly to intercourse with gentlemen only, even as contributors," he wrote. "It would vex me," he continued, "to find that, in spite of this, I have lowered my own character and perhaps even that of my profession by my connection with a publication which I certainly engaged with on very Whig grounds, and have managed, I think, without dirtying my hands in any paltry matters." But if schizophrenia it was, it was a very mild attack. Jeffrey passed to the deanship of the Faculty of Advocates and relinquished the *Review* as a natural and inevitable next stage in his life. Cockburn was right when he concluded his account of the *Edinburgh* with the reflection that whatever influence it had upon the age, that influence was to be more ascribed to him [Jeffrey] than to any other individual connected with it.[6]

Whatever the basis of the reputation of the *Edinburgh* under Jeffrey, and many were quick to attack the myth and to stress the flimsiness and the lack of durability of its early criticism, Leslie Stephen was right to point out in his article on "The First Edinburgh Reviewers" that the great age of the *Edinburgh* as a political organ began after Jeffrey's departure and came into its own in the age of the Reform Bill and with issues such as Catholic emancipation when it was in the hands of Macvey Napier. Jeffrey's famous remark to Scott that "the Review in short, has but two legs to stand on, and Literature no doubt is one of them, but its right leg is politics"[7] is the one that stays in the mind, but Jeffrey himself had very little to do with the political side of the *Review*. It was Napier who laid the *Review's* solid reputation as the organ of the Whigs. Jeffrey did give him some advice on the matter:

There are three legitimate considerations by which you should be guided in your conduct as editor generally, and particularly as to the admission or rejection of important articles of a political sort. 1. The effect of your decision on the other contributors upon whom you mainly rely; 2. its effect on the sale and circulation and on the just authority of the work with the great body of its readers; and 3. your own deliberate opinion as to the safety or danger of the doctrines maintained in the article under consideration, and its tendency to promote or retard the practical adoption of those liberal principles to which, and their practical advancement, you must always consider the journal as devoted.[8]

The difficulties inherent in Napier's task are all too clearly reflected in his correspondence, particularly his dealings with Brougham, of whom Morley in his review of the published correspondence commmmented that "no editor had such a contributor as Brougham in the long history of editorial torment since the world began." Yet throughout, whether it was in his dealings with Brougham, Carlyle, Macaulay, or with politicans, the tradition of the strong editor continued. Napier cajoled, placated, comforted, and expostulated, but he remained on top. It was again in connection with Napier and the *Edinburgh* that Morley compared an editor of what he called "a periodical of public consideration" to the manager of an opera house, an occupation "usually supposed to tax human powers more urgently than any position save that of a general in the very heat and stress of battle."[9]

Napier was succeeded in 1847 by Jeffrey's son-in-law, William Empson, about whom very little is known. In 1853 the editor's chair passed to Sir George Cornewall Lewis, a man far better known for his political offices than his literary activities and yet one who epitomized the link beteen politics and literature that became the *Edinburgh's* hallmark. The biographer of Lewis's successor, Henry Reeve, claimed that the critic William Bodham Donne was offered the job late in 1852 but declined on the grounds that he was not in the current of public opinion. Lewis had been financial secretary to the Treasury in the latter years of Russell's government and secretary of the Board of Control prior to that. Throughout his parliamentary career he had contributed steadily to a range of periodicals, including the *Edinburgh,* and while holding ministerial office had kept up a steady stream of publications. He was a man of such industry that he carried small volumes of his favorite classical authors around with him and if confronted by a spare moment, he promptly pulled out a volume and committed a passage to memory. Russell resigned in February 1852, and Lewis found himself out of office, a situation that did not change with Aberdeen's forming a cabinet in December. Lewis wrote to his friend Sir Edmund Head matter-of-factly in January:

> Since I wrote to you last two events have happened, one of which is important to me individually; the other is important to the public at large. One is, that I have accepted the Editorship of the *Edinburgh Review;* the other is, that there has been a change of government.[10]

Henry Reeve was less flattering when he noted in his journal:

> Amongst other novelties of this new year I may record that George Lewis succeeds Mr. Empson as Editor of the Edinburgh, having mady up his mind that this, or any other task, is preferable to the drudgery of subordinate office.[11]

Lewis's contacts naturally enhanced the political sphere of the *Edinburgh,* but he found it difficult to secure persons who wrote well on literary and general subjects mainly, as he told a friend, because his acquaintances lay chiefly among politicians. Several of the issues under his charge were sold out as a result of a particularly influential political article. Meanwhile he continued his own prodigious output, including a long-projected Roman history and a Treatise on Politics (1852), and took on various commissionerships. His brand of editorial control had some novel elements. He told Whitwell Elwin that he rarely altered articles but always curtailed them. Prolixity, he was heard to moan, was the *bête noire* of the editor. But his more irritating habit was that of readily accepting articles, setting them in print, and then, having held them for some time, rejecting them. He was always puzzled, he told Elwin, that contributors regarded this as an injustice. It explains why more than one other quarterly editor found himself accepting an article from Nassau Senior and other Edinburgh reviewers in the form of Edinburgh proofs.[12] Early in 1855 Palmerston formed a ministry, and Lewis was offered the chancellorship of the Exchequer. Again Lewis wrote blandly to his friend Head:

I had the Edinburgh Review for April on my hands, and the last part of my volumes on Roman history; I had been out of Parliament for two years, and I did not know the present House of Commons. I was to follow Gladstone whose ability had dazzled the world and to produce a War Budget with large additional taxation, in a few weeks. All these circumstances put together inspired me with the strongest disinclination to accept the offer.[13]

He didn't, and Henry Reeve found himself temporarily at least holding the fort. In the eyes of some, Reeve brought a new cosmopolitan brilliance to the *Edinburgh*. Others such as J. S. Mill saw in the appointment the signs of the *Review's* decline. Yet Reeve remained the editor for the next forty years, becoming the longest-serving editor of a quarterly.

According to his biographer, Reeve was "a man whose writings exercised a profound influence on social and political life, whose judgements and whose counsels had a large but unreported share in the decisions of cabinets; a man who for upwards of sixty years, as Clerk of Appeals, Registrar of the Privy Council, as critic, leader writer on the *Times,* editor of the *Edinburgh Review,* literary adviser of a great publishing firm, lived . . . with his fingers on the keys of public opinion, directing it, leading it, guiding it with a power which was none the less real because few recognized it or knew of it, none the less vast because he himself was not fully aware of it."[14] Reeve would, I suppose, be described as a man of letters who hovered on the fringes of the world of affairs. He was also one of those people who knew everybody. He undertook to educate himself in continental affairs by living abroad for some time when he was a young man and upon his return to England assiduously cultivated, as he had done abroad, the prominent and the privileged both in the world of politics and literature. At one point he wrote to his mother: "I am sure in writing to you I may be pardoned for noticing my own position with *les personnages;* but it is strange that at twenty-six I should find myself on terms of acquaintance with the whole Cabinet except Lord Melbourne and Baring." It was Reeve's position as a leader writer on *The Times,* writing as many as four or five articles a week, that gained him the greatest influence in the forties and the fifties. He said of his fifteen years at the *Times* "During a great portion of these years I lived on terms of confidential correspondence and intercourse with several of the leading ministers of England and of France . . . and I question whether there was any person out of the Cabinet more correctly acquainted with the course of affairs; indeed some things reached me which the bulk of the Cabinet did not know."[15]

Reeve took on the *Edinburgh* as a temporary arrangement in February 1855 out of personal friendship with Thomas Longman, but in July his journal recorded that he had "definitely" accepted the editorship. He was torn between writing for the *Times* and writing for the *Review* and at first refused to commit himself to retiring from the *Times.* Longman had "behaved very handsomely" over this, he recorded, and he continued to write for both until October, when G. W. Dasent, acting as the editor in place of Delane, interfered with one of his articles, and Reeve, in a fit of pique, resigned. He later claimed that had it not been for this incident, he would probably have stayed with the *Times* in preference to the *Edinburgh,* "for I enjoyed the power it conferred of governing public opinion." Instead, as he put it, he "fell back on the Edinburgh Review, which is a sort of peerage as compared with the tumult of the Lower House."[16]

Reeve made the change without too much difficulty. He inherited a backlog of contributions accepted by Lewis, no doubt all set in print, and he promptly sent back the lot. A notebook that forms part of the Longman archives lists pages of authors and titles marked with comments such as "failed entirely, returned," "too objectionable to publish." One by J. A. Froude was marked "set up in type but it appeared undesirable to publish it." Another by Nassau Senior was "declined for differences of opinion." One by Trollope was marked "to be considered," and another by W. R. Greg was marked "conditional—to have refusal of it."[17] Reeve clearly had no compunction about offending old contributors or about making it clear that there was a new broom. Unfortunately, Longman's letterbooks for this period have not been preserved, and so we have no record of the day-to-day routine of Reeve's editorship. He did claim to offer no book for review that he had not read himself and later in his editorship gained a reputation for excessive alteration. E. A. Freeman, who must have suffered from this, noted with relief that the *British Quarterly,* with which he had begun an affiliation, did not "sin Reevishly" and told the editor that there must be few people who hold "like Reeve that they know more of all branches of human knowledge than the people who have severally got them up."[18]

Reeve was an immensely hard-working editor, moving up to London for the two or three crucial weeks before the publication deadline each quarter and returning home with relief ten days before the actual date of publication, a rhythm of life that most quarterly editors submitted to with alternating dread and elation. He read most of the articles in manuscript, superintended all the stages through to proofs, which he again read himself, declining the appointment of a deputy. The political articles were often the products of eleventh-hour labors, but Reeve, like Lewis, chose his reviewers carefully and, like Lewis, was able to secure contributors with impressive governmental connections if not themselves the holders of office. In these he claimed always to take care to discriminate between the functions of a daily newspaper and a quarterly review, the old upper chamber-lower house contrast again.

On the face of it, Reeve too was in the Napier-Jeffrey tradition. The correspondence that remains records political association and influence at an extremely high level and an editorial control, which Freeman claimed, left everyone "disgusted with Reeve."

The one thing that was new with Reeve's editorship was the influence of Longman. In a famous fracas in 1857, soon after he took over, Reeve published an article by Robert Lowe that was highly critical of Lord John Russell. Longman stepped in over Reeve's head, insisted that no republication should take place and that an apology should be made to Russell. The correspondence between Russell and Longman on this makes interestng reading.[19]

No amount of cosmopolitan brilliance or political connections, however, could counteract the change in public taste that occurred in the forty years that Reeve remained the editor. The heyday of the quarterlies was over largely by the end of his first decade. Nevertheless, it is clear that Reeve remained in the *Edinburgh* editorial tradition to the end, but that one instance of the presence of Longman working over his shoulder and indeed over his head serves to illustrate the way in which the *Edinburgh* differed from the *Quarterly*.

The publisher of the *Edinburgh,* first Constable, then a brief partnership of Constable and Murray, then a partnership of Constable and Longman, and then eventually Longman alone, was almost entirely a figure in the background. The exact opposite was true of the *Quarterly*. It was very much John Murray's project from the beginning, and he, followed by his son, regarded the operation of the *Review* as one of his major concerns. Lip service, however, was always paid to the appointment of the editor, with the stress on the privacy of the role. "The office of Editor is of such importance," Scott told William Gifford, "that had you not been pleased to undertake it, I fear the plan would have fallen wholly to the ground. The full power of control must of course be vested in the editor for selecting, curtailing and correcting the contributions to the Review."[20] It was also essential, he continued, that channels of communication be effected with those who had the power to supply the reviewers, through the editor, with accurate points of fact, topics of great national interest, in other words, so that the *Quarterly* should fulfill a role for the Tory party similar to that which the *Edinburgh* did for the Whigs. Gifford was singularly ill equipped at the outset either for the task of magisterial editor, on the one hand, or mastermind of a party organ, on the other. He was thought to have been selected chiefly through the influence of Canning, but most of the *Review's* major supporters and Murray himself were quick to point out that although a man of "learning and wit," he had lived too little in the world. He was, Murray assured Scott, "the most obliging and well meaning man alive—perfectly ready to be instructed in those points which his seclusion renders him ignorant."[21] His interests, in other words, were essentially literary, not political, and this factor was crucial to the operation of the *Quarterly* not only under Gifford but under his successors. It meant that from the beginning there was a split between the political and the "literary" activities of the *Review,* leaving the editor at the mercy of a number of influential contributors, notably, John Wilson Croker who more or less controlled the political section of the *Quarterly.* It also meant that there was not a single chain of command, and more than one editor was to complain of the "interference" not only from the publisher but from the political writers.

The relationship between Gifford and Murray improved over the years until the former came to be regarded as a trusted adviser by the publisher, but in the beginning Murray was virtually the editor, soliciting new writers, selecting books for review, finding reviewers to match the books. In some instances the reviews were actually printed before Gifford was consulted, although it was alleged that everything had his approval before it was eventually published.

Gifford also suffered from poor health. Each number left him progressively more exhausted, and he had to repair to the seaside for a fortnight to rest before, he put it,[22] "I could put on my spectacles and look about me." He was also notoriously unpunctual, some said indolent, so that early numbers of the *Quarterly* were a month and a half late in appearing.

On the other hand, Gifford was punctilious in the extreme with editorial detail and altered the work of his literary contributors without compunction. Southey winced and fulminated over what he termed Gifford's "mutilation." George Ellis, another of the *Quarterly's* major supporters, felt that Gifford spent too much time "attempting to elicit a rational meaning from the shapeless lumps of criticism laid before him." What was needed was "wit and variety, a selection of spirited and playful articles, rather than those of scholarship and profundity." "We must veto ponderous articles," he warned; "they will simply sink us."[23]

Gifford's health continued to decline, and he clearly found the burden of the *Review* unsupportable and talked of giving up and yet refused to do so. Murray even bought him a chariot to aid in his recovery at the seaside, a characteristically generous gesture. It was alleged at one point that he had even printed one of Southey's articles without corrections, which was widely regarded as a melancholy and menacing symptom of decay.[24]

The line of succession for a time was unclear. Southey had threatened to found a rival *Quarterly* with John Taylor Coleridge as the editor. Murray promptly appointed Coleridge Gifford's successor at a time when he was advancing rapidly in the legal world, and, as Andrew Lang put it, "no wise barrister would prefer an editorship to such prospects of success as now lay before him."[25] The status of the editor of a quarterly review—this was 1825—was still an ambivalent one. Gifford at an early point in 1812 had written reassuringly to Murray that "you are to consider that we have not hacks in pay like the Monthly and Critical Review and that we are at least dealing with gentlemen."[26]

The man Murray sought to succeed Coleridge was John Gibson Lockhart, who had been, of course, closely involved with

Blackwood's, an association that by no means redounded to his credit. Murray's initial plan was to recruit Lockhart to head a newspaper, the brainchild of the young Disraeli, and interestingly, Lockhart's correspondence refers to the "loss of caste in society" that would occur if he edited a newspaper and of the "impossibility of my ever entering into the career of London in the capacity of a newspaper editor." The editorship of a review, however, was clearly a different matter. A friend advised him that "your accepting of the editorship of a newspaper would be infra-dig, and a losing of caste, but not so, as I think, the accepting of the editorship of the Quarterly Review. An editor of a Review like the Quarterly is the office of a scholar and a gentleman, but that of a newspaper is not."[27]

Lockhart, like Coleridge, was a lawyer by profession, but Andrew Lang commented that literature, more than law, was his real province, though his pride appeared to have resented his official connection with literature as an editor. But he accepted Murray's offer of the editorship. Significantly the appointment was opposed by several of the *Quarterly's* old reviewers, including Sir John Barrow and Croker, and those whom Lang referred to as the "junta in the Admiralty," whom Murray apparently did not consult.

The situation was thus fraught with difficulties, including the quick appointment and retirement of Coleridge. Against Lockhart was his total inexperience on the political front. According to Lang, Lockhart felt trammeled and troubled in his new office. "On the whole it seems very desirable," he commented, "that the proprietor of a serial should either be his own editor, as Blackwood was, with irresponsible assistants, or that he and his friends should leave a responsible editor entirely alone." Lockhart found neither of these cases applicable. He was not, Lang concluded, entirely his own master as the editor. The editing of a quarterly review demanded incessant intercourse with people in power, or, crudely, "lobbying," and for this Lockhart had no taste. He was far more interested in his own literary activities, and even Murray's handsome financial rewards could not, as Lang said, make him into a political partisan. Disraeli, in a waspish mood, told Macvey Napier that the *Quarterly* was beng edited by a tenth-rate novelist.[28]

Despite the sense of disengagement that he managed to convey, Lockhart's routine labors were onerous. His biography records the endless reading of contributions in manuscripts, of books in manuscripts, interminable consultations over articles, corrections and interpolations of articles. Lockhart had a reputation for interpolating, some of which was unjustified, but he once told Murray there were only three contributors whose articles could be printed without revision. Correspondence with the writers of articles, reading new books, and accomplishing new articles on new books, often trash, engaged the daily life of Lockhart, as of able editors in general. A man in his position, Lang said, is engaged "in a kind of intellectual egg dance" among a score of sensitive interests. Lockhart claimed that whenever anyone was civil to him, especially one not habitually so, "I always ask myself for the first question, is he or she big with book or big with article."[29]

Lockhart early grew weary of the job, declaring in 1830 that he could not see the *Quarterly* as a stepping-stone to any permanent benefits for him. He gathered around him a small number of faithful reviewers, Henry Hart Milman, Lady Eastlake, Sir John Barrow, and, of course, Croker, and submitted himself to what he called the "business of article making." His own articles, few of them worth reprinting, reflected that weariness. The picture that emerges from Lang's albeit partisan biography is that of an industrious but disengaged editor who was constantly having his authority challenged if not by Murray then by Croker, hence his adaptation of an early ditty by Gifford:

Overworked, over worried
Over Crokered, Over Murray'd.

Gifford had added:

Over Southeyed, Over Waltered,
Fain I would that I were altered.[30]

Lockhart's health declined rapidly in the 1850s, and there was
no heir apparent. As a temporary measure he was given some
assistance by a recent acquisition to the reviewing staff, the Rev.
Whitwell Elwin, a country clergyman of a near mythical
variety—an unworldly, eccentric, bookish man—on the surface
of things the most inappropriate candidate for the editorship of a
quarterly review. And yet in the same essay in which he offered
Walter Bagehot as a candidate for "the Greatest Victorian,"
G. M. Young suggested that anyone who wished to understand
the Victorian mind should turn away from remembered names
and study three men, among them Whitwell Elwin, "reflecting
. . . on the breadth of their interests . . . and the quiet and
substantial permanence of what they did."[31] This unlikely man,
who had been reluctantly drawn into the fold to relieve the ailing
Lockhart, turned out to be an outstanding editor. Elwin was vicar
of Booton in Norfolk, and spent his life mainly reading, punc-
tuating this with a gentle round of parochial duties. He spent a
great deal of his time reading in bed, taking huge piles of books to
his bedroom each night in preparation for the morning, and he
perfected a technique for reading large folio volumes while lying
down. He and his wife built a large vicarage that they never
bothered to have finished. The rooms were neither papered nor
painted, and visitors, some twelve years later, asked in a puzzled
fashion if the Elwins had recently moved in. Carriages got stuck
trying to negotiate unmade-up roads that served as a drive. The
village of Booton did not have a post office until Elwin took over
the *Quarterly,* whereupon one was created. The irony of this was

that Elwin was notoriously dilatory about answering his post. Manuscripts lay unopened, an introductory letter (unopened) would be followed by a second inquiring as to the receipt of the first. Neither would be attended to until the whole thing acquired nightmarish proportions.

Elwin, like Reeve, began by agreeing to help out on a temporary basis and took on the job full time when no one else could be found. He did so reluctantly. He hated London. He went there each quarter for the crucial ten days before the deadline, staying at a hotel, working feverishly, often carrying the proofs around in his coat pocket, and returned home as soon as possible, claiming that "When I got between the Booton hedgerows they were as grateful to my eyes as if they had been the hedgerows of the Garden of Eden."[32] Like Gifford, he was often physically ill at the end of each of these sessions. Henry Reeve, having met him early on one of these sorties, remarked on the coincidence that the two major quarterlies were edited by Norfolk men but commented that "Nothing, however, can be more unlike than this editor and myself. He is a Norfolk parson of immense reading, great knowledge of books and great ignorance of the world; evidently unversed in politics and in society."[33] Elwin described the responsibilities of the *Review* as going about with "a clog on my leg,"[34] and yet the world of affairs was not as unattractive to him as he pretended. He was genuinely interested in some political questions and contributed articles on the Crimean question in particular. His famous boast that he had not a drop of party feeling in him led the Duke of Bedford to declare in 1856 that the *Quarterly Review* had become distinguished for truth. Elwin found that he was far better at dealing with difficult contributors than Lockhart had been and even persuaded Croker not to proceed with an article on the Crimean situation strongly favorable to Russia. He reverted to Gifford's widespread practice of using books merely as pegs on which to hang original articles. His own practice in this was exemplary. He went to enormous pains to secure the right contributors for subjects, and at times became so concerned for accuracy that he found it necessary to study the subjects himself to protect the *Review* from error. In rewriting he was remorseless, claiming to rewrite three out of every four articles in proof. One irritated contributor returned his check, claiming that the article that had appeared was not his at all.

As in the days of Gifford, the *Review* was chronically late. Warwick Elwin, Elwin's son and biographer, at the end of his memoir of his father, draws a comparison with Gifford, which is in fact striking to anyone who reads about both men.

What one sees in Elwin, I think, is the continuation of the tradition of a scholar-editor. He had fewer contributors. He wrote a large number of articles himself. Distasteful as he claimed to find the world of affairs, he secured contributions from Gladstone and others, and yet one does not have the sense, as with Lockhart and Reeve, of an editorial office that undertook political lobbying of any kind or that the *Quarterly* was quite so much at the center of things politically. Some of the old guard found this distressing and, unlike the Duke of Bedford, saw a falling off of the old acerbic, partisan quality of the *Quarterly* as a change for the worse.

Eventually Elwin too wearied of editorship. He murmured the need to resign. In 1860 Murray took the matter out of his hands by announcing that he had found a successor. If he was hurt, Elwin did not show it but said, "I feel like a man who has been transported for seven years and whose time is up."³⁵

The *Quarterly* had a succession of editors after Elwin, none of whom was able to put a personal stamp on the review in the way their predecessors had done.

If one looks at the succession of editors of the two quarterlies, I think there are some generalizations that can be drawn. The emphasis on the "gentlemanliness" of the position is significant.

They saw themselves, I suggest, in a tradition of amateur scholarship, a tradition begun by Jeffrey, with his prodigious amount of
reviewing, and carried on by Lewis and Reeve and by Napier and
Empson. Gifford himself did not contribute to the *Quarterly,* but
Lockhart did, and Elwin, as I have indicated, epitomized the
tradition. None of them, I think, made a clear distinction between
the function of the editor and that of a contributor, or at least they
did not see themselves solely as managers, as newspaper editors
might have done.

The actual power they wielded depended on a number of factors. The *Edinburgh* tradition from the start was that of the strong
editor, with the publisher in the background. The *Quarterly* pattern was the reverse, with John Murray, the publisher and the
proprietor, playing a significant role in his own publication and in
appointing the kinds of editors he did, creating a split between the
literary activities of the review and its political role.

If their powers in terms of policymaking were curtailed, the
editors were assiduous in the technical aspects of their job,
rewriting, if not interpolating, keeping a close eye on the material
offered to them, if not always going to the extremes of Reeve and
Elwin in making themselves experts on every subject. I have
argued elsewhere[36] that editors of the new generation of
quarterlies had far less self-confidence than their eminent
predecessors, that they simply accepted what was offered to
them, gladly making room for the sweepings from under the
worktable of the *Edinburgh* and the *Quarterly,* with very little
view of forming a cohesive policy or taking a firm line on issues.
For an *Edinburgh* or a *Quarterly* editor such a procedure would
have been unthinkable.

Finally and very briefly, I suggest that the last of the great
quarterly editors was Bagehot at the *National Review* between
1855 and 1864. The *National* was the successor to the *Prospective Review,* but it was determined to move intellectually

upmarket from the *Prospective,* retaining loosely the latter's Unitarian affiliations but attracting around itself a galaxy of talent as reviewers. Richard Holt Hutton and Bagehot shared the editorship for most of the nine-year period, with Hutton taking charge of the nuts and bolts of the enterprise and Bagehot responsible for what Mrs. Barrington, his biographer, termed the "intellectual side" of the management. Bagehot's correspondence with Henry Crabb Robinson and with James Martineau shows him as the moving force behind the venture, and if he did not actually draw up the prospectus, he certainly established the principles behind it. The *National* became almost a personal organ for Bagehot. Some of his best literary criticism was published in it, along with political articles that essentially made him a national figure.

Bagehot differed in two respects from his predecessors on the *Edinburgh* and the *Quarterly.* He would not, I think, have described himself as a "man of letters." He took some pride in pointing out, while engaged in planning the *National,* that he was a man of business, literally, a banker. His prominence in the world of affairs was earned by his abilities as an economist and as a political observer and theorist. As G. M. Young points out in his essay "The Greatest Victorian," his influence on his time was almost inestimable, and it began during his years at the *National.* Second, both he and Hutton, having a foothold in the weekly press (Bagehot as a director and eventually the editor of the *Economist,* Hutton, first working for the *Economist* and then as the long-serving editor of the *Spectator*), differed from the other editors of the quarterlies. This situation, I think, illustrates the new position of the quarterlies in the latter half of the century. It was Reeve's Upper House versus the tumult of the Lower Chamber yet again. It meant that the quarterly became the forum for the long, considered view, and the weekly entered into the cut and thrust of regular political debate. The old political role of the quarterlies, as Macaulay and Croker recognized it, was a thing of the past.

182   Joanne Shattock

The *National* came to an end in 1864. Mrs. Barrington for one linked its demise to Bagehot's changing fortunes and interests. "Bagehot's interest in it had been great," she wrote. "It brought him congenial work when he had felt a special need of it. That need no longer existed, but he felt parting with it as from an old friend."[37] The *National's* recognized heir on its general side was the new *Fortnightly Review,* published more frequently and containing shorter articles signed by its distinguished contributors. That in itself was a comment on the changing status of the quarterlies.

And so to the quotation in my title. None of the quarterly editors discussed here was flamboyant enough to be described as a showman. There was a sufficiently hard core of egotism in each that, I think, disinclined them toward lion-hunting of the deferential sort practiced by James Knowles, although none was against maneuvering for a prize "catch" in the form of notable contributors. Given their considerable abilities, none, I think, could be described as a hack. They were distinguished editors in the best sense of the term, representative of a tradition that, I suggest, has long deserved attention.

NOTES

1. Walter Bagehot, "The First Edinburgh Reviewers," *Literary Studies* I (London, 1895): 175; Sir Frederick Pollock, *For my Grandson: Reminiscences of an Ancient Victorian* (London, 1933), p. 93, quoted by Christopher Kent, "Higher Journalism and the Mid-Victorian Clerisy," *Victorian Studies* XIII (1969): 196.
2. Henry Cockburn, *Life of Lord Jeffrey* (Edinburgh, 1852), I, pp. 295, 302.
3. Cockburn, I, p. 301.
4. Samuel Smiles, *A Publisher and His Friends: Memoir and Correspondence of John Murray* (London, 1891), I, p. 105.
5. Quoted by John Morley, "Memorials of a Man of Letters," *Studies in Literature* (1901): 313.
6. Cockburn, I, pp. 280, 303.
7. Quoted by Leslie Stephen, "The First Edinburgh Reviewers," *Hours in a Library* II (London, 1899), p. 245n.

8. Morley, p. 306.

9. Morley, pp. 292, 287.

10. *Letters of Sir George Cornewall Lewis,* ed. the rev. Sir G. F. Lewis (London, 1870), p. 258.

11. J. K. Laughton, *Memoirs of the Life and Correspondence of Henry Reeve* (London, 1898), I, p. 270.

12. See my article, "Spreading It Thinly: Some Victorian Reviewers at Work," *Victorian Periodicals Newsletter* IX (September, 1976): 84.

13. Lewis, p. 293.

14. Laughton, I, p. vi.

15. Ibid, I, pp. 110, 338.

16. Ibid, I, pp. 333, 337, 339.

17. Longman Archives, University of Reading Library.

18. Henry Allon, *Letters to a Victorian Editor,* ed. Albert Peel (London, 1929), p. 82.

19. Longman Archives, University of Reading. Some of the correspondence is published in A. R. D. Elliott, "The *Edinburgh Review,* 1802-1902," *Edinburgh Review* 196 (October, 1902), pp. 275-318.

20. Smiles, I, p. 105.

21. Ibid., p. 109.

22. Ibid., pp. 154, 156.

23. Ibid., p. 163.

24. Andrew Lang, *The Life and Letters of John Gibson Lockhart* (London, 1897), I, p. 354.

25. Ibid., p. 163.

26. Smiles, I, p. 260.

27. Lang, I, p. 367.

28. Ibid., I, pp. 132, II, 77.

29. Lang, II, p. 283.

30. Quoted in *Memoir of Whitwell Elwin,* preface to *Some XVIII Century Men of Letters,* ed. Warwick Elwin (London, 1902), I, p. 76 n.3.

31. G. M. Young, "The Greatest Victorian," in *Today and Yesterday* (London, 1948), p. 241.

32. Elwin, I, p. 70.

33. Laughton, I, p. 353.

34. Elwin, I, p. 95.

35. Ibid., I, p. 238.

36. "Editorial Policy and the Quarterlies," *Victorian Periodicals Newsletter* X (September 1977): 130-39.

37. *The Works and Life of Walter Bagehot,* ed. E. I. Barrington (London, 1915), X, p. 366.

Charlotte C. Watkins

Editing a "Class Journal": Four Decades of the *Queen*

The periodical once known as the *Queen* is incorporated today in the magazine known as *Harpers and Queen*. A century ago the *Queen* would have been recognized as the title of an influential, illustrated weekly paper for women. In its Victorian form, the paper was a period piece, like the tastes of the readers for whom it was designed. Its appeal, unlike the wit of *Vanity Fair,* has not survived. Yet the *Queen* is of considerable interest. Its pages of fashion plates, more delicately executed than Godey's ladies, are valuable for historians of costume and for theater arts, and its illustrated patterns and directions for crafts in a period style—from crochet to woodworking—are still practicable. Its record of new books and theater and musical events and its descriptions of pastimes are cultural documents; and its leaders and articles, including its well-written obituaries, are overlooked resources for historians and for biographers of minor—and major—women and men. An additional historical value may be the illustration it presents of the making of a periodical of its kind. Reading through a rare almost complete run of the early decades of the journal provides the occasion and the means of identifying the editors and their roles and of recovering some of the history of the management of a "class paper" in the context of changing Victorian journalism.

The *Queen* was a "class journal" in the sense understood by H. R. Fox Bourne and other Victorians, a periodical designed to meet the special interests of a particular segment of the reading public. Its prospectus, issued in 1861, announced "a new sixpenny weekly newspaper . . . about the same size as the *Illustrated News,* and . . . especially addressed to ladies," and advertisements defined the readership to which, as a "class" journal, it was addressed:

THE QUEEN, an Illustrated Journal and Review. – Men of all classes in England – the clergyman, the student, the schoolmaster, the man of letters, the artist, the merchant, the artizan – have each a journal written especially for them; but for the whole mass of educated women not a single paper of value exists. Under the title of 'The Queen,' a journal for Englishwomen is now in preparation. The first number will appear on Saturday, September 7. 'The Queen' is simply intended to be for educated women what certain high-class journals are for men – recording and discussing from week to week whatever interests or amuses them. There will be a large number of original articles on the daily life of society, its manners and morals; on books, music and the theatre. Considerable space will be devoted to the amusements which ladies most pursue, at home and abroad; while as for *la mode*, 'The Queen' will be the earliest and most accurate chronicler of all its changes. The engravings in 'The Queen' will really illustrate the events of the day, and give point to whatever topics happen to engage the public mind. No expense and no trouble will be spared in their preparation. . . .[1]

As a weekly paper written for "educated women," the *Queen* had in fact been anticipated by *The Lady's Newspaper and Pictorial Times,* which had been founded in 1848 and was already well established. In format it closely resembled *The Illustrated London News,* and as Herbert Ingram had chosen an engraving of St.

Paul's Cathedral for the heading of the *Illustrated London News,* Windsor Castle furnished the subject for a pictorial heading for the *Queen.*

The first number of the *Queen* was issued on September 7, 1861. The founder and proprietor was Samuel Orchart Beeton, and Frederick Greenwood was the editor. It was Greenwood's first editorial post. Under Beeton the paper was not profitable, and in less than a year Beeton sold it "on very easy terms," it was said,[2] to Edward William Cox. Cox was a barrister who had established a reputation for shrewdness and financial skill in journalistic enterprises "as numerous as the armies of the Czar," a reviewer in the *Athenaeum* once wrote spitefully.[3] He had established or acquired more than a dozen "class" periodicals, including *The Field; the Country Gentleman's Newspaper,* to which a counterpart—in a different "class"—was now provided by the *Queen.* The *Queen* acquired a new editor. New contributors were added and new departments developed, and on April 12, 1862, its offices were moved to 346, Strand, to join those of the other Cox enterprises. "The *Queen,* the ladies' newspaper," it was announced, "will henceforth be edited by a lady, and neither pains nor expense will be spared to make it the most attractive and useful ladies' journal ever published. Political news will be omitted from the *Queen,* as such news can best be obtained in papers devoted to it. The speciality of the *Queen* will lie in all matters which interest ladies at home and abroad."[4] In the following year, on July 4, 1863, Cox acquired and merged with the *Queen* its competitor, *The Lady's Newspaper and Pictorial Times.* Horace Cox, already associated with his uncle, Edward William Cox, became in 1865 the business manager of the *Queen.*

The conductors of the *Queen* were the proprietor and the editor. Except for the announcement that the *Queen* would "henceforth be edited by a lady," the editor's name was obscured by the anonymity that Greenwood was to call "the inflexible rule

of journalism then"[5] reinforced by a house rule that communications be addressed "to the editor and not to the name . . . of any
person who may be known in connection with the paper." The
new editor of the *Queen* can be identified as Helen Lowe. Helen
Lowe was the daughter of Thomas Hill-Lowe, the dean of
Exeter. Her father had published a volume of her juvenilia in
1840 under the title of *Poems, Chiefly Dramatic*. His name was
given as the editor; the poems were ascribed to "a young and
inexperienced writer." A second volume of her poems, entitled
Prophecy of Balaam and Other Poems, appeared in the following
year. She had also published anonymously two travel books with
the distinctive titles *Unprotected Females in Norway; or, The
Pleasantest Way of Travelling There, Passing through Denmark
and Sweden: With Scandinavian Sketches from Nature* (1857) and
*Unprotected Females in Sicily, Calabria, and on the Top of
Mount Aetna* (1859). The commencement of "An Unprotected
Female's Tour in Switzerland; or, a Lady's Walk across the
Sheideck and Wengern Alps," was advertised by the new conductors of the *Queen* as a series of weekly articles to begin on April
12, 1862, written "By the Editress."

Helen Lowe lacks the fame of Frederick Greenwood, and
references to her life and works are now scattered and fragmentary. The first of her travel books was dedicated to Hepworth
Dixon; both were reviewed in the *Athenaeum* on their appearance, as was a subsequent volume of poems, *Taormina and
Other Poems*, in 1864.[6] The reviewer of *Taormina* noted briefly
that the title poem was partly poetry and partly travel chronicle
and commented on the author's knowledge of classical languages.

The reminiscences of a later contributor to the *Queen* record
that in the late 1880s the editor of the *Queen* was "Miss Lowe."[7]
Helen Lowe held a long tenure as the editor of the *Queen*, from
1862 until 1894, when Percy Stuart Cox, the son of Horace Cox,
assumed the post. Her role as the editor of the *Queen* was limited

by that of the proprietor. It was not that of the "well paid clerks" that Clement Shorter once complained was all but universally the role of a Victorian editor,[8] but Cox's style as a proprietor is discernible in the copious advertising—the largest in any weekly paper, it was said[9]—and in the subsidiary projects it generated, *The Queen Lace Book* and the annual *Queen Almanac and Calendar,* and the extension of one department into a new weekly paper, the *Exchange and Mart,* beginning on May 13, 1868, and continuing from 1871 as the *Bazaar, Exchange, and Mart.* It was also characteristic of Cox as the proprietor that responsibility for the "class" content of the journal was delegated to the editor.[10]

The editor of the *Queen* was responsible for the substance of the paper, its "class" aspects, that is, its "feminine" features. Wilfrid Meynell, writing of the *Queen* in 1880, said that it was "presided over by a most able editress, under whose conduct the paper has risen to its present eminent position."[11] The contents of the paper were organized into leaders, departments (each with its own heading), occasional serial fiction, and miscellaneous articles of "class" news and notes. The leaders were anonymous. The author of a leader, wrote one contemporary, "is not known by name to one of his readers out of a thousand. . . . Only when he dies, perhaps a friend—one of the initiated few—may in a necrological notice mention that he was once a contributor to some periodical or daily paper."[12] From obituaries and biographical notes, there is some evidence that the editors of other Cox journals—John Henry Walsh of the *Field,* James Lowe of the *Critic,* Edward William Cox as the editor of his *Law Times*—contributed to the *Queen,* and their contributions may have been leading articles. Many leaders were in a style reminiscent of the content and the vocabulary of Helen Lowe's travel books and poems.

Each department had its subeditor or staff. Departments in a typical issue in 1866 included "The Library Table," "Music and the Drama," "Pastimes," "Our Plants and Flowers," "The Exchange," "The Court Chronicle," "The Upper Ten Thousand," "Dress and Fashion," "Our Boudoir," "The Work Table," and "Domestic Economy," each of the last four departments, it was noted, "edited by a lady." An innovative feature was the introduction within departments of queries and answers, to which Horace Cox attributed in large part a rapid increase in the circulation of this new "class" paper. Responding much later to an interviewer, Horace Cox said, "I think we owed much to our querists and our replies to them; and coupling this with the best fashion plates obtainable and a series of departments interesting to women helped to give us the position we hold."[13] Articles, sometimes signed, sometimes unsigned, were written by staff correspondents or outside contributors, whom the *Queen* acquired a reputation for paying well.[14] Except for the annual Christmas numbers, few articles were signed in the early decades of the *Queen*. As a writer in the *Critic* remarked in 1861, "In France journalism is public by law, and in the United States by custom. In England it is anonymous; few of us ever know the name of the writer who pleases or vexes us in a brilliant article, and we read our favourite paper year after year and never take a thought about its editor."[15] There were "office signatures"—"Emerald" writing from Ireland and "Thistle" from Scotland—and occasionally identifiable initials or pseudonyms of contributors. "Cavendish"—Dr. Henry Jones—wrote not only on whist but also on chess, word puzzles, and other pastimes for that department. Edmund Yates, as "Mrs. Seaton," anticipated his later "personal journalism" in a brief epistolary series in 1872. Henriette Corkran, a daughter of Fraser Corkran, was probably the author of an article on Browning in 1889, which was signed simply "C."[16] But the *Queen* was not a literary journal: Throughout its first three decades its serial fiction and its book notes were subliterary for the most part. Edward Walford's signed essays on "Tales of Our Great Families" carried regularly in the *Queen* for over a decade were reprinted under that title, the first series dated 1877, a second, 1880.

Certain contributors can be identified with the help of their books based on articles that originally appeared in the pages of the *Queen*. Some of these books were widely read and today are most interesting because they—and the original articles in the *Queen*—present analogues to contemporary Victorian tendencies of mind and art. The shibboleths of the day reappeared applied to fashion and the practical arts, including the "aesthetics of dress" and "Pre-Raphaelite dress" and "beautiful homes" and "artistic houses"; and injunctions against "useless ornament" and "servile copies" recorded how quickly doctrine was translated into cliché.

A particularly important series of twenty articles by Charles Locke Eastlake was the basis for his immensely popular *Hints on Household Taste in Furniture, Upholstery and Other Details.* Charles Locke Eastlake, the nephew of Sir Charles Lock Eastlake, had written an anonymous article, "The Fashion of Furniture," for the *Cornhill* in March 1864. The editor of the *Queen* saw beyond the rather trivial essay the possibilities of the subject, applying contemporary ideas to the practical interests of the readers of this class journal; and she sought out the author of the essay. As Eastlake explained in his preface to the first edition of the book in 1868, the article in the *Cornhill* led "to my being invited by the Editor of the *Queen* to write for that journal a series of articles on the same subject." The articles, which appeared between June 24, 1865, and June 15, 1867, were signed "Jack Easel," a pseudonym already familiar to readers of Eastlake's columns in *Punch*. [17] In 1868 Eastlake recast and augmented the articles from the *Queen* and published them in book form. The book bore his name, and successive editions of *Hints on Household Taste*—four within ten years—established the reputation of the author, now better remembered for his *History of the Gothic Revival.* They also form part of the history of the emerging arts and crafts movements of the second half of the century. The circumstances under which Eastlake's articles were originally commissioned for the *Queen* illuminate the editor's methods of creating the content of the journal in its most interesting and influential days.

A signature that recurred in the columns of the *Queen* in the late 1870s and early 1880s was that of M. E. Haweis, occasionally initialed "M.E.H." or sometimes simply "Mrs. Haweis." Mary Eliza Joy, the wife of the Rev. Hugh Reginald Haweis, contributed many signed and unsigned articles to the *Queen* in those years. Many were on the subject of dress; many more were on home decoration. In *The Art of Beauty* in 1878, she called attention to Eastlake's *Hints on Household Taste,* "which is so extremely good, practical, and interesting, that I cannot do better than to recommend it. . . ."[18] Like Eastlake, she connected architecture, interior decoration, and fashions in apparel and in manners, and like him, she quoted or echoed Ruskin, Morris, and Rossetti on occasion and related their principles to those subjects. Her book *Beautiful Houses* published in 1882 was based on articles contributed to the *Queen,* as she acknowledged in her "Forewords" to the book: "In the present *Renascence* of art in *England,* when dress and decorations of every kind are again studied with scientific ardour, I have thought it well to reprint some descritpions of a few well-known artistic houses, which appeared originally in the *Queen,* 1880-1."[19] Her informed and detailed descriptions of the exteriors and interiors of houses, including the homes of Sir Frederick Leighton and Sir Lawrence Alma-Tadema, among others, and the British embassy in Rome, serve well historians of Victorian architecture, industrial design, and taste.

Few of the writers for the *Queen* in its first three decades can now be identified. The contributors who signed their work, however, were often authors who enjoyed some contemporary reputation in the fields in which they wrote. The women often followed conservative social custom in signing their work: Mrs. Haweis, Mrs. Aria, Mrs. Talbot Coke, Mrs. C. S. Peel, for example. Mrs. Aria—Eliza Davis—wrote on women's fashions for several periodicals, including her own short-lived journal, *The World of Dress,* which she edited.[20] Mrs. Talbot Coke— Charlotte Fitzgerald before her marriage to John Talbot Coke—wrote on various subjects and for two years (from 1886 to 1888) directed the department of home decoration in the *Queen* with memorable success, as the *Queen* noted a few years later (1892) in reviewing her book, *The Gentlewoman at Home.*[21]

Mrs. C. S. Peel's association with the *Queen* in various capacities was to span a long period through the time of her public life in the years of the First World War and of her considerable and varied writing, which includes the chapter on "Homes and Habits" in G. M. Young's *Early Victorian England.* As a young woman, before her marriage to Charles S. Peel, Constance Dorothy Evelyn Bayliff joined the *Queen* apparently as a staff writer in what was called dress and shop journalism. Sketchy references to those early days in her autobiography, *Life's Enchanted Cup,* provided rare glimpses of the editing of the paper in the late 1880s. Her sister, Charlotte Mary Augusta Bayliff, was already illustrating the articles on home decoration written for the paper by Mrs. Talbot Coke, who was their cousin. "I now wrote for the *Queen,*" Mrs. Peel recorded, "which was then edited by dear old Miss Lowe, who wore a mushroom hat tied under her chin and looked like Queen Victoria." (The reference was to Queen Victoria's style of wearing "in the country . . . a mushroom-shaped hat secured on a broad black ribbon fixed on the crown, and tied in a large bow under Her Majesty's chin.")[22] As for the paper, Mrs. Peel continued: "The *Queen* had a great prestige. Advertisers humbly asked for space in the paper. Once I, going to a certain shop to write a notice of its wares, was kept waiting and not too politely received. I told Miss Lowe what had happened. She struck the bell on her desk. 'Ask Mr. Dash (the advertising manager) if he will be good enough to speak to me.' 'Will you kindly tell Messrs. So and So that we are unable to accept their advertisement. I require that representatives of *The Queen* shall be treated with consideration.' " In the 1890s Mrs. Peel followed Mrs. Talbot Coke and Mrs. Aria to *Hearth and Home,* and she also served an apprenticeship under Arnold Bennett who undertook to teach her something of the techniques of journalism. "He said," she recalled in her autobiography, "that . . . authorship was a trade as well as an art."[23]

The contents of the *Queen* included much that justified Arnold Bennett's later observation that papers of this class—which included *Woman* as well as the *Queen*—assumed that "the chief interest of educated women was the doings of exalted social circles."[24] Court news (approved by Buckingham Palace) and "The Doings of the Upper Ten Thousand," as the caption ran, were regular departments; but there was more substance in the "class news" of the *Queen.* Theodora Bostick's study of the practical politics of the early woman's suffrage movement records the role of the *Queen.*[25] There is material in the articles and leaders of the *Queen* for a study of the higher education of women, identified by a leader in the *Queen* in 1881 as "one of the more important facts in the political and social state of this, the latter part of the nineteenth century."[26] The admission of women into professions, especially medicine, and the opening of universities and university degrees to women became recurrent subjects; and potential biographers of Millicent Garrett Fawcett and Dr. Elizabeth Garrett Anderson and Emily Davies will find primary material in the class news and in the leaders of the *Queen.* The balance between manners and ideas in the contents of the paper may account in part for its continuing growth in prestige and in circulation, which, although reliable figures are sparse, seems to have more than doubled within the first decade of Cox's proprietorship.[27]

By the time Percy Stuart Cox became the editor of the *Queen*, the style of the paper was changing noticeably. These changes are illuminated by Christophe Campos's new introduction to Holbrook Jackson's *The Eighteen-Nineties*.[28] Campos presents the end of the century as a heterogeneous but coherent decade, with origins in the tensions that underlay the surface of mid-Victorian conformity. In addition, what Campos calls a small publishing revolution was occurring. Changing cultural patterns were being reflected by corresponding changes "in the very organization of cultural transmission." These changes affected the history of the *Queen*. The class of readers for whom the *Queen* had been designed now included a growing number of women whose tastes and interests were quite modified. As new ideas in literature and the arts and crafts produced new magazines side by side with the "new journalism," the editorial policies of the *Queen* were modified in the fourth decade of its history.

The Cox papers had been incorporated after their founder's death in 1879 as a family business, and Horace Cox had become managing proprietor. Percy Stuart Cox, his son, was named the editor of the *Queen* in 1894. The paper had already begun to change to resemble not so much the newer periodicals in its class — *Woman,* for example — as certain of the new literary and artistic magazines. Literary topics and book reviews increased. New signatures began to appear, including popular writers of fiction — Eliza Lynn Linton, James Payn, Sabine Baring-Gould, Robert Louis Stevenson, and, much later, Arnold Bennett — and a coterie of outside contributors. The *Queen* especially came to resemble a group of new periodicals to which these authors also contributed: *Author,* the *Idler, To-Day,* and the *Sketch.* One writer in the *Queen* raised the question whether, as was widely held, "all literature in London reduces itself to one or two cliques."[29] Clique journalism was institutionalized in the "*Idler* teas," open house held every Friday for contributors and their literary and artistic friends in the offices of the *Idler,* which had been founded in 1892 by Jerome K. Jerome. (Jerome was also the founder and the editor of *To-Day.*) The connections of three contributors with the *Queen* may illustrate the effect of coterie journalism on the editorial style of the paper. These three are Walter Besant, Clement K. Shorter, and Douglas Sladen.

Besant and Shorter are considered, of course, somewhat eminent Victorians. Beginning in 1892 Walter Besant contributed to the *Queen* a signed weekly column of *ephemerae* entitled "Voice of the Flying Day," which stood immediately after the leader in each issue. His name lent prestige, for he was already well known as a journalist and a novelist. Besant had founded the Society of Authors, and he served as its chairman. Although the Society was an organization devoted to the professional interests of its members, it may have lent itself to the patterns of coterie journalism, for Douglas Sladen remarked (in the *Queen*) that the Society included "every single author of quite first class rank."[30] Besant also edited *Author,* the journal of the Society, from its establishment in 1890. Percy Stuart Cox's name is not prominent in the reports and news of the Society of Authors, but Horace Cox was an active member both of the Society and of its offshoot, the Authors' Club, which Besant had also founded ("being a clubbable man," as Francis Gribble described him in his *Reminiscences.*) Beginning in 1892 Horace Cox was listed as the printer and the publisher of *Author.* In that same year, Besant's "Voice of the Flying Day" began to appear in Cox's *Queen* as a regular feature. It was never memorable writing and is recalled only as an illustration of changing policies within class journalism.

Clement K. Shorter was considered one of the ablest of the younger journalists in London in the 1890s. Besant had invited him to the dinner that marked the founding of the Society of Authors. Shorter was attracting attention as a successful regular contributor to T. P. O'Connor's *Star,* when, as he recorded, an invitation came "from the proprietor of the *Queen* and his editor and for some years I wrote a weekly column in that journal, and found Horace Cox, the managing proprietor, the kindest of friends."[31] Shorter's column, "Literature—a Causerie," signed with his initials, contained some of the best sustained writing in the *Queen.* After Shorter became the editor of the *Illustrated London News* and in 1893 founded the weekly *Sketch,* which he also edited, he had no regular connection with the *Queen;* but in 1895 he published in the *Sketch* an interview with Horace Cox, in a series, "Journals and Journalists of To-day." The article was not, unfortunately, written by Shorter himself; signed "M.P.," it was probably by Max Pemberton. It recounts briefly the history of the *Queen* within that of the other Cox periodicals, focusing on the *Law Times, Field,* and *Queen,* Cox's most financially successful journals. Commenting on the fact that his son, Percy, was now the editor of the *Queen*—"I venture to believe that he inherits the true journalistic faculty"—Horace Cox insisted, in agreement with his interviewer, that the position of the paper in the mid-nineties continued to be, despite its competitors, "unassailable."[32]

The most copious writer for the *Queen* in the nineties and a prime exammple of coterie journalism at work was Douglas Sladen. Besant had made Sladen honorary secretary of the Authors' Club; and through Jerome's *Idler* teas, Sladen gained introductions to other London literary gentlemen. Jerome advised him, "If you wish to make your way as an author, lose no opportunity of getting to know people. If an editor is a friend, he will see you, if you have anything to offer him, and publishers are impressed."[33] Sladen began to write a column of literary gossip for Jerome's *To-Day* and to write for the *Pall Mall Budget* another feature that he called "The Diner-Out" and signed with the pseudonym "St. Barbe." Sladen's connection with the *Queen* began when Percy Cox, now its editor, commissioned a series of travel articles on Canada. Sladen succeeded Shorter as "a sort of literary editor," he said, and he wrote weekly reviews, including a signed review of a "Book of the Week." He also transferred to the *Queen* his "Diner-Out" column, which, he recorded with pride, Queen Victoria was reported to have read to her each week.[34] Signed articles by Sladen on various subjects abounded in the pages of the *Queen* in the nineties.

The editorial policies of coterie journalism did not serve the fortunes of this class journal well. The historian of the *Field* notes that the circulation of the *Queen* fell from 23,500 in 1890 to 16,000 in 1900.[35] For its Edwardian readership, the journal began to revert to its earlier emphases, as writers such as Mrs. Aria and Mrs. Peel reappeared on the staff and in editorial capacities. Nevertheless, the paper never regained the prestige it had occupied in Victorian class journalism. A centenary volume entitled *The Frontiers of Privilege,* edited by Quentin Crewe, was an anthology and a summary of the contents of the periodical throughout its first one hundred years. The history of the making of the paper, however, lies in the policies of an editor who fashioned a class paper in its first three decades into an emblem of a cultural style.

NOTES

1. *Critic,* July 27, 1861; August 24, 1861.
2. John C. Francis, *John Francis, Publisher of the Athenaeum* (London: Richard Bentley and Son, 1888), II, p. 430.
3. *Athenaeum,* October 28, 1854.
4. *Critic,* April 5, 12, 1862.
5. J. W. Robertson Scott, *The Story of the Pall Mall Gazette, of Its First Editor Frederick Greenwood and of Its Founder George Murray Smith* (London: Oxford University Press, 1950), p. 164.
6. *Athenaeum,* July 18, 1857; January 8, 1859; December 31, 1864.

7. Mrs. C. S. Peel, *Life's Enchanted Cup: An Autobiography (1872-1933)* (London: John Lane, 1933), pp. 63-64.

8. *C. K. S.: An Autobiography: A Fragment by Himself,* ed. J. M. Bulloch (privately printed, 1927), p. 68.

9. Francis, II, p. 430, n.

10. R. N. Rose, *The Field, 1853-1953* (London: Michael Joseph, 1953), p. 57.

11. John Oldcastle [Wilfrid Meynell], *Journals and Journalism* (London, 1880), pp. 125-26.

12. *Athenaeum,* May 17, 1851.

13. *Sketch,* March 27, 1895.

14. E. A. Bennett, *Journalism for Women: A Practical Guide* (London: John Lane, 1898), p. 87.

15. *Critic,* September 7, 1861.

16. *Queen,* December 21, 1889.

17. M. H. Spielman, *The History of Punch* (London: Cassell and Company, 1895), p. 362.

18. Bea Howe, *Arbiter of Elegance* (London: The Harvill Press), p. 93.

19. Mrs. Haweis, *Beautiful Houses: Being a Description of Certain Well-Known Artistic Houses.* (London: Sampson Low, Marston, Searle, & Rivington, 1882), p. [i].

20. Mrs. Aria, *My Sentimental Self* (London: Chapman and Hall, 1922), pp. 33-38.

21. *Queen,* June 18, 1892. On Mrs. Coke, see John Talbot Coke, *Coke of Trusley* (London, 1880).

22. "The Queen at Home," rpt. from *Madame* in *To-Day,* May 25, 1897, p. 540.

23. Peel, *Life's Enchanted Cup,* pp. 61-65. On Mrs. Peel, see *Times,* August 8, 1934, and entry in *Who Was Who, 1929-1940.*

24. "Editing a Woman's Paper," *The Savour of Life: Essays in Gusto* (New York: Doubleday Doran, 1928), pp. 175-76.

25. "The Press and the Launching of the Woman's Suffrage Movement, 1866-1867," *Victorian Periodicals Review* 13 (Winter 1980): 125-31.

26. *Queen,* September 3, 1881.

27. The parliamentary returns for the year ending June 30, 1866, record for the *Queen* 28,000 stamps at 1d. and 18,000 at 1½d.; for the year ending June 1870, 16,500 at 1d. and 79,500 at 1½d.

28. Humanities Press, 1976.

29. *Queen,* September 1, 1894.

30. *Queen,* December 28, 1895.

31. C.K.S.: *An Autobiography,* p. 53.

32. " 'The Queen,' 'The Field,' 'The Law Times,' and Mr. Horace Cox," *Sketch*, March 27, 1895.

33. Douglas Sladen, *My Long Life* (London: Hutchinson and Company, 1939), p. 143.

34. Douglas Sladen, *Twenty Years of My Life* (New York: E. P. Dutton & Company, n.d.), pp. 188-90.

35. Rose, *The Field*, p. 138.

Part Three

SOME LEADING PRACTITIONERS

Robert A. Colby

Goose Quill and Blue Pencil: The Victorian Novelist as Editor

"As an author who has written long, and had the good fortune to find a very great number of readers, I think I am not mistaken in supposing that they give me credit for experience and observation . . . and having heard me soliloquize, with so much kindness and favour, and say my say about life, and men and women, they will not be unwilling to try me as a Conductor of a Concert, in which I trust many skilful performers will take part." So Thackeray addressed his unknown readers of the newly launched *Cornhill Magazine* in January 1860.[1]

By then Thackeray was but the latest in a long line of novelist-editors reaching back to the birth of the periodical in the eighteenth century. Among his more illustrious predecessors, Defoe was a polemical journalist who evolved into a novelist; Fielding seized upon periodical journalism, along with judicial posts, to help eke out an insecure career as a novelist and a dramatist, and Fleet Street fed into his fiction as much as Westminster; Smollett

204 Robert A. Colby

introduced the practice that became a commonplace in the next century of utilizing a journal he was editing to launch one of his own novels (his poorest, *Launcelot Greaves,* as it happened). Once the magazine became the leading medium for fiction, as it did by the Victorian period, it increasingly attracted novelists to editorial posts for a variety of reasons: most obviously for the large captive (that is, subscription) audience that was guaranteed for their books but also for the opportunity afforded to test the market for their future product, and—hardly the least consideration—security during periods of lagging creativity.

Dickens is, of course, the most celebrated of Victorian writers who turned to journalism, but a full catalog of novelist-editors would have to include Thackeray and Trollope, along with Theodore Hook, Bulwer-Lytton, Harrison Ainsworth, Charles Lever, G. W. M. Reynolds, R. S. Surtees ("Jorrocks"), Joseph Sheridan Le Fanu, Francis E. Smedley, Alfred Austin, Edmund Yates, George Augustus Sala, James Payn, Walter Besant, Oscar Wilde, and among the "singular anomalies," the evangelical Charlotte Elizabeth Tonna, the churchy Charlotte Yonge, those two grand mistresses of the sensation novel, Mary Elizabeth Braddon and Mrs. Henry Wood, as well as others who might be named, such as Florence Marryat and Mrs. Riddell. (Mrs. Oliphant, the most prolific of Victorian women novelists, importuned her publisher, Blackwood, in vain to put her in charge of a magazine.) I will confine myself here to four representative figures whose careers extended from the early to the late Victorian period: Ainsworth, Lever, Thackeray, and Trollope. All four, highly esteemed novelists in their day, exemplify in their grapplings with editorial responsibility the tribulations of what Thackeray once referred to as "the corporation of the goosequill." Furthermore, typical of the reciprocal logrolling that characterized the Victorian marketplace, their careers touched at various tangents. In particular they illustrate the mutual influences of periodical journalism and fiction during this period as well as the ways in which novelists "used" periodicals.

Each of the four, to begin with, became an editor at a different stage of his career and under varying circumstances. The only "professional" journalist of the four was Harrison Ainsworth. By the time he launched *Ainsworth's Magazine* (in February 1842) he was already an experienced editor *(Bentley's Magazine)* as well as a famous novelist *(Jack Sheppard)*. The quarrel with Bentley that led him to resign from that magazine in December 1841 left him with the determination to own as well as edit a magazine, an ambition realized with the magazine that bore his name and subsequently with the *New Monthly Magazine*. For much of his professional life Ainsworth's proprietary zeal led him to own two magazines simultaneously (first *Ainsworth's Magazine* and the *New Monthly Magazine,* then the *New Monthly* and *Bentley's,* which he bought back).[2] For Charles Lever, on the other hand, the editorship of the *Dublin University Magazine,* which he took up in 1842, constituted part of his apprenticeship as a writer. Initially the outlet for his first successful work of fiction, *Harry Lorrequer,* "Dea" eventually provided Lever with an opportunity to return to Ireland, which overcame his reluctance to give up his medical practice in Brussels.[3] For Thackeray the editorship of the *Cornhill Magazine,* launched at the beginning of 1860, a position that he had some hesitation about accepting, marked the capstone of his career, a kudo bestowed upon him by George Smith, the publisher of *Henry Esmond,* who counted on Thackeray's prestige to lend luster to this new venture in a shilling magazine. Having suffered two failed journalistic enterprises in his youth and two futile efforts to acquire prestigious journals later on, Thackeray found in *Cornhill* the belated fulfillment of an ambition he had expressed in his paradoxical fashion early in life to head "a slashing, brilliant, gentlemanlike, sixpenny aristocratic literary paper."[4] Editorship came late also to Trollope, though at midcareer when he was at the apex of his prestige and popularity as a novelist. He had flirted casually with journalism in Ireland during his period as a postal inspector (when he met Charles Lever, among others). When he was established as a novelist, he helped found the *Fortnightly Review* and turned down an offer to edit the *Pall Mall Magazine*. Not until his resignation from the post office in 1867 did he accept the responsibility of an editorship, though, like Thackeray, with some misgivings.[5] *Saint Paul's Magazine,* offering Trollope a haven once he decided to leave St. Martin's-le-Grand behind him, actually constituted his first professional literary situation.

Their journals served these novelist-editors as springboards in diverse ways. Ainsworth, obviously no believer in the subliminal approach, was the only one of the four to name a magazine after himself as well as to print his portrait (by Daniel Maclise) on the frontispiece. (Lever inherited his title; Thackeray and Trollope both refused to allow their magazines to carry their names.) *Ainsworth's Magazine,* although varied in content, was quite openly the vehicle for the latest romances by the editor as well as his refurbished old ones. Although he aimed at a readership not up to the level of the prestigious reviews such as *Blackwood's* and *Fraser's,* Ainsworth assured subscribers that he and his contributors were striving "to advance the solid and the permanent, no less than the light and the temporary purposes of literature."[6] Lever's editorship was driven by a combination of ego gratification and patriotism. During the years when he was at its helm, the *Dublin University Magazine* continued to prove a lucrative organ for his fiction, which at first delighted his readers, and his political commentary, which soon alienated them. But his highest hope was to make his magazine bound ahead of its English and Scottish counterparts, *Fraser's* and *Blackwood's*[7] (the nickname of *DUM,* "Dea," was attached by analogy with "Regina" and "Maga"). For Thackeray, unlike the others, the primary inducement to accept an editorial post was the financial security it brought. George Smith's offer of £1,000 a month, in addition to what he had contracted for serial stories, was one, as he said, that he could not refuse.[8] As it turned out, *Cornhill Magazine* brought him the largest simultaneous readership he had ever enjoyed, affording him the opportunity to extend that "conversation with his readers" begun with his first novel *Catherine.* Essentially the pages of *Cornhill* provided Thackeray with the typographical equivalent of the lecture platform that he had trod with profit during the preceding years. For Trollope *Saint Paul's Magazine* during the brief period (1867-70) that he guided it served mainly as a platform for his "conservative liberal" political views as well as a launching pad for his own (unsuccessful) campaign for a seat in Parliament.[9] As with Lever, periodical journalism enabled Trollope to unite his vocation with his avocation.

Periodical journalism not only offered ready vehicles for the novels of these gentlemen of letters, as for those of many of their confreres, but also outlets for the justification of their calling in an age when fiction was widely associated with "the diffusion of useless knowledge" (in the words of a forgotten novel of the 1860s).[10] Ainsworth alone made fiction preeminent — openly proclaiming the first journal he owned *A Monthly Miscellany of Romance, General Literature, and Art.* For the most part *Ainsworth's Magazine* served as a proving ground to try out his ideas for domesticating and historicizing the Gothic romances of Horace Walpole, Mrs. Radcliffe, and "Monk" Lewis (i.e., Windsor Castle substituted for the Castle of Otranto, Revelations of London instead of the Mysteries of Udolpho). However, he also thought of himself as "illustrating" history in the manner of Scott and John Galt and prided himself as well on reviving interest in national monuments (e.g., the titles of his best known romances: *Windsor Castle, Old Saint Paul's, The Tower of London, Saint James's*). Significant in this connection is his initial editorial greeting to his readers wherein he announced himself as the breaker down of the barrier between past and present, his tales serving to "exhibit many of the pictures and manners and of social habits in the byegone time, by which the Magazine may become the happy instrument of introducing every young reader to his great-grandfather."[11] Generally it was a lurid picture that Ainsworth gave his readers of their ancestors, but interspersed among his tenebrous melodramas illuminated in chairoscuro by the graver of Cruikshank were some bright patches such as "The Great Paris Fêtes," and pieces on architecture and archaeology disciplined his antiquarian zeal.

For Lever, although he lacked Ainsworth's experience, the transition from novelist to editor was relatively easy since he carried over the pseudonym "Harry Lorrequer" already familiar to his readers in his opening "Editor's Address" ("A scarcely interrupted acquaintance of more than three years emboldens me thus to address you," he began).[12] Lever obviously thought of his fiction as fitting in with the nationalistic ideas of *DUM,* which he recapitulated in his first editorial: "benefitting our native country—illustrating its antiquities—elevating its literary tastes—fostering its arts—and encouraging its industry, . . ." his contribution being to illustrate the characters, customs, and culture of his native land and to bring his countrymen to a better understanding of themselves. Although it is evident that fiction was lucrative for Lever, he actually took more pride in his "serious" writing. Summing up his prodigious output for 1842, the first year of his editorship, he estimated that he had contributed 336 pages to the magazine, "making 21 sheets in a quantity equal to the matter of a three-volume octavo." The point he was making was that it was not all fiction. In his log for 1843 he called specific attention to his social commentary (the series entitled "Nuts and Nutcrackers"), travel writing, and reviews of medical books, taking well-merited pride in his versatility.[13]

As far as his fiction went, Lever's editorial post, particularly his involvement in Irish politics, had the effect of deepening it, turning him from the comic novelist of *Harry Lorrequer* and *Jack Hinton* to the more somber one of *St. Patrick's Eve* and *The O'Donoghue*.

Thackeray, arguably the greatest novelist of the four, was the most halfhearted about fiction writing by the time he assumed the editorial post that proved his swan song. "I often say I am like the pastrycook, and I don't care for tarts, but prefer bread and cheese," he wrote to Trollope in a letter inviting the author of *Barchester Towers* to become a contributor to *Cornhill*, "but the public love the tarts (luckily for us) and we must bake and sell them."[14] Jaded and with his great work behind him, Thackeray confided to Trollope his desire for "getting out of novel spinning and back into the world." It is true that the novels contributed by Thackeray to *Cornhill—Lovel the Widower, The Adventures of Philip*, and the half-told *Denis Duval—*are now his least read, whereas his most enduring contribution to his magazine has proved to be the series of reflective essays he called "The Roundabout Papers" (modeled after his beloved *Spectator*). Here he spoke out *in propria persona* as a "weekday preacher" to a captive audience that began at 125,000 and continued to average close to 85,000 throughout his editorship. However, novels and "essaykins" actually fed each other, with readers becoming sounding boards for the author-editor. As Thackeray had already remarked in his opening "Letter" inviting contributions, his readers were used to hearing him verbally "soliloquize . . . and say my own say about life, and men, and women, . . ." an indication that the novel was always for him a form of meditative discourse. Sometimes the papers introduced ideas explored in greater depth in the novels: social hypocrisy (Thackeray's perennial theme), the sinister fascination of evil, the changes wrought by time, the persistence of childhood into adult life, human versus divine judgment.[15] Now and then he discussed a novel in progress (particularly *Denis Duval*, with which he was obviously making a bid for popular success).[16] Among the most poignant of "The Roundabout Papers" are those in which Thackeray let down his silver hair, confiding his personal fears of waning creativity or deploring the ephemerality of fame.

Like Thackeray, Trollope regarded the publication of fiction in his magazine as a compromise with reader demand. Oddly enough, as one of its founders, he had opposed the inclusion in the *Fortnightly Review* of a serialized novel in every issue, though he was persuaded to run *The Belton Estate* in its initial number.[17] In his editorial introduction to the first number of *Saint Paul's Magazine* (October 1867) he downplayed fiction mainly because he was concerned to refute the common association of periodicals with "light literature." Denying that the magazines of the day were made up, as had been alleged, of "novels and padding," he pointed out that the likes of Arnold and Carlyle were not ashamed to write for them. "Novels we will have and syllabubs," he went on to assure his readers with a note of condescension, "but we will not believe that our guests will be content with no other dishes at the banquet." Trollope made it quite clear toward the end of his introductory address that he himself did not regard fiction as merely the dessert course. "The preaching of the day is done by the novelist, and the lessons which he teaches are those to which men and women will listen," he affirmed in anticipation of his famous lecture on "English Prose Fiction as a Rational Amusement." But in the next breath he lauded politics as "the first and finest" of all studies to which men and women attach themselves. *Phineas Finn*, which made its debut in the first number of *Saint Paul's Magazine*, obviously united its author's dual preoccupations. Although composed before Trollope became the editor of *Saint Paul's*, this second in his Palliser series happened to coincide in the course of its run with Trollope's own unsuccessful campaign as the Liberal candidate for Beverley in the general election of 1868, and woven into the tissue of the novel are topics dealt with in Trollope's political articles, such as "On Sovereignty," "The Uncontrolled Ruffianism of England," "Whom Shall We Make the New Leader of the House of Commons?" and "The Irish Church Debate."[18] It is no coincidence that *Ralph the Heir,* the last work of fiction published by Trollope in *Saint Paul's Magazine,* has for one of its characters Sir Thomas Underwood, a lawyer who suffers defeat in his campaign for the seat from Percycross (read Beverley), becomes disillusioned with politicians, and retires to a quiet life to complete a work in progress.[19]

As for their general conduct of their magazines, all the novelists-editors started out with high hopes and noble purposes and, far from showing condescending attitudes, tended to idealize their readers. Ainsworth, the least pretentious of them, nevertheless professed to serve "some moral end" while entertaining his subscribers. He hoped to attract the so-called gay-hearted readers without scaring off "Philosophy . . . looking with face severe, yet neither scornful nor ashamed upon her frolicsome companions." Above all, Ainsworth prided himself on reaching all generations: "In a word we would render our work in the best moral and literary sense, a FAMILY MAGAZINE."[20] Lever was not so concerned with reaching young ears, but he presumed that he was speaking out to the entire nation, "seeking to induce on the common ground of literature and science, a bond of union between all parties and denominations. . . ." Addressing this wide constituency as "Harry Lorrequer" in his editorial greeting, he extolled the *Dublin University Magazine* for its "bold and upright career unblemished by a stain, unshaken by a doubt," a tradition he stood pledged to carry on.[21] Thackeray thought of himself and of his colleagues at *Cornhill* along the lines of his hero Arthur Pendennis's associates on the fictitious *Pall Mall Gazette,* "gentlemen speaking to gentlemen." "If our friends have

good manners, a good education, and write in good English,"
wrote Thackeray in his open letter to contributors that greeted the
readers of the first number of *Cornhill Magazine,* "the company,
I am sure will be better pleased; and the guests, whatever their
rank, age, sex, will be glad to be addressed by well educated men
and women." Moreover, Thackeray spread his net wide: taking
in the learned academic, the retired curate, the artisan at leisure,
"a schoolmaster or mistress when the children are gone home, or
the young ones themselves when their lessons are over. . . ."[22] It
is doubtful whether *Cornhill* ever embraced this wide a universe,
but Thackeray's hope to attract and hold young ladies and
children may in particular have accounted for the certain
squeamishness he betrayed in his editorial decisions. Of the four,
Trollope was the most conscious of what Wilkie Collins dubbed
"The Unknown Public"—the "increasing thousands of readers
whom the progress of education is producing"—in the first
number of *Saint Paul's Magazine.* These were the readers,
Trollope recognized, who gained most of their knowledge from
periodicals. To this flock waiting to be fed he felt obligated to
"see that the article produced is as good of its kind as it can be
made." Hence his justification of fiction as lay sermon, his self-
conscious defense of periodicals as adding to, not superseding,
the prose of ideas. As he put it in his shilly-shallying editorial:
"We hope to conciliate the graver sisters, but shall not do so by
turning up our noses at the laughter-loving Muse."[23]

"It has sometimes been thought well to select a popular literary
man as editor, first because his name will attract, and then with
an idea that he who can write well himself will be a competent
judge of the writing of others," wrote Trollope in 1879 in his
critical biography of Thackeray commissioned for the *English
Men of Letters* series.[24] Thackeray, of course, was long dead by
then, and Trollope's own experience with *Saint Paul's* was well
behind him, so that he was looking back with wry detachment. In

his usual laconic way he seemed to suggest that the great expectations of magazine publishers who employ great writers may well be disappointed. For those whom we have been considering, the verdict is mixed.

Of the four, Thackeray was the most successful in attracting writers of comparable distinction. His most famous acquisition, of course, was *Framley Parsonage,* to which he gave pride of place in the first number of *Cornhill*—his own *Lovel the Widower* relegated to the third spot. ("I sang purposely small; wishing to keep my strongest suit for a later day, and give Trollope the honours of *Violono primo,*" he wrote to Charles Lever at that time.)[25] *Framley Parsonage,* as Trollope later recalled in his *Autobiography,* marked a turning point in his economic fortunes as well as reputation. Ironically one of Trollope's worst novels, *The Struggles of Brown, Jones, and Robinson,* also appeared under Thackeray's editorship (not owing to Thackeray, however, but to George Smith out of enthusiasm for Trollope's first contribution),[26] whereas another of his better ones, *The Small House at Allington,* did not come out in *Cornhill* until after Thackeray had resigned. The luring away of George Eliot from *Blackwood,* considered a coup at the time, was not Thackeray's doing either, but George Smith's—again prompted, as it happened, by the failure of Thackeray's *The Adventures of Philip* to hold readers. (By another quirk of destiny, *Romola* too proved a limited success as a serial.) Thackeray for his part did try to follow through on his plan announced in the first number to encourage unknown writers, but finding them broken reeds, he ultimately found it necessary to lean on "names" in order to carry on. Fortunately, these included John Ruskin, James Fitzjames Stephen, George Henry Lewes, Henry Sumner Maine, and Mrs. Gaskell. Undoubtedly his prize was Tennyson's "Tithonus."

When it came to the recruitment of authors, the others do not stand up as well in retrospect. Lever's biographer, W. J.

Fitzpatrick, has recorded that although "Harry Lorrequer," like Thackeray, "found many thrones in the editorial chair," he did take real pleasure in discovering and developing new talent.[27] But presumably having served their temporal purpose of awakening their fellow Hibernians to their heritage, these nova have proved ephemeral. The same can be said of the writers who shared the fiction pages of Lever, such as G. P. R. James *(Arrah Neill)* and Mortimer O'Sullivan, the true author of *The Nevilles of Garratstown: A Tale of 1760*, once falsely ascribed to Lever. Lever's own better novels of this period, such as *The O'Donoghue* and *St. Patrick's Eve*, were not published in the magazine, Lever by now feeling uncomfortable about appearing in it.[28] Probably the best of *DUM* during the Lever years is to be found in the articles on Irish poetry and culture.

Ainsworth did succeed in attracting Thackeray to *Ainsworth's Magazine* but with one of his trifles, the pseudo-Arabian Nights tale "Sultan Stork" (enhanced by Cruikshank's drawing of a dancing stork).[29] More characteristic of his stable were G. P. R. James, Martin Tupper, and Carolyn Bowles. Like Lever, Ainsworth prided himself on encouraging neophytes, but his discoveries were Eliza Lynn Linton, Ouida, and Mrs. Henry Wood (whose *East Lynne*, destined to be one of the most popular novels of the century, was introduced, practically unnoticed, in the *New Monthly Magazine)*. R. S. Surtees is the one name that stands above this ruck. With more reason Ainsworth boasted of his gallery of illustrators: George Cruikshank, Tony Johannot, Alfred Delamotte. These gave to his magazines what panache they could claim.

As for Trollope, none of the fiction that ran in *Saint Paul's Magazine* during the years of his editorship measured up to his own contribution. He did recruit Charles Lever (who had befriended him when he was in Ireland and helped him publish articles in *DUM* after Lever's own editorship) but with an inferior work, *Paul Gosslette's Confessions,* which might have attracted Trollope by its subtitle: *In Love, Law, and Civil Service.*[30] Unfortunately, the redoubtable Mrs. Oliphant, whom literary historians have tended to join with Trollope in subject matter as well as productivity, also delivered of her less than best with *The Three Brothers.* The other fiction writers whom Trollope commandeered have hardly stood the test of time: his sister-in-law Frances Eleanor Trollope *(The Sacristan's Household);* Marie Blaze de Bury *(All for Greed* appeared in the first issue, Trollope consigning his own *Phineas Finn* to a middle position); Annie Hall Thomas Cudlip *(For a Year).* George Macdonald was represented by a short story, but his *Wilfrid Cumbermede* did not appear until the editorship of Trollope's successor, Alexander Strahan, who also procured Nathaniel Hawthorne's *Septimus Felton.* More to Trollope's credit, he published the first poems of Austin Dobson (though letters indicate that he had difficulty persuading the poet to write so as to be clearly understood by "ill-instructed, uneducated, but perhaps intelligent minds").[31] It has recently been suggested by one of Trollope's detractors that he deliberately selected second-rate novelists who would select lower payments in order to keep his own ante up,[32] but it is more likely that he treated fiction with his left hand in order to concentrate his own as well as his readers' attention on the current parliamentary and social issues that engaged him more at that time. At any rate, the articles by eminences such as Edward Dicey ("Ethics of Trade Unions"), Peter Bayne (a series on statesmen, including Lord Palmerston, Disraeli, Sir Robert Peel, and Daniel O'Connell), Sir Austen Henry Layard ("How to Settle the Eastern Question"), William Rathbone Greg ("Disposal and Control of the Criminal Classes"), and Leslie Stephen ("Anonymous Journalism," "Alpine Climbing"), together with Trollope's own political articles, constitute the real substance of *Saint Paul's Magazine* under his direction.

Caricature of Harrison Ainsworth, by Linley Sambourne, from PUNCH, September 21, 1881.

W. HARRISON AINSWORTH.

TO THE GREATEST AXE-AND-NECK-ROMANCER OF OUR TIME, WHO IS QUITE AT THE HEAD OF HIS PROFESSION, WE DEDICATE THIS BLOCK. *AD MULTOS ANNOS!* *Reproduced from "Punch" (September 21st, 1881) by kind permission of the Proprietors and of the artist, Mr. Linley Sambourne.*

Original cover of CORNHILL MAGAZINE, designed by Godfrey Sikes, executed by W. J. Linton.

Thackeray's open letter to readers of CORNHILL MAGAZINE (January, 1860).

"THE CORNHILL MAGAZINE," Smith, Elder and Co.
65, *Cornhill,* 1st *November,* 1859.

A LETTER FROM THE EDITOR TO A FRIEND AND CONTRIBUTOR.

Dear ——, Our Store-House being in Cornhill, we date and name our Magazine from its place of publication. We might have assumed a title much more startling: for example, "The Thames on Fire" was a name suggested; and, placarded in red letters about the City, and Country, it would no doubt have excited some curiosity. But, on going to London Bridge the expectant rustic would have found the stream rolling on its accustomed course, and would have turned away angry at being hoaxed. Sensible people are not to be misled by fine prospectuses and sounding names : the present Writer has been for five-and-twenty years before the world, which has taken his measure pretty accurately. We are too long acquainted to try and deceive one another ; and were I to propose any such astounding feat as that above announced, I know quite well how the schemer would be received, and the scheme would end.

You, then, who ask what "The Cornhill Magazine" is to be, and what sort of articles you shall supply for it ?—if you were told that the Editor, known hitherto only by his published writings, was in reality a great reformer, philosopher, and wiseacre, about to expound prodigious doctrines and truths until now unrevealed, to guide and direct the peoples, to pull down the existing order of things, to edify new social or political structures, and, in a word, to set the Thames on Fire ; if you heard such designs ascribed to him—*risum teneatis?* You know I have no such pretensions : but, as an Author who has written long, and had the good fortune to find a very great number of readers, I think I am not mistaken in supposing that they give me credit for experience and observation, for having lived with educated people in many countries, and seen the world in no small variety ; and, having heard me soliloquize, with so much kindness and favour, and say my own say about life, and men and women, they will not be unwilling to try me as Conductor of a Concert, in which I trust many skilful performers will take part.

We hope for a large number of readers, and must seek, in the first place, to amuse and interest them. Fortunately for some folks, novels are as daily bread to others ; and fiction of course must form a part, but only a part of our entertainment. We want, on the other hand, as much reality as possible—discussion and narrative of events interesting to the public, personal adventures and observation, familiar reports of scientific discovery, description of Social Institutions—*quicquid agunt homines*—a Great Eastern, a battle in China, a Race-Course, a popular Preacher—there is hardly any subject we *don't* want to hear about, from lettered and instructed men who are competent to speak on it.

I read the other day in "The Illustrated London News," (in my own room at home,) that I was at that moment at Bordeaux, purchasing first-class claret for first-class contributors, and second class for those of inferior *cru*. Let me adopt this hospitable simile ; and say that at our contributors' table, I do not ask or desire to shine especially myself, but to take my part occasionally, and to invite pleasant and instructed gentlemen and ladies to contribute their share to the conversation. It may be a Foxhunter who has the turn to speak ; or a Geologist, Engineer, Manufacturer, Member of the House of Commons, Lawyer, Chemist,—what you please. If we can only get people to tell what they know, pretty briefly and good-humouredly, and not in a manner obtrusively didactic, what a pleasant ordinary we may have, and how gladly folks will come to it ! If our friends have good manners, a good education, and write in good English, the company, I am sure, will be all the better pleased ; and the guests, whatever their rank, age, sex be, will be glad to be addressed by well-educated gentlemen and women. A professor ever so learned, a curate in his country retirement, an artisan after work-hours, a schoolmaster or mistress when the children are gone home, or the young ones themselves when their lessons are over, may like to hear what the world is talking about, or be brought into friendly communication with persons whom the world knows. There are points on which agreement is impossible, and on these we need not touch. At our social table, we shall suppose the ladies and children always present ; we shall not set rival politicians by the ears ; we shall listen to every guest who has an apt word to say ; and, I hope, induce clergymen of various denominations to say grace in their turn. The kindly fruits of the earth, which grow for all—may we not enjoy them with friendly hearts ? The field is immensely wide ; the harvest perennial, and rising everywhere ; we can promise competent fellow-labourers a welcome and a good wage ; and hope a fair custom from the public for our stores at "The Cornhill Magazine."

W. M. THACKERAY.

portrait of the editor facing the title page.

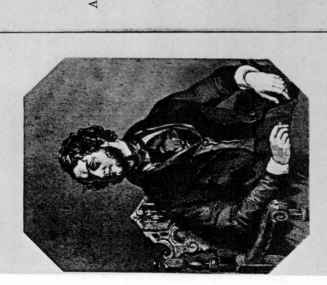

AINSWORTH'S

MAGAZINE:

A MISCELLANY OF ROMANCE,

General Literature, & Art.

EDITED BY

WILLIAM HARRISON AINSWORTH.

ILLUSTRATED BY

GEORGE CRUIKSHANK.

VOL. V.

LONDON:

JOHN MORTIMER, PUBLISHER, ADELAIDE STREET,
TRAFALGAR SQUARE.

MDCCCXLIV.

Whatever is to be concluded about the novelist as an editor in general, ultimately it must be said of the four whom we have been considering that their reach exceeded their grasp. Three of them found editorship a disillusioning experience. The fourth, Ainsworth, though he never seems to have lost his zest for this literary task, proved a poor manager. The reasons for failure in periodical journalism must be at least as various as the reasons for success, and so it is not surprising that although Ainsworth, Lever, Thackeray, and Trollope all met with adverse circumstances in their editorial careers, these were of different sorts in each case.

To start with Lever, his main motive in returning to Ireland from the Continent, apart from touching down again on the old sod, was to realize his youthful dream of taking up the life of a landed squire.[33] Concomitantly he hoped that his visibility as a journalist would yield him a prominent political appointment or a secure medical ˙post. As things turned out, he found the Irish countryside not nearly so idyllic as he had pictured it, the damp climate ruinous to his health, the social life stuffy. Moreover, he was passed over for preferment. As well paid as he was in his post, he never had enough money to suit the extravagant life-style he cultivated. At the same time the conducting of the magazine proved more than he had bargained for. In a euphoric mood at the outset, he wrote in his initial "Editor's Address" with false modesty: "If the coachman on the box be an inferior whip . . . his team is unsurpassed."[34] Shortly afterward the coach had obviously run down, for we find Lever complaining that "the machine [Magazine] was drawn by as groggy a set of screws as ever marched in harness." Unsolicited manuscripts, which he dubbed "the great unknown," were soon dismissed as "the great rejected."[35]

More seriously, his attempts to calm the turbulent political waters only stirred them up more. Prior to his invitation by the publisher, James McGlashan, to edit *DUM,* he had published in the magazine an article defending the newly appointed Irish secretary, Lord Eliot, thereby incurring the wrath of the Tory party, and its organ, the *Evening Mail,* continued to take potshots at him throughout his incumbency as the editor. Although he did succeed in raising the readership of *DUM* to a then unprecedented level (about 4,000), ultimately he brought many of these readers down on his head. Inclined, as he wrote in a letter, to a "moderate government with Tory leanings," he was opposed to the emergent Young Ireland party and the Repeal Movement under the leadership of Daniel O'Connell, making him persona non grata to the Nationalist party in whose eyes he, as a graduate of Trinity, a member of the Church of England, and an advocate of the Ascendancy, was already identified with the traditionalists. Yet his sympathetic tone toward rebels in his novels *St. Patrick's Eve* and *The O'Donoghue* made it seem in conservative circles that he was siding with the advocates of Repeal. From the other side, the *Nation* condemned his stories, intended to make his countrymen see themselves more objectively, as "libels on the Irish character."

In the end, far from conciliating the differences among the parties, Lever succeeded only, like Ibsen's Dr. Stockmann, in antagonizing conservative and radical alike. Not surprisingly, as early as 1844 he was consulting guide books to the Continent. His letter to the Rev. Samuel Hayman, his confidant at the time, said in effect "a plague on both your houses.":

I am off to Brussels and the Rhine, to Dresden, and to Vienna, heartily sick of drudgery, printers, publishers, and small literati, with little brains and much malice. . . . When I shall return, if ever, I know not. My trip is partly for health, to end as God pleases. For myself I am satisfied to seek out a tranquil place in a foreign land, and work away among my children and content to be as thoroughly forgotten as I am now a prominent object for attack.[36]

By the spring of 1845 Lever had left the editorship of "Dea," as well as his birthplace, well behind him, not to return until 1871, the year before his death. However, his connection with the magazine continued, his sketches from Italy and four of his novels running intermittently through the 1850s.

Under Thackeray, *Cornhill Magazine* (a name selected by him under the inspiration of St. Lucius, founder of the Church of St. Peter of Cornhill) got off to a flourishing start with its black and orange cover—designed by a protegé Godfrey Sikes and executed by W. J. Linton—personifying Plowing, Sowing, Reaping, and Threshing. But soon Thackeray, like Lever, chafed under the drudgery of routine editorial burdens. Some years earlier he had proposed to George Smith an essay journal modeled on Addison's *Spectator* and Johnson's *Rambler* but pulled back in fear of the responsibilities. When he agreed, persuaded by George Smith, to undertake the editorship of *Cornhill,* it was with the assurance that he would have no responsibility for its financial affairs. From the outset Thackeray's eighteenth-century ideal of a genteel critical review was incompatible with the brisker pace of the nineteenth-century miscellany.[37] But his main tribulations issued from relations with contributors. Early on he had the painful task of rejecting a story by his friend Trollope because of an allusion to a man with illegitimate children. Later he felt impelled to turn down a poem by Elizabeth Barrett Browning in which a wife feigns infidelity. Desiring to avoid controversial issues, he terminated Ruskin's *Unto This Last* in response to protests by readers and outraged editorials in various papers. As for the small fry, Thackeray's famous essay "Thorns in the Cushion" offers poignant testimony to the harrassment he suffered from unsung governesses and other aspiring literati whose manuscripts found their way to his Kensington home, despite the clear admonition: "Contributions are only to be sent to Messrs. Smith, Elder & Co. . . ."[38]

Not recorded by Thackeray is a sheaf of beseeching letters (now in the Beinecke Library at Yale) from miscellaneous candidates for fame, responding all too eagerly to his open letter of invitation in the first number of *Cornhill.* There are the fawners, like the would-be contributor who hailed the editor of *Cornhill* as the equal of Solomon and Shakespeare. "I heard you make several speeches when you put up for Oxford. I thought you seemed a jolly fellow," wrote another seeking the "distinguished honour" of placing some poems in the magazine.[39] Numerous are the tugs at the heartstrings (what Thackeray called the argument *ad misericordiam):* "I hope I may live long enough to do my yet unborn son the same good you have me," wrote a lady from Florence offering a bounty of "seventy-five or eighty ballads of various authors" translated from the German; a lady from Taunton, expecting a nephew home from India after a twenty-year absence, was "desirous to convert the furniture of my brain into parlour or even kitchen furniture"; a down-at-heels Eton graduate, supporting a wife and seven children in Ostend on an income of £200 a year, emboldened by a nod from Carlyle, hoped that the editor of *Cornhill* would consider his tragedy and his novel worthy of attention and offered as a bonus to do a monthly piece on politics or philosophy. "Don't hit a fallen man—I implore—Try me. If unworthy, *cast* me," added this tragedian. "But give me a trial—thus casting a ray of hope upon a dissolute and disconsolate family." "A Respectful Servant" from Glasgow, "cultivating literature upon a little oatmeal," perked up momentarily by an acceptance from Mr. Dickens from *All the Year Round,* approached Dickens's chief rival with the assurance that "you share with that gentlemen a sympathy towards ardent, and it may be obscure, followers of letters." A somewhat pricklier thorn was the letter from a Miss Leigh-Spencer of Bromley College, addressed to "Friend of Charlotte Brontë (with whom she clearly identified herself), concluding with a coy and none too subtle hint that she could be available to "Mr. Batchelor"—the name that Thackeray adopted as the narrator of *Lovel the Widower*—as more than a contributor to the magazine. Not all the letters were ego gratifying. One correspondent accused Thackeray of returning a manuscript unread because the writer found that some leaves deliberately left gummed together to test the editor were still stuck. Nor could Thackeray have been elated by a letter asking him to settle a controversy among the writer's acquaintances as to who were the authors of *Lovel the Widower* and *Barchester Towers*.

In his obituary tribute to Thackeray in *Cornhill* (February, 1864), Trollope paised him as the "kindest of guides, the gentlest of rulers." It is obvious that Trollope did not consider these characteristics necessarily virtues in journalism, for in his later biography he contended that Thackeray lacked the tough-mindedness and firmness to be an effectual editor. The way in which Thackeray carried out his duties during his brief editorial career more or less bears Trollope out: his impatience with detail, his absentmindedness in handling correspondence, his frustrations over the interruption of his own writing, and above all the pain and anguish it cost him to reject even the most unworthy manuscripts that came his way. It is not surprising under these circumstances that Thackeray considered withdrawing from the editorship as early as the middle of 1861 – a year and a half after he assumed the post. The decrease of circulation after the conclusion of *Framley Parsonage* – with a consequent lowering of Thackeray's editorial salary – along with differences with George Smith over editorial content, precipitated his decision.[40] Actually Thackeray's tenure as the editor of *Cornhill* lasted a little over two years. The March 1862 issue carried his farewell to his readers in the guise of a sea captain (to whom he had likened himself in the first "Roundabout Paper") by now "careworn, oppressed, uncomfortable," doffing his gold lace and epaulets and retiring to land. His last story, *Denis Duval,* left unfinished at his death and published posthumously in *Cornhill,* had for its hero, appropriately enough, a sailor looking back in serene old age to his stormy youth.

Trollope assumed the editorship of *Saint Paul's Magazine* under the strong persuasion of James Virtue, a printer and publisher of an art magazine eager to launch a literary magazine as an outlet for his own publications, following the path successfully pursued by such publishers as Smith and Elder, Macmillan, and Tinsley.[41] With Trollope he was counting heavily on the prestige of a famous name (as alluded to wryly by Trollope in his *Autobiography).* Trollope betrayed his own lukewarm attitude toward the magazine in his introductory address that appeared in the first number: "[The editor] begs to assure such of the public as will kindly interest themselves in the matter that *Saint Paul's Magazine* is not established . . . on any rooted and mature conviction that such a periodical is a great and pressing want of the age." Apparently Trollope was prevailed upon to assume the editorship mainly by Virtue's generous terms (£1,000 per year, besides £3,200 for *Phineas Finn)* and the stipulation that he would have full editorial control. Initially Trollope was at cross-purposes with Virtue in conceiving the magazine as primarily political, whereas Virtue had wanted a literary publication, but Trollope had his way. Along these lines Virtue proposed *Trollope's Magazine* for the title, a suggestion immediately vetoed by Trollope.[42]

The lack of experience on the part of both the proprietor and the editor did not bode well for *Saint Paul's,* and indeed, Virtue's sanguine hopes for it were not realized. It never reached a circulation above a marginal 10,000 perhaps because of the competiton from other magazines similarly titled, such *Temple Bar, Cornhill,* and *Belgravia.* We do not know how typical was the reaction of the *Spectator,* which, in reviewing its first issue, thought it lacking in "variety and veracity" and something of a "blanc mange" altogether,[43] but it is certain that *Saint Paul's* did not take hold of the magazine public. To account for its failure the suggestion has been made that in the face of the rapid

changes brought about by the elections of 1866-68, Trollope's
conservative liberalism was undercut and lacked clear focus. His
problem presumably was compounded by the dashing of his own
political prospects in the Beverley election.[44]

On the literary side, T. H. S. Escott contends that Trollope's
editorial procedures "fell between two stools" as he tried, on the
one hand, to liven up the more high-brow manuscripts that came
to him to suit what he thought of as average taste and, on the
other, to raise the level of ordinary fare in accordance with his
own standards of excellence. Trollope himself was cryptic on the
matter in his *Autobiography,* attributing his failure not to poor
editing but to too much editing. "I was too anxious to be good," he
recalls, "and did not think enough of what might be lucrative."[45]
As for Trollope's relations with contributors, in the absence of
such primary evidence as has survived for Thackeray, we must
infer what we can from the six stories collectively entitled *An
Editor's Tales* in which Trollope intermittently unburdened
himself in the pages of *Saint Paul's Magazine.* "We are much
given to speculations on the characters and probable circumstances of those with whom we are brought into contact,"
admitted the editor at the beginning of one of the tales, "The
Turkish Bath," adding that "our editorial duties require that it
should be so."[46] Trollope thus established the motif of all the
stories that have for their common theme the involvement of the
editor in the lives of various literary aspirants, to his grief. In
"The Turkish Bath," for example, the editor is hoaxed by a
loquacious Irishman into believing that he is in poverty and has a
sick wife on his hands; the editor discovers eventually that he
(Molloy by name) is a madman actually being supported by his
wife. The editor decides not to print any of Molloy's manuscripts
but continues to visit him and to supply him with paper, "which
he continues to use — we presume for the benefit of other editors."
The heroine of "Mary Gresley," another Charlotte Brontë in all

but literary ability, so engages the editor's sympathies that he helps her with her novel in progress, even going out of his way to get it placed. Miss Gresley, however, gives up novel writing out of religious conviction, eventually marries a missionary (a fate that Jane Eyre escapes), and moves to Africa where she dies. In still another story, "Josephine de Montmorenci," the editor is fooled by a series of letters into thinking the authoress is a pretty young lady, only to be confronted by an ugly cripple who bears the unromantic name of Maryanne Puffle. Although he thinks her novel is uneven, he uses his influence to get it publisheld.

"The cowardly professional reader indeed, unable to endure those thorns in the flesh of which poor Thackeray spoke so feelingly, when hard-pressed for answers, generally lies," commented Trollope's alter ego when faced with Miss Montmorenci's manuscript. "He has been asked to be candid, but he cannot undertake a duty so onerous, so odious, and one to which he sees so little reason that he personally should perform it." Trollope gave the impression that he was every bit as much the bleeding heart as he said that Thackeray was. Even more revealing is this *cri de coeur* from "The Turkish Bath": "The butter boat of benevolence was in our hand, and we proceeded to pour out its contents freely. It is a vessel which the editor should lock up carefully; and should he lose the key, he will not be the worse for the loss." Since "The Turkish Bath" was the first, not the last, of *The Editor's Tales,* this particular editor apparently did not "lose the key." Trollope in short may have won his readers' and contributors' goodwill, but he could not make his magazine pay. But then neither could anybody else, for *Saint Paul's* ceased publication in 1874.[47]

The "butter boat of benevolence" was dispensed generously also by Harrison Ainsworth, for whom the milk of kindness mixed quite well with printer's ink and elbow grease. If diligence and consideration for writers sufficed, he should have been a model editor. He was a prodigious worker, insisting on reading all the manuscripts submitted to him, even while continuing to produce works of fiction of his own at a steady clip. He also took a paternal interest in fellow writers who sought him out, giving them careful advice on revision, sometimes even helping them place their work elsewhere if it was not deemed suitable for one of his magazines.[48] It can be argued, as it has been by Ainsworth's biographer, S. M. Ellis, that this frantic industry proved deleterious to his career, rather than enchancing it, by causing him to spread himself too thin. In fact his critics have detected a falling off in the quality of his fiction after 1842 *(Old Saint Paul's)*, the year that he launched *Ainsworth's Magazine.*

Unfortunately, Ainsworth's geniality and industry were not accompanied by much business sense. Ownership of his own publications, so successful for Dickens, proved a disaster for him. His attempt to run *Ainsworth's Magazine* and the *New Monthly Magazine* simultaneously was particularly foolhardy, for it was impossible for him to maintain both at the same quality. Finding that the *New Monthly* was more solvent, he tended to give it more favored treatment, propping up the magazine that bore his name with reruns of his old romances and rejects from the *New Monthly.* Much as he boasted about his ability to keep a faithful fold of authors about him, his outstanding contributors fell away as his rates of pay decreased. Moreover, when he was forced to cut down his expenses, he had to sacrifice the feature he was proudest of, the illustrations. On top of all this, he bought and sold his magazines impetuously, losing on every transaction. Although no more competent an editor than his colleagues whom we have already considered, Ainsworth differed from them in persisting longer at the desk. In time, though, he had to give up: His paper empire collapsed around him. To make a long, sad story short, *Ainsworth's Magazine* ceased publication in 1854; *Bentley's Magazine,* which he bought from Bentley when *AM* folded, was sold back to the proprietor (at a severe loss) in 1868; in 1870 Ainsworth turned over the *New Monthly Magazine* to his nephew.[49] Thus ended an editorial career that extended over more than thirty years but not Ainsworth's literary activity that continued virtually up to his death in 1881. Shortly before his death he was caricatured in *Punch,* decked out in Elizabethan costume, the wood engraving bearing the caption "To The Greatest Axe-and-Neck Romancer Of Our Time, Who Is Quite At The Head Of His Profession, We Dedicate This Block."[50] Nothing was said about his having been an editor.

Looking back over his own career in his *Autobiography,* Trollope concluded that in the long run publishers are the best editors of magazines. He pointed specifically to *Blackwood's* and to *Cornhill* between the editorships of Thackeray and Leslie Stephen, when it was largely under the supervision of George Smith. "The proprietor, at any rate, knows what he wants and what he can afford," declared Trollope, "and is not so frequently tempted to fall into that worst of literary quicksands, the publishing of matter not for the sake of readers, but that of the writer."[51] Trollope undoubtedly simplified the situation, but in his commonsensical way put his finger on the essential incompatibility between the mercurial temperament and the self-centeredness that we associate with the novelist and the pragmatic shrewdness along with open-mindedness and adaptability demanded of the popular journalist, as brought out by the four careers that we have briefly traced. However, whatever generalization we are tempted to make, there is always a paragon such as Dickens to refute it.

"As to my project—it is not exactly like the existing order of weeklys [sic], but a union of the best qualities of all, and . . . 'something more,' " wrote one of our novelists to an unknown correspondent, "something to combine the terse smartness of the Examiner in politics (albeit not of the same tone); the pleasantry of Punch (acclimatized to the atmosphere of gentlemen and ladies); the racy honesty and vigour of Blackwood (when Ebony was racy and vigourous); with features all its own. . . ." This projected weekly furthermore was to contain urbane political commentary independent of sect and party; criticism without flattery or puffery; and discussion of topical matters in general—home, foreign, and colonial—in the manner of the smartest after-dinner table talk, addressed to Britons domestic and abroad. Last, but by no means least, each issue was to offer a serialized story easily detached from the rest of the publication, allowing for it to be bound up eventually in a volume all its own.[52] Such was the plan offered by Charles Lever, whether before or after his unequal struggle with "the small literati, with little brains and much malice," of Dublin is unclear. It is too bad that Lever never realized this dream, but there is no gainsaying the literary imagination when it comes to conceiving what a periodical *should* be.

NOTES

1. "A Letter From The Editor To A Friend And Contributor," *Cornhill Magazine*, (January 1860), inside front cover.

2. S. M. Ellis, *William Harrison Ainsworth and His Friends*, 2 vols. (London: John Lane The Bodley Head, 1911), II, pp. 131, 218-20; Ainsworth, "Preliminary Address," *Ainsworth's Magazine* (February 1842): iii.

3. Lionel Stevenson, *Dr. Quicksilver* (London: Chapman & Hall, 1939), p. 99.

4. Letter to Bradbury & Evans, 26 February 1844, *Letters and Private Papers of William Makepeace Thackeray*, 4 vols., ed. Gordon N. Ray (Cambridge, Mass: Harvard University Press, 1945-46), II, p. 163.

5. Michael Sadleir, *Trollope: A Commentary* (New York: Farrar, Strauss and Company, 1947), pp. 263-67, 282.

6. "Address to Our Readers," *Ainsworth's Magazine* (January 1843): iii.

7. Stevenson, *Dr. Quicksilver*, p. 100.

8. Gordon N. Ray, *Thackeray: The Age of Wisdom* (New York: McGraw Hill, 1958), pp. 293-94.

9. John Sutherland, "Trollope and St. Paul's, 1866-70," *Anthony Trollope* (Critical Studies), ed. Tony Bareham (Totowa, N.J.: Barnes and Noble, 1980), p. 118.

10. Catherine Ellen Spence, *The Author's Daughter* (London, 1868), Chap. 14 ("Novels and Real Life").

11. "Preliminary Address," *Ainsworth's Magazine (February 1842): 1.*

12. *Dublin University Magazine* (April 1842): 38-39.

13. Notebook for *Dublin University Magazine,* MS (V 10 D), Pierpont Morgan Library, New York City (1842, 1843).

14. 28 October 1859, from *Cornhill* office, *Letters,* IV, 158-59.

15. See, in particular, "Ogres," "On a Lazy, Idle Boy," "On a Medal of George the Fourth," and "On Being Found Out." Relationships between the late novels and "The Roundabout Papers" are explored in Robert A. Colby, *Thackeray's Canvass of Humanity* (Columbus: Ohio State University Press, 1979), Chap. 13.

16. See, in particular, "De Finibus."

17. *An Autobiography* (London: Oxford University Press, 1923), p. 178.

18. October 1867; January 1868; February 1868; May 1868 (the attribution of the latter article, "The Irish Church Debate," is less certain than that of the others, but the article is nevertheless germane to *Phineas Finn*); *Phineas Finn* was serialized in *Saint Paul's Magazine* from October 1867 to May 1869. In his *Autobiography* Trollope recalled: "As I was debarred from expressing my opinions in the House of Commons, I took this method of declaring myself" (p. 288).

19. *Ralph the Heir* was issued as a supplement to *Saint Paul's Magazine* from January 1870 to July 1871. Trollope resigned the editorship in March 1870 but stayed on until the July issue.

20. "Address to Our Readers," *Ainsworth's Magazine* (January 1843): iv.

21. *Dublin University Magazine* (April 1842): 38.

22. *Cornhill Magazine* (January 1860).

23. "Introduction," *Saint Paul's Magazine,* (October 1867): 3-4.

24. *Thackeray* (London: Macmillan, 1879), p. 54.

25. Quoted in Ray, *Thackeray: The Age of Wisdom,* p. 303. The full text of this letter (Houghton Library, Harvard University) is still unpublished.

26. *The Struggles of Brown, Jones, and Robinson* began in *Cornhill* with the August 1861 issue and ended with the March 1862 number, the last edited by Thackeray.

27. *The Life of Charles Lever,* 2 vols. (London: Chapman & Hall, 1879), II, p. 61.

28. Stevenson, *Dr. Quicksilver,* pp. 138-39.

29. February 1842. The full title was *Sultan Stork. Being the One Thousand and Second Night,* translated from the Persian by Major G. O'G. Gahagan H.E.C.I.C.S.

228 Robert A. Colby

30. Lever's novel appeared in *Saint Paul's Magazine* (April-July 1868).
31. Letter to Austin Dobson, 7 March 1868, *Letters of Anthony Trollope*, ed. Bradford A. Booth (London: Oxford University Press, 1951), p. 214.
32. John Sutherland, "Trollope and *St. Paul's,*" pp. 122-26. Sutherland conjectures but on no firm evidence that Trollope maintained his policy of anonymity in *Saint Paul's* (contrary to his advocacy of open authorship for the *Fortnightly Review*) in order to conceal his recruiting of lesser names. He also alleges that Trollope deceived Virtue in various ways. For a later and generally more favorable view of their relationship, see Patricia Thomas Srebnik, "Trollope, James Virtue, and *Saint Paul's Magazine,*" *Nineteenth-Century Fiction* (December 1982), (Anthony Trollope Special Issue): 443-63. On the basis of examining records not available to Sutherland, she concludes that Trollope was straightforward with his publisher and that Virtue himself was not the naïf that he had been made out to be in the past.
33. Stevenson, *Dr. Quicksilver*, pp. 98-99.
34. *Dublin University Magazine* (April 1842): 38-39.
35. Edward Downey, *Charles Lever: His Life in His Letters* (London, 1906), p. 160; Stevenson, *Dr. Quicksilver*, p. 102
36. Quoted in Fitzpatrick, *Life of Charles Lever*, II, p. 94. The novels of Lever that appeared in *DUM* after he relinquished the editorship were *Maurice Tierney, Sir Jasper Carew, The Fortunes of Glencore*, and *Gerald Fitzgerald*.
37. Spencer L. Eddy, *The Founding of the Cornhill Magazine* (Muncie, Indiana: Ball State University, 1970), p. 200.
38. Ibid.
39. This and the quotations that follow in this paragraph are taken from a set of unpublished letters entitled "Thorns in the Cushion" in the Beinecke Library (Jerome Kern Collection), Yale University.
40. Ray, *Thackeray: The Age of Wisdom*, pp. 320-21.
41. Sadleir, *Trollope: A Commentary*, p. 278.
42. Ibid, p. 279.
43. October 5, 1867, pp. 1120-21. There is a brief discussion of its contemporary reception in *Wellesley Index*, II, p. 360.
44. "Trollope and *St. Paul's,*" p. 131.
45. *An Autobiography*, p. 262.
46. October 1869, p. 113. "The Turkish Bath" was followed by "Mary Gresley" (November 1869); "Josephine de Montmorenci" (December 1869); "The Panjandrum" (January and February 1870); "The Spotted Dog" (March and April 1870); and "Mrs. Brumby" (May 1870). The entire series has been reprinted by Ayer Press (New York, 1981) with an excellent introduction by Donald D. Stone.
47. For a brief account of its downward course, see *Wellesley Index*, III, p. 362.

48. Ellis, I, p. 390; II, p. 131.

49. Ellis, II, pp. 112, 218-21, 258-59. A useful chronology of Ainsworth's career is found in George J. Worth, *William Harrison Ainsworth* (New York: Twayne, 1972), material preceding Chap. 1.

50. *Punch,* September 21, 1881 (drawn by Linley Sanbourne); reproduced in Ellis, II, facing p. 338.

51. *An Autobiography,* p. 263.

52. Unpublished letter to unknown correspondent, Charles Lever Correspondence (letter no. 150), Pierpont Morgan Library, New York City. This letter is undated and bears no address but has been placed with a group of letters of 1845 from the Continent.

Ann P. Robson and John M. Robson

Private and Public Goals: John Stuart Mill and the *London and Westminster*

The mere fondness a man has for his child, the delight which an idiot is capable of having in the highest possible degree, which we are not sure that the lower animals have not in the highest degree, is to be considered of greater value, than the outward advantages of parental virtue, the man's hard and persevering labours to supply the wants of his child, his perpetual study of its future happiness, the care with which he watches its inward movements, and endeavours to impart to it those habits which are best calculated to render its life a source of happiness to itself and others.

Thus writes James Mill in his *Fragment on Mackintosh*,[1] as though in response to all the criticisms that have been made of his apparent lack of fondness for and delight in his eldest child. But one might also ponder the words in thinking of John Mill's feelings about the child of his fathering, the *London Review* (later the *London and Westminster*). He did indeed at first feel animal attraction toward it, but the hard and persevering labors came to outweigh the fondness and the delight.

Why does any sane person wish to become an editor? In Mill's case let us take the sanity for granted. One reason (perhaps a sign of feeble wits) would be as a profitable occupation. Mill, though not wealthy, was not, so far as one can judge, poor. (His annual salary at the India House rose in 1828—when he was twenty-two—to £600 and reached £1,200 in 1836, after his father's death.) Nor, the record makes clear, was the position thrust upon him; he actively sought it. What impelled him, we shall argue, was a coalescence of private and public motives relating to his view of his own role as a radical and to his assessment of the role the radicals should collectively play in post-1832 England.

In 1830 young men dreamed of the new times acoming. Mill, trained as a political animal but impatient of his elder's guidance, and possessing a sense of what revolution meant to the actors, was excited beyond his normal measure by the French Revolution of 1830. "It aroused my utmost enthusiasm," he said in the *Autobiography,* "and gave me, as it were, a new existence. I went at once to Paris, was introduced to Lafayette, and laid the groundwork of the intercourse I afterwards kept up with several of the active chiefs of the extreme popular party."[2] Returning to England, he began his most concentrated and fullest series of newspaper writings, reporting on the French scene in Fonblanque's *Examiner* for the better part of four years. What especially captured his imagination was the role of young men as journalists; his attention focused on *Le National* and, in particular, on Armand Carrel, under whose direction it became the first political organ in Paris after the July revolution. Having written to Thomas Carlyle, his new ally (new mentor, Carlyle thought), that what England emphatically needed was a *man,* a leader, Mill began to see that personal and public good could be served simultaneously if he could rally around him a corps of political activists who would make the general aims of the *mouvement* known (he began to use the English version of the French word about this time) and also train, by participation and trial, new leaders for itself.[3]

The young Radical members of the reformed House of Commons, especially John Arthur Roebuck, William Molesworth, and Charles Buller, were his friends and allies, and they joined with him first in attempting to take over the *Examiner*, which was in financial difficulties, and then, when the *Examiner* had been saved, in founding a new review that would better reflect their sense of the exciting possibilities of change than did the journals open to them, the *Westminster, Tait's Edinburgh Magazine,* the *Monthly Repository,* and the *Examiner*. Although they, and Mill in particular, vowed to eschew sectarianism, they loved the sense of being bound together in a coherent vanguard promising to lead all people of goodwill out of the dead past, to drag, in current parlance, James Mill into the nineteenth century. Indeed, John Mill had complained to Sterling in 1829 about his loneliness, by which, he said, "I mean the absence of that feeling which has accompanied me through the greater part of my life, that which one fellow traveller, or one fellow soldier has towards another — the feeling of being engaged in the pursuit of a common object, and of mutually cheering one another on, and helping one another in an arduous undertaking."[4]

Though Mill's position in the India House prevented him from taking on the editorship in title, he became the central figure after an aborted attempt to recruit W. J. Fox. One might have expected that Molesworth, the financial piper, would have played some tunes, but he was young and in awe of the two Mills — he was more distressed at James Mill's funeral than any of the other disciples. Some of the tone of the early days of planning was caught in a playful letter Molesworth wrote to Harriet Grote in the early spring of 1835, before the first issue: "I have not been idle; . . . I have an article, *Deo* (John Mill) *volente,* for the Review, which is, I hope, prospering. John is in such spirits that he says he would make it succeed single-handed. Old Mill will write, consequently we shall be "spectable.' "⁵ There is other evidence that the younger Mill was, as Molesworth's biographer says, in "strict control" from beginning to end; perhaps one might cite simply his refusing to accept an article by Molesworth on Lord Brougham.⁶ He was, however, as fully aware as Molesworth of the importance of his father to the enterprise and was personally uneasy about the effect. As he said in the *Autobiography,* the review at first derived "its tone and colouring from him much more than from [me or] any of the other writers."⁷ The full account in the *Autobiography* needs to be read to appreciate the ambivalent feelings Mill had about his father's participation, but one unnoticed clue about the dual purpose involved because of their differences is seen in the two epigraphs for the *London Review.* The first, from Locke, represents the younger Mill's aspirations: "Those who have not thoroughly examined to the bottom all their own tenets, must confess they are unfit to prescribe to others; and are unreasonable in imposing that as truth on other men's belief which they themselves have not searched into, nor weighed the arguments of probability on which they should receive or reject it."⁸ (In Locke the sentence begins, "At least, those, who. . . .") The second, which, we think, reflects James Mill's views more than his son's, is from Bacon: "Legitimae inquisitionis vera norma est, ut nihil veniat in prac- ticam, cujus non fit etiam doctrina aliequa et theoria." Bacon's English version of this passage (augmented by the words omitted from the Latin version in the review's epigraph, which we have italized) reads: *"Again, it tends to the perfection of learning, because* it is the perfect law of the inquiry of truth, *'that nothing be in the globe of matter which has not its parallel in the globe of crystal or the understanding;' that is,* that there be nothing in practice, whereof there is no theory or doctrine."⁹ Certainly the younger Mill, sitting in the editorial chair, felt the presence of another editor—one whose voice spoke as his conscience[10] —looking over his shoulder.

In deciding how to fill that chair, however, John Stuart could by this time draw on his experience of other editors, including John Black, John Bowring, Perronet Thompson, W. J. Fox, and Fonblanque, but though he had respect for some of them (the notable exception being Bowring), the one who influenced him most was Armand Carrel. In 1833 he again visited Paris—this time Harriet Taylor replaced Roebuck, Buller, and others as his companion. And he met Armand Carrel. The event was crucial in Mill's development. He saw in Carrel an ideal, almost a fantasy realized[11]: To be a Carrel would be to answer all his problems, even, one might speculate, the problem of his love. To Carlyle he wrote an intense account of his meeting with Carrel in 1833 in the office of the *National,* an account he later transcribed almost in full into his eulogistic article on Carrel in the *London and Westminster.* His excitement and admiration show through every phrase:

Among the individuals . . . whom I saw & formed an acquaintance with, two made a particular impression upon me; two perfectly self-subsistent men in the best sense, or I am greatly mistaken in them; & in that, honourably distinguished from Frenchmen in general. Both these are republican leaders; . . . or rather, not leaders, but men who follow no other person's lead, and whom every one is glad to follow. These are, Carrel, the editor of the National, & Cavaignac, whose speech when on trial for a conspiracy two years ago I translated & inserted in the *Examiner.* . . . I knew Carrel as the most powerful journalist in France, sole manager of a paper which while it keeps aloof from all *coterie - influence* & from the actively revolutionary part of the republican body, has for some time been avowedly republican; & I knew that he was considered a vigorous, energetic *man of action,* who would always have courage & conduct in an emergency. Knowing thus much of him, I was ushered into the National office where I found six or seven of the innumerable *rédacteurs* who belong to a French paper, all dark-haired men with formidable *moustaches* (which many of the republicans have taken to wearing) & looking fiercely republican. Carrel was not there, & after waiting some time I was introduced to a slight elegant young man with extremely polished manners, no *moustaches* at all, and apparently fitter for a drawing-room than a camp; this was the commander-in-chief of those formidable looking champions. But it was impossible to be five minutes in his company without perceiving that he was accustomed to *ascendancy,* & so accustomed as not to feel it. . . .[12]

In his eulogy of Carrel, after the Frenchman's fatal duel (fought, interestingly enough, over the honor of his mistress), Mill said:

The true idea of Carrel is not that of a literary man, but of a man of action, using the press as his instrument; and in no other aspect does his character deserve more to be studied by those of all countries, who aspire and are qualified to resemble him.

He was a man called to take an active part in the government of mankind, and needing an engine with which to move them. . . . [E]xcluded from the region of deeds, he had still that of words; and words are deeds, and the cause of deeds. Carrel was not the first to see, but he was the first practically to realize, the new destination of the political press in modern times. It is now beginning to be felt that journalism is to modern Europe what political oratory was to Athens and Rome, and that, to become what it ought, it should be wielded by the same sort of men: Carrel seized the sceptre of journalism, and with that, as with the baton of a general-in-chief, [rallied the scattered hosts around him, and] ruled amidst innumerable difficulties and reverses that "fierce democracy," which he perhaps alone of all men living, trampled upon and irritated as it has been, could have rendered at once gentle and powerful.[13]

One other indication of his intense interest in Carrel is of a rather unusual kind. Mill's eulogy originally appeared in the number of the *London and Westminster* for October 1837, under the heading *"Armand Carrel, his Life and Character.* From the French of D. Nisard. Preceded by a Biographical Sketch, abridged from the French of E. Littré. London: Hooper (not yet published)."[14] The account contains many translated quotations from both Nisard and Littré, and in editing the essay for vol. 20 of Mill's *Collected Works,* we sought the reviewed book or pamphlet to collate the passages. No copy could be found, and after an extensive search, we began to look at the evidence a little more closely. In fact, the passages from Nisard are to be found in his article on Carrel that also appeared in October 1837 in the *Revue des Deux Mondes,* and those from Littré are in his introductory

"Notice biographique" to Charles Romey's edition of Carrel's *Oeuvres littéraires et économiques,* which did not appear until 1854. A comparison of the 1837 version of Mill's essay with the revised version in *Dissertations and Discussions* (1859) shows that the initial words of the original version, "This little work is," had been changed to "These little works are" (with other similar changes). Furthermore, in 1837 the named publisher of the as-yet-unpublished work, Hooper, was the publisher of the *London and Westminster.* Our conclusion is that Mill, being in close touch with Nisard, a contributor to the review and a friend of Carrel, and wishing to make Carrel's name and fame better known in England, proposed to Nisard and Littré that he publish their essays in English, made his own translation (as was his practice when reviewing French works), probably arranged to pay the cost of publication, and then reviewed his own translation as a soon-to-be (but in fact never) published pamphlet. Even if these deductions are not exactly correct, Mill certainly treated Carrel rather specially as the subject of an article (he distributed off-prints of this article widely), and here again reveals what would appear to be, if not envy, a desire for emulation. He himself said as much, speaking through Tacitus:

If there be any habitation for the spirits of the just; if, as wise men will have it, the soul that is great perish not with the body, may you rest in peace, and summon us, your household, from weak repinings and womanish tears to the contemplation of those virtues which it were impiety to lament or mourn. Let reverence rather, let unending thankfulness, let imitation even, if our strength permit, be our tribute to your memory. . . .[15]

That the imitative impulse operated strongly in the shaping of Mill's editorial role is demonstrated by a letter from Mill to J. P. Nichol (written the day after his letter describing Carrel and Cavaignac to Carlyle), which explains the radical plans for a periodical. These plans were, of course, primarily political: to make radical thought progressive, eclectic, and attractive; to provide a leader for the radical party in the country; and specifically to guide if not drive the radical parliamentary party. These goals have been treated so well by Joseph Hamburger and, from a different angle, by William Thomas[16] that we need not say much of them here. That Mill saw them in a French light has, however, not been clearly recognized; being progressive and eclectic meant absorbing French ideas. In 1829 he outlined some hopes to Gustave d'Eichthal:

One object which I have in writing to you at present is to inform you of a project which we have formed and which there is some prospect though but a doubtful one of our being able to realize, of starting a morning newspaper, of which Chadwick should be the editor, and almost all your friends in this country frequent writers. The prospects of success would be very encouraging. You know in how low a state the newspaper press of this country is. In France the best thinkers & writers of the nation, write in the journals & direct public opinion; but our daily & weekly writers are the lowest hacks of literature, which when it is a trade, is the vilest & most degrading of all trades, because more of affectation & hypocrisy, & more subservience to the baser feelings of others, are necessary for carrying it on, than for any other trade, from that of a brothelkeeper upwards. We are not in so low a state here, as not to have in some measure found this out; & there is consequently rather a general sense of the needfulness of some newspaper conducted by men really in earnest about public objects, & really forming their opinions from some previous knowledge, & not from the mere appearances of the moment, or the convenience of party advocacy. The old ties of party and the attachment to established opinions have at the same time been so greatly weakened among all the reading classes, that the times are very favourable for starting new opinions, and especially any which hold out sufficient hopes of extensive good, to enlist in their behalf that enthusiasm and *dévouement,* which are now wandering about the world seeking an object worthy of them. We possess moreover the means of rendering this paper the best as a mere vehicle of intelligence; as a mere newspaper in short, which yet exists; & have therefore no doubt of its success provided we can raise the money which of course is doubtful, but of which we have considerable hopes. As this newspaper will pay very particular attention to French affairs, and will endeavour, as one of its grand objects, to make its readers understand not only French politics but the whole social state of France, including all that is doing in the world of literature & philosopphy by that active and important member of the European community, & in short to explain the character of that general movement which is taking place in the human mind all over the Continent of Europe but especially in France, we shall be very anxious to have a first rate correspondent at Paris, capable of supplying, (along with the general news of the day in politics, literature & philosophy) sound & enlarged views on all these subjects.[17]

In 1834 he again contrasted French and English newspapers to the discredit of the latter.[18] And when he began his search for contributors, he looked to Paris as well as London and was specially pleased when the fourth number of the *London Review* included three articles on French thought and politics. In enticing French contributions, he described the aim to d'Eichthal not as advocacy of a *"doctrine générale et unitaire,"* but an attempt to encompass "whatever *vues d'avenir"* they could gather.[19] He expanded the idea further to Tocqueville:

Vous me demandez, mon cher Monsieur, dans quelles limites doit s'exercer la collaboration que j'ai osé vous demander en faveur du *London Review.* C'est une question fort naturelle, mais qu'il n'appartient pas aux rédacteurs de la Revue de résoudre. La Revue n'a pas pour but la propagation d'un système donné, d'une doctrine générale et unitaire; je n'ai pas besoin de vous dire que jusqu'ici cette doctrine est encore à créer. En défaut d'une théorie complète, les fondateurs du *London Review* ont désiré que cet ouvrage périodique devînt un recueil des meilleures idées du siècle, notamment en fait de philosophie politique: et dans ce but ils voudraient obtenir la coopération des plus forts penseurs et des hommes les plus éclairés de notre temps, du moins parmi ceux qui sympathisent avec les tendances dominantes du siècle. Cette seule condition est de riguer, attendu que pour pouvoir travailler utilement avec des amis du mouvement il faut l'être soi-même.

Dans une réunion de pareils hommes il ne vous appartient pas de jouer un role secondaire. Aussi ce que nous vous demandons n'est pas une collaboration en second ordre: nous ne vous invitons pas à mettre votre talent à notre disposition pour exposer ou pour discuter telle ou telle série d'idées ou de faits. Nous vous engageons á fixer, de concert avec nous, ce que sera la Revue elle-même; dans quel esprit, et sous l'influence de quelles idées, elle sera faite. La Revue a la prétention de représenter ce qu'il y a de plus avancé dans les doctrines démocratiques: c'est précisément ce que vous avez, vous-même, ou créé, ou fait ressortir avec une vigueur jusqu'ici inconnue, des faits ou des principes connus. Vous êtes donc fait pour dicter des conditions à la Revue, et non pour en recevoir d'elle. Notre voeu serait que vous vouliez bien vous joindre à nous, et vous servir de la Revue comme organe de vos opinions. Elle est déjà l'organe de ce qu'il y a de meilleur parmi nos hommes du mouvement; mais ces hommes, avec de grandes connaissances spéciales, sont, du moins la plupart d'entre eux, tellement au-dessous de votre niveau quant aux idées générales, que la direction que vous pourrez imprimer à la Revue par vos articles et par l'influence qu'exerceront ces articles sur les autres rédacteurs, décidera peut-être si ce journal servir à éclairer le public anglais sur les questions de haute politique, ou seulement à exciter l'esprit démocratique sans lui donner des principes capables de régler sa marche.[20]

Mill's principal goal for the review—a broad base for English radical opinion—shows more, as might be expected, in his letters soliciting help from his English colleagues:

The spirit of the review will be democratic, but with none of the exclusiveness and narrowness of the Westminster Review; & the plan adopted of individual signatures enables the various writers to indulge the liberty of individual opinion within considerably less narrow limits than are imposed by the plan of most reviews.[21]

He made specific moves to get series on political economy, science, and literature and the arts—in the last case referring rather annoyingly to "light readers,"[22] although he himself had sworn allegiance to the powers of the arts in morals as well as aesthetics. His own articles demonstrate the breadth he sought more than any other test.

The policy of signed articles was designed to avoid accusations of *coterie* and sectarian writing. In 1833 he had praised "Junius Redivivus" (W. B. Adams) for using a consistent signature;[23] he adopted "Antiquus" as his own signature in the *Monthly Repository* (later shortening it to "A"); and he echoed the argument for signed articles elsewhere in letters and in editorial notes to the review. The signed article places the responsibility for opinions on the writer, who should be happy to bear it, allows readers to follow the ideas of an author, and removes the false appearance of unity and *ex cathedra* claims entailed by an editorial "we." Furthermore, the prestige of the review might be enhanced, particularly with the full name and particularly in Carrel's case: "The name of Carrel has done much for us already: his speech before the Chamber of Peers has spread his fame in this country. The editor of one of our best journals, the Spectator, advises strongly that we should request Carrel's permission to print his signature at full length."[24] It is quite possible that, given his state of mind at this time, his lack of system — "only a conviction, that the true system was something much more complex and many sided than I had previously had any idea of, and that its office was to supply, not a set of model institutions, but principles . . ." — more direction could not be forthcoming; such a publication, acting as a forum for all ideas as long as they were advanced, would serve his private needs as well as the public good.[25] All Mill stipulated was that the "general course" of the review's policy should be maintained:

> The plan (Roebuck's & mine, to which all have at once assented) is, to drop altogether every kind of lying; the lie of pretending that all the articles are *reviews*, when more than half of them are not; and the lie of pretending that all the articles proceed from a *corps*, who jointly entertain all the opinions expressed. There is to be no *we*; but each writer is to have a signature, which he may avow or not as he pleases, but which (unless there be special reasons to constitute an exception) is to be the *same* for *all* his articles, thus making him *individually* responsible & allowing his opinions to derive what light they can from one another. The editor answers only for adequate literary merit, & a general *tendency* not in contradiction to the objects of the publication.[26]

On the surface this policy — which probably helped other periodicals move toward signed articles — was successful. There was some cheating: Mill occasionally used the signature "S," and others, especially Robertson, varied theirs probably to disguise the number of articles they had written. But on the whole, as the diligent editors of the *Wellesley Index* have acknowledged, the initials or other symbols (a pound sign for Sterling, e.g.) signaled an identity. It is hard to estimate how widely individual signatures were recognized by readers, however. Mill, as already indicated, had not published any books before this period, and yet at least some people and probably many knew that the articles signed "A" were by him.[27] Unquestionably those closely connected with the review from the beginning were privileged and could break the code, but individual responsibility for articles did not prevent them from becoming increasingly unhappy about the direction the review seemed to be taking; they, like the public generally, were not yet ready for the nonunivocal approach Mill was asserting, let alone for the eldritch shriek of the prophet from Ecclefechan.

Mill certainly ran into trouble over the policy. Some evidence suggests that his own article on Bentham in October 1838 was the principal cause of Philosophic Radical discontent with him, but actually that trouble began earlier over two matters: most obviously, his line on the proper radical action; less obviously but very significantly, his publication of Carlyle's "Mirabeau" in January 1837.[28] The first of these had been so fully treated that we need not repeat the tale here; the second deserves some comment, especially as Mill's editorial style was implicated. That article was troublesome from its first consideration: Mill had solicited it—indeed, he had been urging Carlyle to contribute to the proposed review as early as December 1833; during Mill's illness and absence Thomas Falconer had held it back; Mill then accepted it but with some suggestions, saying to Carlyle:

My annotations, & proposed alterations in phraseology, amount as you will see, to but little; less than I expected—& you will probably think most of them trifling. My object has been to remove, when it can be done without sacrifice, anything *merely* quaint in the mode of expression—but I have very often not ventured to touch it for fear of spoiling something which I could not replace. The only general remark I have to make on the stile is that I think it would often *tell* better on the reader if what is said in an abrupt, exclamatory, & interjectional manner were said in the ordinary grammatical mode of nominative & verb—but on that as on everything else I ask nothing but that you will deal with it as you like, disregarding all my observations if you do not think them just—& in any case that you will not make the thing an annoyance to you.[29]

As usual, he had little sense of what Carlyle actually thought of him, an innocence he shared with all others of Carlyle's acquaintance. To his "dear Wommannie" Carlyle wrote:

. . . I have had my *Mirabeau* returned with a sheet of "remarks" on it. The remarks are of no import or little; in a style of great fear-of-offence; accompanied by a Note that I am not to put myself out of humour . . . with the thing: . . . I let it lie eight and fourty hours; sent it back with a Note that "two" of the things proposed were perhaps improvements; that I kept the "remarks" till the Proofsheets came, but felt as if I could not open "that fatal Manuscript again, for a guinea."[30]

He goes on to say that Mill wishes him to write more (he "forget[s] what more") but that he does not care much if he never writes more in the review, "nor in any beggarly 'dog's-meat cart' like it. . . ."[31]

Though being edited by Mill may not have made Carlyle happy — anyway he always repudiated happiness as a goal — his participation in the review certainly made many of its old supporters, who held to a hedonistic calculus, very unhappy. By Mill's own admission, after the appearance of "Mirabeau," Roebuck, Grote, Nassau Senior, John Austin (and probably Sarah as well), and George Cornewall Lewis were all offended, and Mill's assertion that it was "the most popular article we ever had in the review" and one "that has been extremely useful to us" rings a bit of self-justification.[32] Those who liked the article must, for the most part, have been radicals of a different stamp from Harriet Grote. In April 1837 she commented to Roebuck:

Molesworth wrote a flippant letter in mighty bad taste about our ceasing to write for L. and W., affecting despair, &c. Now, I merely wrote to John, by G.'s desire, a simple refusal to furnish an article on Greek History. M. chuses to book it as a piece of *party feeling,* I suppose, towards T. F. (Thomas Falconer), as he is very sore, I see. I am quite persuaded the Review will cease to be the engine of propagating sound and sane doctrines on Ethics and Politics under J. M. Whether by getting hooks baited with carrion, he attract other sorts of fish than those *we* angle for, and thus render it a better investment, I really am not in a condition to judge.[33]

It is possible that, as in the case of Carlyle, Mill was out of touch with others' feelings and unaware of the annoyance he had caused. His remark to Robertson in July of 1837 does not indicate a full grasp of the enormity of his offense: "The falling off to be guarded against in substantial merit and originality does not arise from our having lost any of our writers, but in our *not using them.* I do not understand the false position you speak of, nor do I know what friends of ours we have attacked."[34]

What with hooks baited with carrion on one side and beggarly dog's-meat carts on the other, Mill was not free from noisome offense — but he did not see either Carlyle's or Grote's letters. Carlyle, of course, expressed his judgments with knowledge of his correspondents' attitudes and so was able in writing to John Sterling, a close friend of Mill's as well as of himself, to express a somewhat less repulsive — even a hopeful — image of Mill's editorial behavior. "Mill himself means really well, and according as you mean, all the way he goes: he is also parting from the Anatomical- preparation Radicals, deadest of men; which is a good symptom."[35]

Carlyle's choice of phrase may have been subconsciously suggested, for the most influential of the anatomical-preparation radicals had just died. Much has been written of the effect his father's death had on John; the change his father's death brought about in Mill's attitude toward the policy of the review was striking. Less than six months later, he wrote (somewhat unfeelingly, one might think) in a letter to Lytton Bulwer:

As good may be drawn out of evil — the event which has deprived the world of the man of greatest philosophical genius it possessed & the review (if such little interests may be spoken of by the side of great ones) of its most powerful writer, & the only one to whose opinions the editors were obliged to defer — that same event has made it far easier to do that, in the hope of which alone I allowed myself to become connected with the review — namely to soften the harder & sterner features of its radicalism and utilitarianism, both which in the form in which they originally appeared in the Westminster, were part of the inheritance of the 18th century. The Review ought to represent not radicalism but neoradicalism, a radicalism which is not democracy, not a bigotted adherence to any forms of government or to one kind of institutions, & which is only to be called radicalism inasmuch as it does not palter nor compromise with evils but cuts at their roots – & a utilitarianism which takes into account the whole of human nature not the ratiocinative faculty only – the utilitarianism which never makes any peculiar figure as such, nor would ever constitute its followers a sect or school – which fraternizes with all who hold the same *axiomata media* (as Bacon has it) whether their first principle is the same or not – & which holds in the highest reverence all which the vulgar notion of utilitarians represents them to despise – which holds Feeling at least as valuable as Thought, & Poetry not only on a par with, but the necessary condition of, any true & comprehensive Philosophy. I know I am writing very loosely & expressing myself very ill – but *you* will understand me – & as I have, through Molesworth's confidence in me, complete power over that review whenever I chuse to exercise it, I hope you will believe, that if the review has hitherto been too much in the old stile of radical-utilitarianism with which you cannot possibly sympathize very strongly (nor I either) it is because the only persons, who could be depended upon as writers, were those whose writings would not tend to give it any other tone. My object will now be to draw together a body of writers resembling the old school of radicals only in being on the Movement side, in philosophy, morality, & art as well as in politics & socialities – & to keep the remnant of the old school (it is dying out) in their proper place, by letting them write only about the things which they understand.[36]

In his *Autobiography* he described more succinctly the effect vis à vis the *Review*.

Though acutely sensible of my own inferiority in the qualities of which he acquired his personal ascendancy, I had now to try what it might be possible for me to accomplish without him; and the review was the instrument on which I built my chief hopes of establishing a useful influence over the liberal and democratic portion of the public mind. Deprived now of my father's aid, I was also exempted from the restraints and retinences by which that aid was purchased: I did not feel that there was any other radical writer or politician to whom I was bound to defer further than consisted with my own opinions: and having the complete confidence of Molesworth, I resolved from henceforth to give full scope to my own opinions and modes of thought and to open the review widely to all writers who were in sympathy with Progress as I understood it, even though I should lose by it the support of my former associates. Carlyle from this time became a frequent writer in the review; Sterling, soon after, an occasional one; and though each individual article continued to be the expression of the private sentiments of its writer, the general tone conformed in some tolerable degree to my opinions. This was not effected without parting company with the nominal editor, Falconer, who, after holding on for some time in spite of differences of opinion, at last resigned [rather on account of an article of Carlyle's].[37]

The *affaire Mirabeau* was, however, the culmination of difficulties with Falconer. From the beginning the review's practical success had been slight. Perhaps Mill lacked the personal qualities—he certainly lacked the time—to make efficient management easy if not automatic. With Falconer's help, it was neither. Most of the details are not preserved, but Mill's letters to Aristide Guilbert, who was retained as French correspondent responsible for conveying articles, soliciting contributions, receiving issues, and so on, indicate the difficulties in a regular London-Paris series of transactions; a letter to Blanco White points to problems with agents and with the printers, the latter theme also appearing in a letter to Sarah Austin. But even with these warnings, Mill's letter to Falconer on 17 January 1836 comes as a bit of a shock. "A strange fatality attends our review," Mill began: "I do not believe there ever was any undertaking in which *every single* thing which ought to be done was so regularly left undone. We advertised the number as out when it was not out, and to make amends (I suppose) I have not been able to find a single advertisement that made known the fact since it actually happened." He continued by quoting Peacock's remark that "the London Review comes out surreptitiously," went on to mention that contributors were not receiving copies and that some copies lacked an index, and concluded with a postscript of despair: "We are the laughing stock of everybody who knows us, for our way of doing business."[38] In a letter to Henry Chapman he described in detail Falconer's weaknesses and then amplified an echo of the postscript to Falconer: "Every person I know is continually complaining to me of the mismanagement; our utter incapacity is become a subject of general sarcasm and jokes, and at length our printers and publishers have such a contempt for us as men of business that they will not attend to a single one of our orders."[39]

Mill had high hopes that Robertson would change *tout cela*. To some extent he seems to have done so, for complaints of this kind lessened, but he caused other worries. After Mill's first flurry of attempts to solicit articles from new sources early in 1837, he appears to have relied fairly heavily on Robertson for such solicitations, many of them self-addressed—Robertson contributed more than a fifth of the articles published under his subeditorship—and also for initial editing. The result was a number of rows, most markedly over an article by Harriet Martineau on the young queen, which had been solicited by Robertson, and one by him on women, especially women writers. Robertson's indiscretion also led to a strong protest by Abraham Hayward, Mill's inveterate opponent, who very properly objected to slanderous comments in one of Robertson's articles that Mill seems not to have seen before publication. Robertson's editorship may have alienated contributors; certainly Alexander Bain, who knew him well, held him in rather low esteem:

Robertson's attainments were of the slenderest description, and his industry very fitful; but he could make a vigorous and brilliant display both in composition and in conversation. . . . His impetus and suggestiveness in conversation drew out Mill, who never talked better than he did with him. But although he made friends in London circles and in the clubs, he was very distasteful to many of Mill's associates and increased the difficulties of carrying on the Review; being in fact, for a *novus homo,* as Henry Mill styled him, somewhat arrogant.[40]

Whether "Mirabeau," James Mill's death, or Robertson's replacement of Falconer had the most effect one cannot say, but of their cumulative effect there is no doubt. Of the sixty contributors (counting the unidentified authors), only eight wrote both pre- and post-"Mirabeau." That eight includes Mill, of course, and Robertson; it also includes Molesworth, who continued to contribute while he was the proprietor, and one of the other founders, Charles Buller, who had been tutored by Carlyle before becoming attached to the Philosophic Radicals—he also, of course, was instrumental in Mill's campaign in 1838 to save Durham's reputation. The others are Lytton Bulwer, subject to special solicitation on Mill's part, J. H. Burton, W. J. Fox, and William Napier, each of whom contributed only two articles, one before and one after "Mirabeau." Twenty-five authors contributed only before Carlyle's accession; twenty-seven only after (in the latter group is Grote, who finally submitted an article, which had been solicited long, long before). A fuller analysis of the division of the review's history into these two parts, taking into the account the personal relations between Mill (and his subeditors) and the contributors, as well as the subjects covered, is desirable but not here practicable. It is worth mentioning just that Mill and others perceived a change; that although Mill could continue his talk of a wider and a deeper radicalism, the implications were different; and that he delegated more authority to his subeditor who had much more self-will and recklessness than Falconer. His aim was still high and still both private and public: To Robertson he wrote, "We want *now* to give a *character* to the Review, as Carrel gave one to the National. . . ."[41] But this renewed burst of enthusiasm in 1837 did not, given the political situation and Mill's relations with his old and new allies, make any more readily attainable the goals he had in mind.

The alienation of actual or potential contributors exacerbated a problem that had plagued Mill—to his great disappointment—from the beginning. He had hoped to build a corps of writers and had had many promises. In a letter soliciting support from John Pringle Nichol, he reported:

The project advances, and if we had a sufficient list of good writers on whom we could *rely* so as to be independent of chance contributions, we could start almost immediately; but, unhappily, "the harvest is great, and the labourers are few". . . . For writers, those we most rely on for regular support are my father, wno, if he continues to be satisfied with the conduct of the *Review,* will, I have no doubt, write frequently; Roebuck, Buller, and myself (the originators of the scheme), Fonblanque, John Wilson, secretary to the Factory Commission, a most valuable man; Fox himself, to whom we have now the pleasure of adding you. Strutt and Hawkins will write occasionally. Many others, some of them most valuable, have promised assistance, but we cannot count upon them to the same extent. With some of the very best it is on the cards whether they will be able to give us much of their time or none; for instance, Chadwick, the poor Law Commissioner, one of the most remarkable men of our time in the practical art of Government, Dr. Southwood Smith, and a variety of others. Can you help us to swell the list?[42]

He must have made many attempts of which no record survives, but those that are recorded are sufficiently numerous to give some sense of how hard Mill tried and how disappointed he must sometimes have been when people on whom he thought he could count failed to respond with printable material. Even before the first issue came out, Mill had moments of foreboding; in January of 1834, he wrote to Nichol:

The Review scheme has been slumbering temporarily for want of assurance of a sufficient number of writers. O for ten men with your ardour of character, and rectitude of intellect! I am not meaning it as praise, but as the expression of a lamentable fact that I know not any three except you, me, and Mr. Fox, who I feel sure will always be moving and could always move together — and I could name perhaps fifty who have every requisite except some *one*. There is always some fatal *want*. Now, by way of beginning, will you say how much you think you could *undertake* to write regularly? I mean on the average, not to tie you to a particular *time*. We want sixteen sheets a quarter or thereabouts — if you will undertake for one sheet in every number, I will do the same, and I will see what others will do — but our poor Radicals! what a miserable figure they make in Parliament!"[43]

There is no point in listing here all Mill's failures, but certain of them are significant. Repeated attempts brought nothing from Albany Fonblanque, even though Mill offered to write material for him to free him for an article for the review (a similar offer worked in the case of W. J. Fox).[44] John Austin, who had an almost pathological inability to finish anything, disappointed Mill. Chadwick, one of Mill's oldest friends, wrote nothing;

given Mill's views, later expressed, about Chadwick's weaknesses as stylist and expositor, perhaps the failure is not to be regretted. Many, also, who might have been expected to write regularly did not do so: Grote, as we have seen, wrote only one article, as did Sarah Austin, Arthur Buller, J.G. Graham, James Martineau, Wakefield, and, most disappointingly of all, one suspects, Tocqueville. Mill's special desire to bring French thought and politics before the English reading public produced, apart from minor materials, only three articles by Nisard and one from Tocqueville. Nothing came from Carrel, on whom such high aspirations had hung. The situation had shortened Mill's temper:

Guilbert's offer, however, promises fair, but I have never found that a Frenchman's promise to do anything punctually could be depended upon. They promise everything and do nothing. They are not men of business. Guilbert is better, being half an Englishman. . . .

The sheets of Mignet will be a catch. Those of Hugo not, because he is exhausted and effete. Châles is a humbug, whom I showed up in a letter intended for the National, but published in the Monthly Repository, and the bare idea of his reviewing George Sand is enough to make one split. I would not give a farthing for the opinion of Galebert, or anybody connected with his review, about writers, for they are mere milksops themselves; and Hugo's opinions, like most French literary men's opinions of one another, are affairs of coterie and puffery.[45]

Our account is not meant to suggest that the review's stable was bare of runners: There were, after all, sixty contributors who collectively produced 180 articles of quite considerable variety and very considerable power. To think of an average of three per contributor is, however, misleading: Almost half the authors wrote only one piece. Indeed, in the long view, Mill's major success in the review, as we have said, lies not in his role as the editor but as an author. He commented in the *Autobiography* that in the initial years of the *Westminster* (from 1824 to 1828), he was the most frequent contributor, supplying thirteen articles. But during his own dynasty he authored twenty-seven articles and parts of at least four more. Robertson may be credited with nineteen, and when one adds Molesworth's eleven or eight (three by the same hand may not be his) and seven each by Buller and James Mill, it is seen that more than one third of the total came from only five hands, and the most indelible of these was Mill's own. There can be little doubt that most of those acquainted with the review, whether friends or foes, knew just how important Mill's role was and identified the review, in success or failure, with him.

Mill's imprint is strengthened by the editorial notes he attached to a number of the contributions. These notes, although not sufficient in number to justify Bain's remark that the review "abounds in editorial *caveats*,"[46] give an indication of the intimate interest Mill took in the editorial function. There are twenty-two that may roughly be categorized as explanations of policy—the sort of thing Bain was referring to—the most frequent (seven instances) and the most interesting; puffery of contributors or of the review (five instances); matters of fact in articles (four instances); retractions and corrections or explanations of editorial actions not relating to policy (three of each); and cross-reference to another article (one). These give a sense also of Mill's difficulties, and since we are giving what must now appear to be a depressing account of failure, a few words of excuse seem called for.

His life was not devoid of episode or interest in the five years of the review. He so seldom complained about overwork that it is with some surprise that one comes across his letter to Nichol of 29 January 1837 in which he says, "I have not needed your caution against *writing* much for the Review, for the mere mechanical drudgery connected with editorship has so filled up the chinks of my time that I have hardly written a line since I returned."[47] He had been ill at the beginning of the previous year; indeed, in Bain's memorably startling phrase, he had been "seized with an obstinate derangement of the brain,"[48] surely enough to fell a lesser mortal. His illness worsened during the course of the year, and after his father's death in June of 1836, he had to travel through Europe until November, seeking relief. When he wrote to Nichol, he was suffering from flu, sufficient in itself to explain the tone. But there is more than tone: He had to catch up on the six-month backlog of work in the India Office; one tends to forget that he was in regular, if undemanding, full employment throughout this period. And still we have seen only part of his travail: He had, when he wrote to Nichol, a large correspondence to bring back to active life (most of his surviving letters have to do with the review, but his political and intellectual activities must have occupied more of his correspondence than has survived); he had to prepare each month for the meetings of the Political Economy Club, and other public matters, such as acting, in his words, as "general referee, and chamber counsel to Molesworth and others of the active Radicals,"[49] absorbed his attention. Further, his private life was not tranquil: Much has been made of his apparent trauma at taking over his father's role as head of the family; whatever weight one wishes to place on the psychological stress and its possible somatic consequences, there were all too many active duties that he could not or did not escape. He was the executor of his father's will and the only male support of the family (all nine children were still living at home); indeed, he was the guardian of the younger ones (four were minors at their father's death); in addition, though he never made much ado about this demand on him, he was their "preceptor," as he said to Nichol, being still tutor to the younger ones; indeed, the two younger boys, Henry and George, had traveled with him and Harriet Taylor—with her children—in the preceding months. Finally, he was still sorting out his relation with his future wife in these years, perhaps helped, perhaps hindered, by the open scandal that surfaced in mid-1835 over the relation between Eliza Flower,

Harriet's closest friend, and W. J. Fox, minister, friend, and – not least – editor. Of course, that year was especially difficult but not untypical of the period 1835-40. There was a further extensive bout of illness (December 1838 to July 1839); his family responsibilities did not diminish; he became more deeply embroiled in radical politics; and, intermittently but with increasing fervor and concentration, he took up again his work on the *System of Logic* and virtually finished what was to be his masterwork during those years. After looking at his busyness, it is, one may say without exaggeration, not amazing, though some without Puritan genes may find it sad, that he defined leisure as "*choice* of work" – of course, he did so in a letter to Carlyle.[50] In the midst of all this, he wrote a great deal for the review, and these articles are an offset to the failures.

He did not claim triumph for them, though he reprinted seven of the most considerable of them and parts of four others. His claims for success through editorship were very modest: His championship of Durham he believed to have been instrumental in turning the tide of opinion; his review of Carlyle's *French Revolution* he thought had first called attention to its greatness; and the trumpeting of Guizot's virtues had made the British public aware of him.[51] Not much, in view of the bounding hopes. No strong body of radicals in or out of the House in 1840; no leader; no widely read and influential periodical; no echoes of Armand Carrel; much personal alienation.

Here we must close. Having lost money, friends, and much reputation, Mill had no sooner passed the *London and Westminster* on to William E. Hickson than he was off to fresh fields and pastures new, mourning, if at all, privately and trying to take with him some of the young shepherds[52] – his new fellow travelers – to the *Edinburgh Review,* which soon published some of his greatest essays. His career as an activist was not over, but it was to be conducted for more than twenty years under the mantle of the sage who won his elevation from the organ tones of the *System of Logic,* not from the caroling of the *London and Westminster.*

NOTES

1. *A Fragment on Mackintosh* (London: Baldwin and Cradock, 1835), pp. 212-13. This work was published, one may note, during the brief career of the *London Review.*

2. *Autobiography and Literary Essays,* ed. John M. Robson and Jack Stillinger, *Collected Works* (subsequently cited as *CW*) 1 (Toronto: University of Toronto Press, 1981), p. 179.

3. *Earlier Letters* (subsequently *EL*), ed. Francis E. Mineka, *CW,* vols. 12 and 13 (Toronto: University of Toronto Press, 1963), 12, p. 210 (17 January 1834).

4. Ibid., p. 30 (15 April 1829).

5. Millicent Fawcett, *Life of the Right Hon. Sir William Molesworth* (London: Macmillan, 1901), p. 63.

6. Ibid.

7. *CW* I, p. 209. The words in square brackets were deleted in the Early Draft; see *CW,* I, p. 208.

8. *Essay Concerning Human Understanding* in *Works,* new ed., 10 vols. (London: Tegg et al., 1823), 3, p. 104 (Bk. 4, chap. 16, sect. 4).

9. *De augmentis scientiarum* in *Works,* ed. James Spedding et al., 14 vols. (London: Longman et al., 1857-74), p. 772 (Latin), 5, p. 59 (English). James Mill's Commonplace Books in the London Library have numerous references to this matter (see vol. 1, f. 185r ff.; vol. 3, ff. 94v, 100r, 103r, 112v, and 114v), on which he wrote a dialogue for the *London and Westminster* (III and XXV [April 1836]: 223-34), and the importance of which he stressed to his young son early in his education (see *Autobiography,* p. 35).

10. See *Autobiography,* Early Draft, canceled passage, p. 208 n.

11. After reading about the French Revolution when he was fifteen or sixteen, Mill recorded that "the most transcendant glory I was capable of conceiving, was that of figuring, successful or unsuccessful, as a Girondist in an English Convention" (*Autobiography,* p. 67).

12. *EL,* 12, pp. 194-96 (25 November 1833). Cf. "Armand Carrel" (1837), *Dissertations and Discussions,* 2 vols. (London: Parker, 1859), 1, pp. 211-83.

13. *Dissertations and Discussions,* 1, pp. 215-16. The words in square brackets were deleted in 1859 and *baton* and *powerful* were substituted for *truncheon* and *formidable.*

14. *London and Westminster Review* XXVIII (October 1837): 66.

15. The translation is from Tacitus, Agricola, in Dialogus, *Agricola, Germania* (Latin and English), trans. Maurice Hutton (London: Heinemann; New York: Macmillan, 1914), p. 250 (sect. 46).

16. Joseph Hamburger, *Intellectuals in Politics: John Stuart Mill and the Philosophic Radicals* (New Haven: Yale University Press, 1965); William Thomas, *The Philosophic Radicals: Nine Studies in Theory and Practice, 1817-1841* (Oxford: Clarendon Press, 1979).

17. *EL,* 12, pp. 38-39 (7 November 1829).

18. "English National Character," *Monthly Repository* VIII (June 1834): 391, 392.

19. *EL,* 12, p. 242 (29 November 1834).

20. Ibid., p. 265 (11 June 1835). Mill and Tocqueville had met in London in May, and Mill's review of the first part of *De la démocratie en Amérique* appeared in the *London Review* I (July 1835): 85-129.

21. *EL,* 12, p. 248 (26 February 1835).

22. Ibid., 13, p. 384 (11 May 1838).

23. "The Writings of Junius Redivivus," *Monthly Repository* VII (April 1833); in *CW,* 1, pp. 370-71.

24. *EL,* 12, p. 254 (19 March 1835).

25. *Autobiography,* p. 169.

26. *EL,* 12, p. 202 (22 December 1833).

27. For example, Dean W. C. Lake of Durham, writing of W. G. Ward's views in the 1830s, says: "In philosophy, he was, or believed himself to be, a thorough Benthamite, and devoted especially to young Mill, whose articles in the *London Review* of those days we all eagerly devoured. . . ." (Wilfrid Ward, *W. G. Ward and the Oxford Movement,* 2d ed. [London: Macmillan, 1890], p. 60). Mill distributed offprints of some of his articles (especially, as mentioned above, that on Carrel) and so made his authorship more widely known.

28. "Memoirs of Mirabeau," *London and Westminster Review* IV and XXVI (January 1839): 382-439.

29. *EL,* 7, p. 307 (20 July 1836).

30. *The Collected Letters of Thomas and Jane Welsh Carlyle,* ed. Charles Richard Sanders et al., (Durham, N.C.: Duke University Press, 1981) 11, p. 21.

31. Ibid.

32. *EL,* 12, pp. 333-34 (26 April 1837).

33. Alexander Bain, *John Stuart Mill* (London: Longmans, 1882), pp. 56n-57n.

34. *EL,* 12, p. 344 (28 July 1837).

35. *Letters of Thomas Carlyle to John Stuart Mill, John Sterling and Robert Browning,* ed. Alexander Carlyle (London: Fisher Unwin, 1924), p. 212. Later, it may be added, when Robertson refused his "Cromwell," Carlyle was

even more himself, writing to his brother, "Having nothing to do with fools; *they* are the fatal species! Nay Robertson withal is 'fifteen years younger' than I; to be 'edited' by him, and by Mill, and the Benthamite formula—O heavens it is worse than Algeirs *[sic]* and Negro Guiana; nothing short of death could drive a white man to it." (26 December 1838; National Library of Scotland, 523/60.) He was also contemptuous of Mill's offer, early in December 1839, to print his *Chartism* in the review *(EL, 13, p. 414);* its inclusion most certainly would have enraged Mill's early associates.

36. *EL,* 12, pp. 312-13 (23 November 1836).

37. Early Draft, *CW,* 1, pp. 212-14; the words in square brackets were canceled by Mill.

38. *EL,* 12, pp. 293-94 (27 January 1836).

39. Ibid., p. 294 ([?] February 1836).

40. *John Stuart Mill,* p. 59 n.

41. *EL,* 12, p. 353 (28 September 1837).

42. Ibid., pp. 210-11 (17 January 1834).

43. Ibid., pp. 222-23 (15 April 1834).

44. Ibid., p. 246 (to Fonblanque, 25 December 1834) and p. 331 (to Fox, 15 March 1837; Mill wrote an article for the *True Sun* of 22 February 1837).

45. Ibid., pp. 343-44 (28 July 1837). The attack on Châles is in the essay cited in n. 18 above.

46. *John Stuart Mill,* p. 57. The notes are reprinted in *CW,* 1, pp. 598-607. Two of them may be quoted to illustrate points made elsewhere in this discussion. To the first word—*We*—of Joseph Blanco White's "Godoy, Prince of Peace," is appended: "It seems desirable, at the beginning of this article, to inform the reader that the plural pronoun is employed in conformity with established custom; and that, as it will be readily perceived, in regard to certain statements, both matters of fact and expressions of sentiment have a direct reference to the personal knowledge and individual feelings of the writer." *(London and Westminster* III and XXV [April 1836]: 28n; *CW,* 1, p. 600).

And (the last note to appear under Mill's proprietorship) appended to the conclusion of Sterling's "Carlyle Works": "In giving our readers the benefit of this attempt by one of our most valued contributors (we believe the first attempt yet made) at a calm and comprehensive estimate of a man, for whom our admiration has already been unreservedly expressed, and whose genius and worth have shed some rays of their brightness on our own pages; the occasion peculiarly calls upon us to declare what is already implied in the avowed plan of this Review—that its conductors are in no respect identified with the opinions delivered in the present criticism, either when the writer concurs with, or when he differs from those of Mr. Carlyle.

"While we hope never to relax in maintaining that systematic consistency in our own opinions, without which there can be no clear and firmly—grounded judgment and therefore no hearty appreciation of the merits of others; we open our pages without restriction to those who, though differing from us on some fundamental points of philosophy, stand within a certain circle of relationship to the general spirit of our practical views, and in whom we recognize that title to a free stage for the promulgation of what they deem true and useful, which belongs to all who unite noble feelings with great and fruitful thoughts." (*London and Westminster* XXXIII [October 1839]: 68n; *CW*, 1, p. 607.)

47. *EL*, 12, p. 322.

48. *John Stuart Mill*, p. 42.

49. *EL*, 12, p. 323 (29 January 1837).

50. Ibid., p. 347 (8 August 1837).

51. *Autobiography*, pp. 221-25; *EL*, 12, p. 427 (16 April 1840).

52. *EL*, 13, p. 430 (to Napier, 22 April 1840); he specifically mentioned John Robertson and George Fletcher as well as his ally of longer standing, Charles Buller.

Joel H. Wiener

Edmund Yates:
The Gossip as Editor

Edmund Yates is invariably considered to be among the pioneers of the "new journalism" in Britain. Though not as well known as W. T. Stead, Frederick Greenwood, and T. P. O'Connor, he has been characterized as the founder of "society journalism" or "personal journalism."[1] Frederick Moy Thomas described him as "a new journalist before the new journalism was ever heard of"[2]; Henry W. Lucy, a collaborator on the *World*, observed: "To him next to Frederick Greenwood . . . is largely due the present improved style of the English daily press."[3] In his *English Newspapers: Chapters in the History of Journalism*, Henry Fox Bourne, though marginally less effusive about Yates, concedes that he was the "most successful adaptor (of journalism) for the present generation."[4] Yates himself evaluated his journalism less highly. He told readers of his memoirs that it was "light and flippant, wanting in dignity and tone . . . personal in the inoffensive sense of the word . . . amusing."[5]

Yates did not suffer from a surfeit of humility. Yet, in this instance, he was being unfair to himself. The new journalism of the late nineteenth century was characterized by innovations, and Yates was responsible for several of them. If Greenwood was the first editor to divide the leading article into three paragraphs and one of the first to introduce into journalism "a style more idiomatic and familiar, unpedantic, flexible,"[6] and if Stead and O'Connor injected a political conscience into journalism together with stylistic and typographical changes, Yates too made his contributions. He "Americanized" the British press by introducing the personal interview to it.[7] He made short paragraphs and tidbits a part of the currency of the press, a decade before the publishing changes initiated by George Newnes. He removed parliamentary politics from the center of newspaper reading and substituted "light literature" for it. He gave his backing to investigative reporting and parliamentary sketch writing. He made "gossip" essential reading because in the *World* and elsewhere it began to compete with the remainder of the paper. In short, Yates was both a creator of the new journalism and, as he conceived it, "a recorder of the floating light gossip of the day."[8] This seeming inconsistency demands closer analysis because in some ways it is typical of the new journalism.

Most of Yates's career was bound up with *The World: A Journal for Men and Women,* which he founded in July 1874 and continued to edit for twenty years until his sudden death after collapsing in a West End theater in 1894. Like many other Victorian pressmen, he was enormously prolific. Besides the *World,* he edited six journals (among them the *Comic Times, Temple Bar,* and *Town Talk*); contributed dramatic criticism and comic sketches to newspapers and periodicals such as the *Daily News,* the *Illustrated Times,* the *Welcome Guest,* and *Household Words;* and wrote more than seventeen novels and nearly as many burlesques and one-act dramas, most of which were acted professionally.[9] Like his close friends Charles Dickens and Albert Smith, he gave public readings and "entertainments." And like another associate, George Augustus Sala, he was the offspring of a prominent theatrical family.[10] In true Victorian fashion, Yates was also a celebrated raconteur and man-about-town. But the gourmandizing, the storytelling, even the writing of fiction, were sidelights for him. It was in journalism that he excelled. And he did so for reasons that must now be examined.

Yates was a product of the 1850s. Born in 1831, he came of age at a critical period in the history of the press. Earlier forms of journalism were beginning to be transformed as the result of technological changes and the dismantling of political controls. In the first half of the century, the great bulk of newspapers and journals were defined by their readership. They included established papers such as *The Times* and the *Morning Chronicle,* whose influence rested on powerful leaders; cheap political journals that were the products of individual efforts; Sunday papers such as *Lloyd's Weekly Newspaper* and *Reynolds's Weekly Newspaper,* which attempted, somewhat uneasily, to combine radical politics and fiction; and a large variety of periodicals ranging from literary quarterlies and monthly reviews to cheap comic papers such as *Figaro in London* and *Punch* to crude scandal sheets such as C. M. Westmacott's *Age* and Renton Nicholson's *Town.*

Few of these papers had a wide readership, and in most cases their price was artificially high before 1855, when the final penny of the newspaper duty was repealed. Only a small number of journals were "classless," and even fewer were read by both sexes. Middle- and working-class readers generally took in different papers, and female readers supported journals (usually edited by women) that were specifically marketed for them. In the 1850s these separate compartments began to break down. Yates came to maturity at a time when the press was beginning to acquire a homogenizing function. His conception of good journalism as consisting of "all the light and gossipy news of the day, properly winnowed and attractively set forth"[11] was fairly typical of the 1850s. The political and economic battles of previous decades seemingly had ended. Artisans, clerks, shopkeepers, and laborers—many of them newly litrate—were calling for reading matter that would cut across traditional lines. Yates was one of the first journalists to give it to them.

An increased concern for respectability was connected to these changes. By the 1850s politics and literature were beginning to be "purified." Writers frequently excised sexual and political references from their vocabulary. There was an increased emphasis on reading matter suitable for the family. In the view of many people, neither troublesome political allusions nor unwholesome sexual innuendos should be allowed to creep into journalism. On the other hand, gossip was perfectly acceptable. As R. D. Blumenfeld, a famous editor of the *Daily Express,* shrewdly commented: "[Gossip is] the currency of speech; without it life would be dull and inexpressive."[12] Gossip of this kind was not to be circulated for personal reasons, as was the case with the earlier scandal sheets, or calculated to set the poor against the rich. Instead, it should convey a moral lesson and be entertaining. Yates and other young men who plunged into journalism in the 1850s (such as Sala, James Hannay, and Angus Reach) had little sensitivity to the condition of poor people. In Yates's words, many of them were "unshorn, unwashed, tattered, woe-begone, dissipated beings."[13] But they deplored the crassness of those people who wielded economic and political power, whether they represented landed or moneyed wealth. In their view a positive overlay of "light literature" and gossip was a useful counterpart to this crassness because it would bind families and classes together. Such a conception of journalism was very different from the traditional one, which, in the words of William

Lovett, was to communicate ideas, assist "moral and intellectual progress" and "advance . . . trade, commerce, and the peaceful arts of life."[14] But it is fundamental to an understanding of Yates and the part that he played in the new journalism.

Influenced by these tendencies toward classlessness and self-censorship, Yates was also deeply affected by literary bohemianism, which he defined as a "delicious sense of lawless freedom."[15] His parents had little money and few connections outside the theatrical fraternity. His formal education ended in 1846, after he attended Highgate School and spent several months in Düsseldorf. He did not go to a university, which was becoming the route to journalism for many aspiring litterateurs. Instead, he took a position in the general post office (with the help of family contacts) and kept it until he retired on a pension twenty years later. Amid these somewhat unpromising circumstances, he began to aspire to literary fame.

The bohemian ideals of Thackeray's *Pendennis* (first published serially in 1848-50, when Yates was not yet twenty) gave him hope. Like Arthur Pendennis, Yates wanted to feel the "sacred flame—a little of the real poetical fire," and "to think that his writings are creating some noise in the world."[16] Within four years reality began to imitate art, and Yates had achieved some success. "So I was Pendennis at last," he recollected in his memoirs.[17] His first important position was the editor of the *Comic Times* (1853), published by Herbert Ingram. When this ld. journal collapsed after a few months, he solidified his literary reputation by becoming the editor of the *Train* (January 1856-June 1858), a "light and flippant" monthly that was run as a "cooperative" and has been described by M. H. Spielmann, the historian of *Punch,* as a "brilliant little journal . . . which was not destined . . . to live as long as it deserved."[18] Yates was now a bohemian literary figure. He presided over weekly suppers of the "Trainband" in different taverns, with such able collaborators present as Sala, Frank Smedley, John Oxenford, Edward Blanchard, and Robert Brough. He also came to be appreciated for his "habits of business, punctuality, steadiness and zeal."[19]

This assertion of romantic freedom unleashed considerable reserves of energy in Yates. And it is a key to his career because it gave him the self-confidence to experiment with new journalistic forms. Two paradoxes follow from this. One is that Yates was a happily married "bohemian" with four children to support and many "tax-paying, church-going, and society-fearing" obligations to attend to.[20] The other is that he worked voraciously, day in and day out, precisely in order to be able to enjoy himself. No great moral or ideological purpose animated him. He eschewed political loyalties. And he rejected the journalism of the "captive audience," by which a writer seeks to convey a specific message to those who are already converted. For Yates gossip was all-important because it alone offered him the means to secure his literary and artistic ambitions.

Before looking more closely at Yates's career as an editor, an additional factor must be taken into account—his urban loyalties. By its very nature, Victorian journalism was a product of urbanization, an analogue to the economic and social changes that were creating an urban world.[21] Yates, who spent almost every night of his working life in a London theater or club, intuitively understood this. He gave expression to it in his huge literary output. And as an editor, he experimented in ways that were particularly suitable to an urban (or a suburban) readership. He created "personal" modes of expression to meet the needs of an expanding audience. And he spoke to this audience in a language it understood, describing the everyday world of London to his provincial readers (in the guise of a "Looker-On in London" in the Belfast *Northern Whig* and a "London Correspondent" in the *Inverness Courier*) and sharing innumerable insights about the metropolis with readers who knew it well. Yates was often critical of London, "this huge locust of civilisation, which is so rapidly devouring every patch of greensward or leafy retreat."[22] Yet, bursting with the vitality of the city himself, he loved it passionately, especially during the "season" when its theaters and concert halls were filled to bursting. Its "always-changing, deeply-interesting panorama" constantly fascinated him.[23] He could not have been a successful editor anywhere else.

Gossip was the unifying element in Yates's journalism. It brought all his strengths and weaknesses together. And although the *World* constituted the pinnacle of his achievements as an editor, it was in Henry Vizetelly's 2d. *Illustrated Times* between 1855 and 1863 that he first created a distinctive style and point of view. His famous gossip column in the *Illustrated Times,* "The Lounger at the Clubs" (followed in succeeding years by the weekly "Flâneur" column in the *Morning Star,* by pages of chitchat in the *Northern Whig* and the *Inverness Courier,* and by the "Five O'Clock Tea" column in the *Queen*), established the pattern of Yates's journalism. The "Lounger" was, in the words of a contemporary, the first example of the "school of public journalistic gossip."[24] It influenced many "new journalists," including Grenville Murray in *The Queen's Messenger* (1869), Henry W. Lucy in *Mayfair* (1877-79), and Henry Labouchere ("Entre Nous") in *Truth* (1877-97).

The "Lounger" introduced the personal element into journalism. Yates shared the first person singular with his readers in a way that no journalist had done previously: "I learn," "I understand," "I hear from private sources," "I do not believe the rumours," and so on. His approach was unstructured. He had "no particular topic to write upon but simply to gossip idly on all."[25] He therefore transmitted "semi-private gossip, those pleasant rumours which originate in cliques, and coteries, and flit from smoking-room to smoking-room."[26] He commented on the week's political events, wrote informal theatrical and artistic

266 Joel H. Wiener

"reviews," described exhibitions and "entertainments," and made innumerable observations about books, concerts, and that peculiarly English obsession, the weather.

In true *Private Eye* fashion, Yates's readers were taken into his confidence about rumored defalcations at the Reform and Junior United Clubs and about the official of a metropolitan railway who was under investigation for fraud ("at present it would be dangerous to say more"). One week he would allude to an unpopular marriage being secretly arranged at court; another time he would reveal (on the basis of a private letter) that an article in the prestigious *Saturday Review* had been plagiarized.[27] Yates's point of view was mildly radical. He advocated military reform, an extension of the franchise, an end to public executions (though not capital punishment), and the employment of women. He condemned sham and hypocrisy, as practiced both by the aristocracy and the rising middle class, whom he referred to as "the suburbans, the Pancras-cum-Bloomsburys."[28] But the content of the "Lounger" column is of little importance. Rather, its tone establishes it as a landmark in the history of journalism. For in the mode of the modern gossip columnist, Yates shared bits of information with his readers. He did not lecture them or present a consistent point of view. On the contrary, he was vaguely populist. He seemed to be saying that since we are all in this together, we should abandon pretense and enjoy ourselves.

Yates continually made a point of discretion. Although his "Lounger" column contains a few references to a homosexual scandal in the Foot Guards and to "disgusting facts, which are talked about in well-informed circles, but will never find their way into print,"[29] these are atypical. For Yates sex was an unwelcome subject outside the context of marriage. The "Lounger" rarely alluded to divorce or adultery. And he eschewed coarseness of expression of the kind resorted to by Westmacott and Nicholson in earlier decades and by Theodore Hook in *John*

Bull.[30] This restraint was even more evident in "What the World Says," Yates's famous gossip column in the *World,* which, notwithstanding its mildness, was the object of several private prosecutions for libel.[31] For one thing, Yates's previous gossip columns were written anonymously, whereas the identity of "Atlas" was well known. For another thing, the concept of the "society journal" as fit for family reading had been firmly established by the time he commenced the *World.*

In the 1850s and 1860s, in the pages of the *Illustrated Times,* the *Morning Star,* the *Weekly Dispatch,* and elsewhere, Yates began to feel his way toward a new journalistic mode; by the 1870s in the *World* he had developed it. A self-assured tone characterized "What the World Says." Most of it was admittedly "persiflage," as Sala, a friendly critic, put it.[32] Yet it was persiflage with a purpose, for Yates set out to present "an amusing chronicle of current history, divested of the nonsense which has hitherto stuck like treacle to public business."[33] And he made clear to his readers that they should not expect more from him. The "In the City" column of the *World,* begun by Henry Labouchere, dealt with financial peccadilloes. Political analyses were the province of Lucy, whose "Under the Clock" series established a new vogue for the parliamentary sketch. And the *World's* leaders, increasingly sympathetic to the Conservative party, were mostly written by Thomas Escott. Yates touched upon everything else.

His forte was gossip, and for more than thirty years he read every newspaper and periodical that he could, trying to extract as much information as possible. He wandered about London, relaying opinion from whatever source he considered to be reliable. He dined regularly at the Arts Club and the Carleton Club, sifting rumor from fact and taking quick note of passing events.[34] In "What the World Says," he also relied increasingly on anonymous correspondents who (as in the case of the modern gossip column) fed him information. When his sources proved to be inaccurate (or when Yates's own instincts failed him), he often withdrew his comments as quickly and as gracefully as he could. Usually he was none the worse for wear because so much was happening and speed was of the essence. Yates bewailed the fact that other newspapers sometimes scooped him before he got into print. He did his best to satisfy his customers, however, by making his province not only London, as in his previous gossip columns, but the "world." "What the World Says" began with foreign gossip and then proceeded to scan domestic and metropolitan events in the same way that a modern newspaper follows a principle of selection in its news coverage.

As a "veteran gossiper," Yates's career moved in a fairly straight path from one column to the next. But his "Five O'Clock Tea" series in *The Queen: The Lady's Newspaper,* written by "Mrs. Seaton," deserves special attention. It ran from February 1872 to March 1873 and was subsequently revived in a modified form for several months. "Mrs. Seaton" was the wife of a Conservative M.P. named "Horace," and the bulk of her political gossip was conveyed through his sources. Other characters appeared regularly: "Mr. Goss, who knows everything diplomatic"; "Selina Pottle," whose interest lies in the arts; "Mr. Bingrove," a denizen of clubland. The usual melange of gossip was communicated by Yates to his predominantly female readers: Did so and so accept ministerial preferment? Has the Earl of D been blackballed at the Marlborough Club? Which "high official" has fled the country after being caught cheating at cards?[35]

The device of transmitting gossip by means of a fictional character enabled Yates to maintain a whimsical style in which he could comment on events with detachment. Upon hearing that the Gladstone government was considering resigning, "Mrs. Seaton" observed: "It would be a horrid nuisance to have society upset just as the season is commencing so pleasantly." When told that servants in London were unhappy because of poor working conditions, she stated tartly: "The creatures declare that they won't work . . . after ten at night, which is positively ridiculous." "Lady Crewkarne," a Mayfair dowager, poked fun at the education of women (which Yates supported): "The female desire for occupying public positions always goes with knobbly foreheads, coarse features, spectacles, and hands and feet the sight of which makes you stagger."[36] Yates failed to make use of the *Queen* as a forum for the discussion of serious issues, notwithstanding his sympathy with the plight of women. But to comment on him in these terms is to be somewhat unfair. He was no more interested in advocating political or social (or feminist) causes in the *Queen* than in the *Illustrated Times,* the *Morning Star,* the *Inverness Courier,* or the *World.* As always, his objective was to purvey gossip, which he believed could have a wholesome, unifying purpose. He did this with exceptional cleverness in the *Queen.*

Gossip can take several forms. And among the significant contributions that Yates made to journalism was to link gossip to the public's interest in famous people. He virtually coined the word *celebrity* in making the "Celebrities at Home" series in the *World* one of its popular features for many years. Providing a peek into the lives of well-known people was the essence of personal journalism, as Yates defined it. It enabled readers to share secrets with the "great." It also extended gossip into more private areas because "Celebrities at Home" was based on the personal interview. From the 1850s on, Yates had begun to understand the potential in this kind of journalism. In the *Train* he had written a series called Men of Mark in which literary and artistic personalities such as W. H. Russell, Shirley Brooks, and Wilkie Collins were sketched in a personal way. His characterizations were light yet revealing in that he seemingly shared confidences with his readers about public figures whom he was acquainted with. For example, he wrote about Brooks: "Any particularly salient hit in the pages of *Punch* may, with safety, be ascribed to his pen."[37] Of John Buckstone, the actor, he stated: "I do not know any other actor who has such a hold over the risible faculties of his audience."[38]

In the "Celebrities at Home" column in the *World,* important elements of the new journalism began to cohere. Yates was influenced by American journalism (he lived in the United States for six months during 1872-73), and he commenced this famous series after considerable advance preparation. It was so successful that "celebrities" vied with one another for the honor of a portrait in the *World.* They were invariably "filmed" in their natural habitats and interviewed whenever possible. Yates wrote most of the sketches (his assistants Bernard H. Pearce and W. Becker did the others), and he captured in print many of the leading personalities of Victorian Britain: Gladstone and Disraeli at Hawarden and Hughendon; John Bright, "the most purely English orator of our time" at One Ash; Tennyson at Haslemere; the Marquis of Salisbury in his mansion at Hatfield ("business-like is the homely term which perhaps conveys the best idea of his undeniably great mental power").[39] No comments overtly critical of the subject were included, and Yates soon adopted the practice of allowing his "celebrities" to amend the proofs. Yet, like the contemporary portraits of Sargent and Whistler, the results were sometimes less flattering than they seemed. The characterization of Wilkie Collins, for example, as "a rapid inventor and a slow producer" does not significantly enhance his reputation.[40] And Anthony Trollope, among others, refused to be interviewed for "Celebrities at Home" because he disapproved of "society journalism."[41] A long line of journalists — beginning with Labouchere in *Truth* ("Anecdotal Photographs") and extending to today's *Observer* reporters who do the weekly "Profile" — owe a debt to Yates.

Yates was a great editor in other ways. He incorporated into newspaper writing the comic literary tradition of Dickens, of *Punch,* and of brilliant journalists such as Grenville Murray, who did the "Roving Englishman" series for *Household Words.* He created a gallery of satirical personalities who successfully made the transition from a weekly humor magazine to a newspaper. He was a talent spotter who gave a lead to creative "new journalists" such as Lucy and Escott. He was himself a writer of considerable substance.

But it was as a gossip that Edmund Yates's reputation will stand or fall. Everything that came from his pen was a function of his ceaseless interest in "news, scandal, tittle-tattle, truth, lies, and *gobemoucheries* alike. . . ."[42] In his own words, he was "club-bish, Carlyleian . . . worldly."[43] He was also extremely super-ficial. If, as Escott perceptively suggests, Yates helped perpetu-ate literary influences in journalism, he did this by giving his middle- and working-class readers of both sexes "an agreeable sensation as of a clever and not too exacting appeal to their intellectual perceptions."[44] By no means was he the worst offender in this regard. Newnes's *Tit-Bits* and Aldred Harmsworth's *Daily Mail* are of lesser quality than the *World.* Yet gossip cannot in itself justify a journalistic career lasting forty years, and too much of what Yates left behind consists of fleeting images and innovation for its own sake. To a considerable extent, he provided what the times demanded, "mental food given to (the newspaper reading public) in minces and snippets, not in chops and joints."[45] His career illustrates some of the important ways in which popular journalism changed in the second half of the nine-teenth century and how one influential editor responded to these changes. It also demonstrates that what Yates wrote about Albert Smith in describing the latter's successes on the public platform may be applicable to himself: "His entertainment was based on the strictest rules of demand and supply . . . his audience wanted amusement, and he gave it to them—he wanted money, and they paid him. . . ."[46]

NOTES

1. Laura Smith, "Society Journalism: Its Rise and Development," *Newspaper Press Directory for 1898* (London, 1898), p. 80; *Athenaeum,* 26 May 1894.

2. Frederick Moy Thomas, ed., *Fifty Years of Fleet Street: Being the Life and Recollections of Sir John R. Robinson* (London: Macmillan and Co., 1904), p. 205.

3. Henry W. Lucy, *Nearing Jordan* (London: Smith, Elder & Co., 1916), p. 167. T. H. S. Escott, who worked with Yates on several journals, described him as "the chief and most capable creator of a new school of journalism." ("Edmund Yates: An Appreciation and a Retrospect," *New Review* XI (1894): 91.)

4. Henry R. Fox Bourne, *English Newspapers: Chapters in the History of Journalism* (London: Chatto & Windus, 1887), II, p. 300.

5. Edmund Yates, *His Recollections and Experiences* (London: Richard Bentley and Son, 1884), II, p. 307.

6. J. W. Robertson Scott, *The Story of the Pall Mall Gazette, of Its First Editor Frederick Greenwood, and of Its Founder George Murray Smith* (London: Oxford University Press, 1950), p. 129.

7. In an important article Joseph O. Baylen overstates the case for Stead by crediting him with the introduction of the personal interview. ("W. T. Stead and the 'New Journalism,' " *Emory University Quarterly* XXI (1965): 204.)

8. *Illustrated Times,* 19 July 1856.

9. There is an excellent bibliography of Yates's writings in P. D. Edwards, *Edmund Yates, 1831-1894* (St. Lucia, Australia: University of Queensland, 1980).

10. Frederick Yates, his father, was the manager of the Adelphi Theatre. His mother, Elizabeth Brunton, was a well-known actress whom a contemporary described as "the most perfect personator of what may be called domestic drama that ever walked the stage." (Serjeant Ballantine, *Some Experiences of a Barrister's Life* (London: Richard Bentley and Son, 1882), I. p. 29.)

11. Edmund Yates, *Fifty Years of London Life: Memoirs of a Man of the World* (New York: Harper & Brother, 1885), p. 246.

12. R. D. Blumenfeld, *The Press in My Time* (London: Rich and Cowan, 1933), p. 93.

13. *Illustrated Times,* 16 April 1859.

14. Cited in Joel H. Wiener, *The War of the Unstamped: The Movement to Repeal the British Newspaper Tax, 1830-1836* (Ithaca, New York: Cornell University Press, 1969), p. 135.

15. *Illustrated Times,* 3 September 1859.

16. William Makepeace Thackeray, *The History of Pendennis,* chapters 31 and 35.

17. Yates, *Recollections,* I, p. 235.

18. M. H. Spielmann, *The History of "Punch"* (London: Cassell, 1895), p. 313.

19. The words are by Charles Dickens. (*The Letters of Charles Dickens,* ed. Walter Dexter (Bloomsbury: The Nonesuch Press, 1938), III, p. 519.)

20. Edmund Yates, "Summer Days," *Temple Bar* III (1861): 411.

21. This point is made by Joanne Shattock and Michael Wolff, ed., *The Victorian Periodical Press: Samplings and Soundings* (Leicester: Leicester University Press, 1982), pp. xiii-xix.

22. "Summer in the Suburbs," *Tinsley's Magazine* II (1868): 625. Elsewhere he referred to London as possessing a "combined odour of stale fruit and vegetables, rotten eggs, foul tobacco, spilt beer, rank cart-grease, dried soot, smoke, triturated road-dust, and damp straw." Ibid. V (1869): 211.

23. "Soothing the Savage Breast," *Train* V (1858): 39.

24. Joseph Hatton, *Journalistic London: Being a Series of Sketches of Famous Pens and Papers of the Day* (London: Sampson Low, Marston, Searle, & Rivington, 1882), p. 86.

25. *Illustrated Times,* 27 February 1858.

26. *Inverness Courier,* 2 September 1858.

27. *Illustrated Times,* 23 May 1857, 8 December 1855, 13 February 1858, 14 November 1857.

28. "Hotspur Street, W.," *Train* IV (1857): 239.

29. *Illustrated Times,* 13 February 1858.

30. There is a fine article on Nicholson by Donald Gray, "Early Victorian Scandalous Journalism: Renton Nicholson's *The Town,"* in *Victorian Periodical Press,* ed. Shattock and Wolff, pp. 317-348.

31. Yates was imprisoned in Holloway Gaol for two months in 1885 after being sued for criminal libel by the Earl of Lonsdale.

32. *The Life and Adventures of George Augustus Sala, Written by Himself,* 3d ed. (London: Cassell, 1895), I, p. 270.

33. *World,* 8 July 1874.

34. Perhaps the most famous incident involving Yates was his expulsion from the Garrick Club in 1858 at the instigation of Thackeray whom he had attacked in *Town Talk.* For two contrasting points of view about this incident, in which Yates was supported by Dickens, see Edmund Yates, *Mr. Thackeray, Mr. Yates, and the Garrick Club: The Correspondence and Facts* (London, privately printed, 1859), and Gordon Ray, "Dickens vs. Thackeray;: The Garrick Club Affair," *PMLA* LXIX (1954): 815-832.

35. *Queen,* 13 April, 16 March, and 6 July 1872; 7 March 1874.

274   Joel H. Wiener

36. Ibid., 27 April and 4 May 1872; 8 November 1873.
37. *Train* IV (1857): 40.
38. Ibid., 41.
39. *Celebrities at Home* (London: Office of the *World*, 1877-79), I, pp. 35, 194
40. Ibid., III, p. 145
41. Yates, *Recollections*, II, pp. 232-233.
42. *Inverness Courier*, 8 July 1858.
43. *Illustrated Times*, 4 August 1855.
44. T. H. S. Escott, "Literature and Journalism," *Fortnightly Review* XCVII (1912): 127.
45. Edward Dicey, "Journalism Old and New," *Fortnightly Review* LXXXIII (1905): 917.
46. *Mont Blanc by Albert Smith: With a Memoir of the Author by Edmund Yates* (London: Ward and Locke, 1860), p. xxiv.

Mary Bostetter

The Journalism of Thomas Wakley

Thomas Wakley, the founder and the editor for thirty-nine years of the *Lancet,* the reformist medical magazine, did not begin his working life as a journalist. Instead, he was catapulted from a medical practice into the editor's chair after he had been mysteriously attacked and left for dead in his burning house. While recovering from the traumatic experience of the fire, his injuries, and a subsequent court case against his insurance company, Wakley was working as a general practitioner on the Strand in the spring of 1823 when an American from Boston, Dr. Walter Channing, dropped into his surgery on a warm May evening. The two men began to talk and soon discovered that they shared the same dedication to the cause of medical reform. When a medical student, Dr. Channing had spent some time studying surgery at St. Thomas's, Wakley's old hospital, and he understood the problems a medical reformer faced in London where the Royal Colleges of Surgeons and Physicians considered all medicine their monopoly.

Totally absorbed in their conversation, the two doctors talked the rest of the night, and just as the sun was rising over the steeple of St. Clement Dane across the street from Wakley's house, Channing told his host about a medical magazine called the *New England Journal of Medicine and Surgery,* which he and a group of Boston doctors had founded twelve years earlier in 1811. Dr. Channing added that he would be the coeditor of the *Journal* in 1825, and he hoped to publish reports of unusual cases, new medical research, innovative surgery, and monthly surveys of what was being done in the fourteen medical schools that were burgeoning in the United States. To Thomas Wakley, who had been marking time for the last three years as he looked for an enterprise into which he could throw all his energies, a medical magazine like the one Dr. Channing was describing seemed made to order for him also. When he tentatively suggested the possibility of his starting such a journal in London, Dr. Channing, who was nine years older than Wakley and equipped with much more business experience, greeted the idea with enthusiasm as a financially feasible project. With encouragement, advice, and considerable financial help from Dr. Channing, the first *Lancet* was published on October 5, 1823.[1]

Although in makeup and contents it was very different from the other three medical journals already in existence in London, the little blue-coated sixpenny magazine, which was to have such a violent history, began innocently enough with short news items designed to stimulate medical shoptalk. There was, however, more than a hint of the turbulence to come in the editor's declared intention of publishing some London hospital lectures so that the practitioners and medical students all over the country could share in the latest medical scientific knowledge with their London colleagues. Wakley ensured the success of his journal when he chose as his first lecturer his old teacher, Sir Astley Cooper, who was easily the most competent and professionally knowledgeable surgeon practicing in London in 1823.

When Sir Astley attacked Guy's Hospital's irresponsible use of mercury for diseases that did not require it, calling this practice "infamous and disgraceful" and destructive to the health of the patient, Wakley had actual proof that the publication of the lectures was accomplishing reform. The Guy's Hospital surgeons knew that Sir Astley disapproved of the practice, but since it was favored by their dictatorial treasurer, Benjamin Harrison, they had not done anything about it. Now when Sir Astley's frank words were published in the *Lancet,* so much controversy was stirred up in medical circles that the Guy's surgeons were focused to discontinue it.

Wakley was so jubilant over this victory that the baronet took offense and replied that he had no wish to hurt the feelings of the Guy's Hospital surgeons to whom he was closely attached. "Why!" he said disarmingly, "I do not want to injure these men. Mr. Travers was my apprentice, Mr. Green is my godson, Mr. Tyrrell is my nephew, Mr. Key is my nephew!"[2] Sir Astley had naively admitted to the very nepotism that was high on the list of medical abuses Wakley proposed to remove. In the *Lancet* of May 22, Wakley commented wryly on this cosy little group of surgeons "united to each other, not only by the amiable ties of consanguinity, but by the no less delightful *vinculum* of a common participation in the £3,600 which they annually extract from the students!" The day after the *Lancet* bearing this gibe came out, Wakley was excluded from St. Thomas's, his old training hospital, by three of Sir Astley Cooper's "boys," Travers, Green, and Tyrrell, all surgeons at St. Thomas's.

Wakley hit back in a vicious attack. Reviving the old eighteenth-century term of opprobrium, he nicknamed the three men the "Ninnyhammers", and he contemptuously referred to the kind of medicine they practiced as "Hole in the Corner" surgery.[3] He continued to visit the operating theater and wards of St. Thomas's whenever he liked, daring the Ninnyhammers to throw him out. Wakley was almost six feet tall, a trained boxer, and in good physical condition. The last thing the three Ninnyhammers wanted was a physical confrontation with him.

Wakley's plan of action for the *Lancet* became even more apparent when he announced that the next lectures to be published would be those of John Abernethy, a surgeon at St. Bart's. If Sir Astley was the best lecturer in London, Abernethy was one of the worst; his lectures were silly and unprofessional and held together only by expletives and witticisms, many of which were as obsolete as his medical knowledge. His lectures had been delivered unchanged for thirty-seven years.[4] Putting medical incompetents such as Abernethy under the *Lancet* searchlight and letting them reveal their own inadequacies was one of Wakley's most effective journalistic techniques.

When his first lecture was published, Abernethy yielded to pressure from his colleagues, who did not want the *Lancet* spotlight shining into their class rooms, and wrote a complaining letter to the *Morning Chronicle,* declaring that a cheap weekly publication had run abstracts of his lectures. Wakley replied with a strong defense of the *Lancet,* saying that he had not published abstracts but the lectures themselves exactly as they had been delivered, omitting nothing and adding nothing.

For his next lectures, Abernethy had the gas lamps in the lecture hall turned off, and he lectured in the dark so that the *Lancet* reporter, whoever he might be, could not take notes. In spite of these precautions, the lectures continued to appear in the *Lancet* every week. It was unimportant to Wakley whether the lights were on or off because William Lawrence, assistant surgeon to Abernethy, with ready access to his supervisor's lecture notes, was also working as a secret reporter for the *Lancet.*[5]

At last Abernethy resorted to the same tactics that many other opponents of the *Lancet* were to employ: He filed in the Court of Chancery for an injunction to keep the printers from publishing the rest of his lectures. Lord Eldon refused the injunction on the first try because Abernethy was unable to produce any formal lectures except what the *Lancet* had published. He did, however, advise Abernethy that he might appeal if he wished on the basis of trust or implied contractual relations with his students. Abernethy did just that, and after a long consideration of the case, Lord Eldon granted the injunction on the basis that "persons attending an oral lecture have in an implied contract with the speaker no right to publish it." Publications by the *Lancet* the judge considered to be "fraud in the third party."

Wakley announced that if the new decision was upheld in the second hearing, he would carry the case to the House of Lords because in that court witnesses could be questioned, which they could not be in Chancery, so that pertinent facts that Lord Eldon did not know could be brought out. Wakley ceased publication of the lectures in mid-June when the injunction went into effect, but on October 1, 1825, opening day for the hospital schools, Wakley defiantly published Abernethy's opening lecture, just as he did those of all other hospital surgeons with the significant exception of Mr. Mayo who was a private lecturer and therefore, Wakley wrote, had the right to refuse publication.

Wakley did not need to go to the House of Lords after all. He settled the matter himself. In November Abernethy played into his hands by making the very mistake that Wakley was expecting him to make. He tried to resign as hospital surgeon while retaining his lucrative position as a lecturer. The governors of St. Bartholomew's told him that he could not resign as a surgeon without also resigning his appointment as a lecturer. Wakley immediately sent an affidavit to Lord Eldon reporting the governor's decision and saying that since the Royal College of Surgeons had passed a bylaw giving only London hospital surgeons the right to lecture medical students and take their fees, "These men have by their own acts constituted themselves a public functionary for a public purpose. They cannot now seek protection due to the other private lecturers to deprive the public of the means of judging whether their duties as hospital surgeon are properly discharged." Thinking no doubt of Abernethy's nervous colleagues who complained that the publication of the lectures might ruin the reputation of the lecturer, Wakley wrote at the end of his affidavit: "If such a publication *did* injure the reputation of a lecturer, he would be incompetent to fill the situation of a Hospital Surgeon. No Court of Equity would protect an incompetent Hospital Lecturer by granting an injunction against the publication of lectures delivered by him." Lord Eldon dissolved the injunction as soon as he finished reading Wakley's affidavit.[6] This was the first legal victory won by Wakley for his *Lancet*. There would be many more.

Up to this point Wakley's journalism had been based on his assumption, not too unlike the one Jeremy Bentham abandoned late in life, that "people only wanted to know what was bad in order to throw it out."[7] Colorful, vigorous, and straightforward as his writing was, it was far too dependent on declamation rather than exposition for effect. By 1825 he had learned that his audience could be moved to action by an appeal only if it was well supported by evidence, composed of concrete and accurate information.

After the Abernethy injunction was removed, Wakley came out openly for medical reform. He let his 8,000 subscribers know that he intended to improve medical education and force the raising of medical performance standards in the lecture halls and the operating theaters, in the surgeries and in the hospitals, not only in London but in the rest of the country as well. He started his campaign with a series of leading articles in which each indictment was soundly backed by the kind of evidence that would stand up in a courtroom if necessary.

Wakley began with the cynical and inadequate medical education that the Royal College of Surgeons was selling and on which it held a tight monopoly. The twenty-one members of the College Council appointed themselves and their relatives and apprentices to all the anatomy and surgery lectureships, and they pocketed all the fees. Wearing still another hat, they also functioned as examiners, taking large fees from the qualifying examinees. Wakley published the curriculum, which had never been made available to the students, pointing out significantly that there was no attempt to teach all the courses a student needed to practice medicine. Then the *Lancet* searchlight rested on lecturers who cut classes, surgeons who charged double fees for "clinical lectures" that were really only "walking the ward" sessions, and officials who scheduled required lectures at the same hour and then kept the money paid by the students who registered before the hours had been announced. Wakley named names, mercilessly creating considerable discomfiture. The *Lancet* was particularly hard on the corrupt system whereby, for all practical purposes, the students purchased their degrees with the certificates they bought for each lecture and which they had to present when they came up for their qualifying exams. No roll call was ever taken in classes, and no exams were given before the qualifying exam. As Wakley pointed out, it was possible to buy certificates, never attend a class, and still pass the perfunctory exam for qualification. Under such conditions, the RCS graduate might be almost as inadequately prepared as the out-and-out quack.[8]

Wakley also took up the case of the younger medical men, both surgeons and licentiate physicians, who had no vote in their colleges and no voice in the way the huge dues that were semiannually extracted from them were spent. These men deeply resented the ruling of both Royal Colleges that no doctor who practiced midwifery was eligible to serve on the governing board of either organization. Indignation had reached a boiling point among the young doctors when the RCS enforced two arbitrary bylaws that cut off all competition not only from the private medical schools in London but also from the large provincial hospitals in the country. By these rulings, every English medical student had to come to the RCS hospitals for his anatomy and surgery. In open rebellion, 1,200 medical students and reformers crowded into Freemason Hall on February 25, 1826. There was much discussion, many resolutions were passed, and a protest was sent to the RCS and a petition to the House of Commons. At last the *Lancet* had raised a standard of reform, and an ever-increasing number of young doctors and scientists were rallying to it.[9]

Preceding Wakley there had been reformers who had advocated the same reforms and attacked the same abuses, but they had no voice and no one heard them.[10] Thousands of people all over the country heard the *Lancet* in 1826. Even the magazine's enemies could not afford to ignore it. Wakley wrote his reports in a direct, say-it-like-it-is manner, which soon found their way into gossip and shoptalk, so that when he attacked a lecturer by name, even the victim's colleagues who may very well have hated the *Lancet,* would remark at their clubs with that satisfaction people show on such occasions, "Did you see what the *Lancet* did to old Freddy today?" Like it or not, the *Lancet* by 1828 had become a power, a fact that the RCS soon had to recognize.

As soon as Wakley had won the right to publish the medical lectures, he announced "the next distinguishing feature of the *Lancet* is the publication of Hospital Reports . . . our reports will have this advantage over any that might be published by the surgeons of the different institutions in that while they would have an interest in concealing many circumstances which might reflect discredit on themselves and the institutions to which they belong, we cannot be influenced by any such considerations." After sounding this alarm bell, Wakley did publish reports of hospital cases, but there was nothing sensational about them and the excitement raised by the announcement subsided. Suddenly in the early months of 1828, Wakley began publishing a succession of reports of incompetence and malpractice in the hospitals, which were deliberately arranged to arouse public indignation: Each new set of facts became more horrifying than those presented in the previous issues of the *Lancet*. At last Wakley had found just what he was looking for: a case sensational enough to be reported by the newspapers all over the country in which the main character was a borough hospital surgeon who owed his appointment to nepotism and who was guilty of malpractice. This time Wakley's culprit was no unknown sawbones from one of the obscure hospitals but one of the sacred inner circle! The *Lancet's* brief, straightforward account left little doubt in any reader's mind that Bransby Cooper, surgeon at Guy's and nephew of Sir Astley Cooper, had, through incredible surgical bungling, killed a patient in what should have been a simple operation for kidney stone.

James Lambert, a *Lancet* reporter, had written the report initially, but Wakley had added the introduction: "It will be useful to the country 'draff' to learn how things are managed by one of the privileged order—a Hospital surgeon—nephew and surgeon, and surgeon because he is a nephew." At first the operation seemed to follow the usual routine. The patient, a sturdy Sussex laborer of 53, was bound to the table in the uncomfortable position customary for a lithotomy, hands tied to feet and knees to neck. Bransby Cooper made a quick incision, tried the forceps unsuccessfully, and, saying that he must enlarge the opening, called for his uncle's knife. There was another cut, another thrust with the forceps, the staff was jammed into the opening, a gorget was pushed in, then the forceps and a blunt gorget were applied, and finally a scoop. Meanwhile Bransby Cooper complained, "I can't reach the bladder with my finger. It is a very deep perinium. . . . I really can't conceive the difficulty. . . . Hush! Hush! Don't you hear the stone?" Then he asked the bystanders if anyone had a long finger? "Give me another instrument. Now I have it! Good God! I can hear the stone but the forceps won't touch it—Oh! Dear! Oh! Dear!" Meanwhile the poor patient—it would be eighteen years before a general anaesthetic would be used in a London hospital—kept crying, "Oh! Let it go—pray let it keep in!" The *Lancet* did not publish Cooper's reply, which came out in the testimony at the subsequent trial: "You were brought here to have the stone removed and removed it shall be if you die upon the table."[11] In light of future developments, this was a most unfortunate remark, to say the least.

After spending fifty five minutes on an operation that seldom took more than ten minutes, Cooper finally did get the stone that he flourished triumphantly in the forceps, turning from side to side so that everyone in the theater could see it while he subjected his shocked audience to a long, involved explanation, leaving the now unconscious patient still bound upon the table. That unfortunate man died the following evening without ever regaining consciousness. The postmortem showed that the perinium was not particularly deep, that the tissue surrounding the bladder was lacerated, and that an opening had been made between the bladder and the rectum.

Bransby Cooper was persuaded by his colleagues to sue Wakley for malicious libel, damages at £2,000. Just before the trial, Wakley announced that he would defend himself in person with the advice and help of his lawyer, Henry Brougham. Bransby Cooper's counsel was Sir James Scarlett, the former Tory attorney general who had led the government fight against the radical press, filing more charges against it than any of his predecessors or successors. When Scarlett stepped forward to open the case for the plaintiff, Wakley stopped him. Turning to the judge, Lord Tenterden, Wakley said that in cases in which the defendant admitted guilt but pleaded justifications without pleading the general issue, the defendant had the right to begin. He then referred the judge to three cases in which his claim had been upheld. Lord Tenterden went out of the courtroom to consult some of his colleagues and soon returned, deciding in Wakley's favor.

Quite apart from the Cooper case, this was a real triumph for Wakley and his fellow journalists. Lord Tenterden's ruling gave press defendants the right to open their cases and have the general replies. No longer would the Scarlett forces be able to denigrate public journalists without being subject to reply and exposure.[12] Wakley crowed with pleasure in the *Lancet:* "We maintained our point of law not only against Sir James Scarlett but against the opinion of our own counsel and we gained it!"[13] After an exciting trial, the jury gave the plaintiff £100, a verdict that was almost more insulting to Bransby Cooper than an out-and-out decision for Wakley would have been.

The Hospital Report of March 29, 1828, hit the London surgeons with an impact that was in a sense far greater than that produced by the load of German bombs that destroyed the Royal College of Surgeons Hall on the night of May 10, 1941. Yet when we look at the report today, it is difficult for us to understand why it was so shocking. By twentieth-century standards, it is a clever piece of journalism that could appear just as it was written in any news-magazine today. It was brief, and the tone, considering the literary excesses of the period, was usually restrained, even objective, yet because it was the first defiant challenge to the privileged surgeons who considered themselves above public criticism and even above the law, its impact was so powerful that it still reverberates in Harley Street more than a century and half later. The uproar it aroused shook London.

These protesters did not know it, but they were reacting against a completely new kind of investigative journalism and one that

Wakley used from 1828 onwards to publicize all his reform campaigns. His decision to print the Bransby Cooper case came not
by chance but as an essential step in his overall plan. According
to his specifications, the case he was looking for had to involve
either important people or sensational events, preferably both,
and it had to culminate either in a court action, as did the Cooper
case, or in a House of Commons Select Committee investigation,
as did his most spectacular exposé, the Andover workhouse bone-
crushing scandal. His method had an obvious flaw in that a
suitable case might not present itself after a painstaking and time-
consuming buildup. Yet when it did work, it was enormously
effective, producing a large audience that had been informed,
influenced, and often moved to action. On the whole, Wakley had
a good batting average. His method ultimately achieved the
appointment of eleven Select Committees from whose delibera-
tions came ten recommendations for measures that were
introduced in the Commons and later became the law of the land.
His method also equipped him with an enormous repertory of
accurate and usable information for which he became so well
known during his seventeen years in the House of Commons.[14]

Immediately after the Cooper case, two medical issues that
were vitally important to Wakley were subjected to the *Lancet*
investigative treatment. The first was concerned with the question
of how to get legal corpses for medical students and surgeons
without using those that the Burkites killed in slums or the Resur-
rection Men brought in from the graveyards. Wakley wanted a
Select Committee that would recommend the repeal of the anti-
quated government ruling that only the corpses of murderers
could be legally dissected, hardly a realistic solution to the problem since in 1828 only thirteen murderers were executed in
London, where the anatomy schools needed at least 2,000 bodies
a year. The *Lancet* campaign did get a Select Committee for
which Wakley, although he was not yet an M.P., named most of

the members and set many of the questions.[15] Wakley sabotaged the first Anatomy Bill in the House of Lords because it did not repeal the murderers' clause, and he accepted the second only after he had forced through enough legislation to prevent the RCS from monopolizing the sale of corpses to the medical students and anatomists.

The second issue was the uncontrolled operation of quacks of all kinds but particularly the untrained male and female midwives who were flooding the country, their ignorant blundering resulting in the deaths of thousands of women and infants.[16] In the Select Committee on Medical Education in 1834, Wakley set a question for the president of the RCS, asking what he thought should be done about quacks. George Guthrie proposed that quacks should pay fines for the privilege of practicing medicine and "also pay an annual license as a person takes out to shoot game,"[17] an answer so outrageous that it is difficult to take it seriously. Guthrie was, of course, simply reflecting the incredible legal ruling that held at that time that a British citizen should be protected in his right to choose untrained and unqualified practitioners if he so desired. There was no register of qualified doctors in Britain until 1858.

Although he hammered away at the issue in hundreds of pages of the *Lancet,* Wakley never did get an antiquack bill through the House of Commons. He did, however, by his own efforts, bring down one of the major quacks, the fashionable John St. John Long, who had killed two young women by painting their breasts and backs with lye. There ensued two dramatic, if incongruous, inquests and one court case, fully reported in the *Lancet,* in which Wakley, representing the two victims, became the prosecutor, challenging the lawyer-coroners, the judge, and Long's defense attorneys. Although Long was found guilty by the first coroner's jury, he got away with token fines because both the judge and the coroner had been bought off by Long's friend, the unsavory Lord

Slingo, whose collection of rare torture instruments was some years later purchased by Monckton Milnes for his museum of erotica. Wakley finally put Long out of business by hounding him in a long vindictive campaign in the *Lancet,* but he could never get a conviction of the quack through the law courts. He did make good use of the Long case as a terrible example when he campaigned for the election of doctors instead of lawyers as coroners. Long was certainly in his mind when he began his long struggle for a national register of all qualified doctors, the only effective weapon for ridding the world of quacks.

The fact that Wakley had neither been able to push through a decent Anatomy Bill on the first try nor to get parliamentary consideration for any legislation that would curb quacks who were such a grave threat to the public made him realize that in a country whose government was so little concerned with the medical safety of its citizens political reform would have to come first before anything could be done about medical reform. In January 1831 he turned his attention to the Reform Bill, establishing another weekly newspaper called the *Ballot,* which gave the public all the news of the bill's progress through Parliament as well as information about the newly organized national political unions. The *Ballot* was a stamped publication, something that annoyed the radicals who thought Wakley had betrayed the cause of the unstamped press. They forgot that Wakley never made any secret of the fact that he was a strong supporter of law and that he was constantly advising the public that "members of a civililzed society will ever find it more prudent to attempt to alter the law than obstinately to violate the law."[18]

Since Wakley never reported in the *Lancet* political news that did not relate to specific medical problems, he needed the *Ballot* to herald his now firm intention of running for the House of Commons. He may even have been planning to use the *Ballot* as a political *Lancet,* reporting in it the many other causes that he would later push in Parliament, causes unrelated to medical reform such as the secret ballot, the extension of the franchise, the abolition of flogging in the Army and Navy, and the reversal of the illegal transportation of the Tolpuddle Martyrs. In any event, Wakley ran short of money and time, and the *Ballot* ceased publication in November 1832, having been in existence just a month less than two years.[19]

On the night of October 16, 1834, a spectacular fire damaged the House of Lords and completely destroyed the House of Commons in ancient St. Stephens. It destroyed as well some of the adjacent buildings, one of which was the meeting place of Wakley's Committee of Medical Education. Two thirds of the incriminating evidence against the RCS, which had been wrung out of the witnesses by Wakley's searching questions, was burned or ruined by water from the fire engines. Wakley had worked ten years in the *Lancet* for that Committee, and he decided that from now on his reforms had to move faster than the *Lancet* could propel them.

In January 1835, three months after the fire, Wakley made his fourth try for a seat in the House of Commons. This time he triumphed, winning the place of member for Finsbury, one of the large new boroughs created by the Reform Act, a seat he filled for seventeen years. Henceforth the *Lancet* would continue to spearhead the movement for medical reform, but its campaigns would be reinforced by the direct actions of its editor. No longer would Wakley be working behind the scenes, setting up Select Committees and determining the scope of the questioning. He would be out on the floor of the Commons, presenting and defending his bills as they emerged from the committees.

In 1839 Wakley became the first doctor to be elected coroner of West Middlesex. For the next twenty-two years he worked ceaselessly, juggling his three great spheres of action, publicizing in the *Lancet* any cases from his coroner's court that he thought required legislation. These he presented himself in the House of Commons. His most famous case to which he gave this treatment was that of Private Frederick John White, the soldier who died in 1846 as the result of a particularly brutal military flogging. The facts about the flogging,[20] which Wakley brought out in his investigation as coroner, were publicized widely in the *Lancet* and later were used as the basis for another bill to stop flogging in the Army.

Wakley said he had named his magazine the *Lancet* because "a lancet can be an arched window to let in the light or it can be a sharp surgical instrument to cut out the dross and I intend to use it in both senses."[21] The *Lancet's* dual aim combined with Wakley's emphasis on reform and the need for professionalism had a strong impact on many forward-looking medical men—doctors, technicians, and scientists—who were trying to do nineteenth-century scientific work in a medical world still controlled by two medieval guilds, the Royal College of Surgeons and Physicians. For these men the *Lancet* opened the door to a new world. Every copy ran lively articles about what was being done in all aspects of medicine in the United Kingdom, France, Germany, and the United States. Some of these articles were written by well-established authorities, but many others came from young men who were still unknown. From its beginning the *Lancet* had been a meeting place and a wailing wall for men such as John Elliotson, the first physician to use the stethoscope, Erasmus Wilson, pioneer dermatologist, and William Farr, the founder of modern statistics, all of whom found in the journalism of Wakley the sense of professional identity so necessary to their work. Wakley encouraged them by lending them money and purchasing their articles for the *Lancet.* Much later on many of these beneficiaries returned the favor by lending their not inconsiderable skills to the *Lancet.*

It seems fitting to conclude this essay with the compliment paid by Lord Chancellor Eldon in 1825, which so pleased Wakley: "I feel it my duty to state that the *Lancet* appears to me to be a work of great utility, certainly of very great utility!"[22]

NOTES

1. Dr. Walter Channing correspondence in Wakley legal file from Potter, Sandford, and Congrove in possession of the author; see pamphlet "Hands Across the Sea," welcoming lecture given by Dr. Channing to the Anglo-American Society of Obstetricians, July 4, 1850, Countway Library of Medicine, Boston, Mass.

2. S. Squire Sprigge, *The Life and Times of Thomas Wakley* (London: Longmans, Green and Co., 1898), p. 109.

3. Ibid., p. 111.

4. Abernethy entry in *Dictionary of National Biography*, I, pp. 49-52; *Biographical Dictionary of the Society for the Diffusion of Useful Knowledge* (London: Longman, 1842), vol. 1, pp. 112-114.

5. Charles Brook, *The Battling Surgeon* (Glasgow: Strickland Press, 1945), p. 41.

6. Lord Eldon wrote Wakley a letter immediately after he dissolved the injunction. Unfortunately, it has not turned up.

7. Bentham said that he assumed people "only wanted to know what was good in order to embrace it." *The Works of Jeremy Bentham*, ed. J. Bowring (London, 1843), vol. 10, p. 66.

8. See Wakley's testimony in the *Select Committee for Anatomy* hearings, 1828, government publication, May 16, 1828, 1348-1384; *Lancet*, vol. 1834-35: 69-71.

9. This group formed the nucleus of support for all the House of Commons medical reform committees in 1837, 1838, and then later in the 1840s.

10. See references to Edward Harrison in S. W. F. Halloway, "The Apothecaries' Act of 1815: A Reinterpretation," Part I, 107-29; *Medical History* IO: 20 (1966); See p. 114.

11. *Lancet*, vol. 1827-28: 959-960; *Lancet*, vol. 1828-29: 353-373; J. F. Clarke, *Autobiographical Recollections of the Medical Profession* (London: Churchill, 1874), p. 56.

12. F. A. Carrington and J. Payne, *Reports of Cases of Nisi Prius* (London, 1841), vol. 3, pp. 474-480.

13. *Lancet*, vol. 1828-29: 376.

14. G. H. Francis, *Orators of the Age* (London: G. W. Nickisson, 1847), p. 316.

15. Warburton to Wakley, undated and unsigned, Wakley legal file, *Lancet* Diary for March-April 1828, with Sprigge Papers in the possession of the Macnemeny Foundation, Pasadena, California.

16. Ruth G. Hodgkinson, *The Origins of the National Health Service* (London: Wellcome Historical Medical Library, 1967), p. 137.

17. *Select Committee on Medical Education,* 1834 (602-II) XIII, 357, (RCS); III, George Guthrie, 4902 on page 26.

18. *Ballot,* June 26, 1831, p. 3.

19. The *Ballot* was succeeded by the *Voice from the Commons,* which was not a newspaper but a series of six pamphlets published weekly from April 23 to May 28, 1836, containing arguments for the removal of the stamp on the press.

20. Harry Hopkins, *The Strange Death of Private White* (London, 1977).

21. This statement has always been used as the motto of the *Lancet.*

22. *Lancet,* vol. April-September 1825: 379; also *Lancet,* vol. 1828-29, Introductory Address to Readers, p. 1.

George Spater

Cobbett, Hazlitt, and the *Edinburgh Review*

An interesting example of the historian's nightmare—a misstatement of fact that has been carried along uncorrected from generation to generation—came to light during the writing of my life of William Cobbett.[1] Those principally involved, in addition to Cobbett, were William Hazlitt and the *Edinburgh Review*.

In 1807 Hazlitt submitted three articles to Cobbett's *Register* and in 1810 a fourth one.[2] They were all on the same subject: They all attacked Thomas Malthus for his proposal that the government issue a regulation denying poor relief to children born from any marriage taking place after the expiration of a year from the issue of the regulation. According to Malthus, the poor man should be taught that the "laws of nature, which are the laws of God, had doomed him and his family to suffer for disobeying their repeated admonitions, that he had no claim of right upon society for the smallest portion of food beyond that which his labour would fairly purchase."[3] Malthus was convinced that cutting off relief for future offspring would slow down the increasing population. Cobbett had attacked Malthus, claiming that his proposal was illegal, cruel, and unwise, and Hazlitt wrote in support of Cobbett's position.

Hazlitt agreed with Cobbett on other issues as well and was a great admirer of Cobbett in general. A recent Cobbett biographer offers this explanation:

It is possible that the quarrelsome Hazlitt, so given to retrospection and so full of truculent honesty himself, understood Cobbett so well because he resembled him.[4]

Hazlitt's pen produced one of the finest descriptions of Cobbett written by any of his contemporaries:

People have about as substantial an idea of Cobbett as they have of Cribb. His blows are as hard, and he himself is as impenetrable. One has no notion of him as making use of a fine pen, but a great mutton-fist; his style stuns his readers. . . . He is too much for any single newspaper antagonist, 'lays waste' a city orator or Member of Parliament, and bears hard upon the Government itself. He is a kind of fourth estate in the politics of the country.

He is not only unquestionably the most powerful political writer of the present day, but one of the best writers in the language. He speaks and thinks plain, broad, downright English. He might be said to have the clearness of Swift, the naturalness of Defoe, and the picturesque satirical description of Mandeville; if all such comparisons were not impertinent. A really great and original writer is like nobody but himself.

The essay continues with further praise of Cobbett until one comes upon this strongly worded negative assessment:

Mr. Cobbett is great in attack, not in defence: he cannot fight an uphill battle. He will not bear the least punishing. If any one turns upon him (which few people like to do) he immediately turns tail. Like an overgrown school-boy he is so used to have it all his own way, that he cannot submit to any thing like competition or a struggle for the mastery: he must lay all the blows, and take none. He is bullying and cowardly; a Big Ben in politics, who will fall upon others and crush them by his weight, but is not prepared for resistance, and is soon staggered by a few smart blows. Whenever he has been set upon, he has slunk out of the controversy. The *Edinburgh Review* made (what is called) a dead set at him some years ago, to which he only retorted by a eulogy on the superior neatness of an English kitchen-garden to a Scotch one.[5]

This reference to the controversy with the *Edinburgh Review* is the only example Hazlitt cited in support of the assertion that Cobbett ever "slunk out" of a controversy, and although I have read the twenty or thirty million words making up Cobbett's published works, I have found no other situation that could reasonably be construed as slinking away from controversy.

This blot on Cobbett's character has stuck to him for the past century and a half. Cobbett himself never gave any sign that he had read Hazlitt's essay. And, strangely, all the principal Cobbett biographers have steered clear of Hazlitt's charge, although they have frequently quoted the good things Hazlitt had to say about their subject. No one apparently has ever made an effort to examine the facts behind Hazlitt's statement. If they had, they would have found that Hazlitt was completely wrong, and it is about time that the blot be removed.

First, a bit of background. During its early years the *Edinburgh Review* was only incidentally concerned with politics, although all four of its principal authors at the outset were staunch Whigs.[6] But by 1806 two of the four, Francis Horner and Henry Brougham, had left Edinburgh for London and had benefited from Whig patronage.[7] Prior to that time Cobbett had referred to the *Edinburgh Review* as a "very able, and, in many respects, excellent work."[8] But after Horner and Brougham entered the political arena, Cobbett began to express his disapproval of migrant Scots and, above all, migrant Scots who had fastened themselves on the government or who were endeavoring to do so and were promoting their ambitions by means of anonymous writings published in the *Edinburgh Review*. To Cobbett, who had an almost religious attitude toward the obligation of the press to remain uncontaminated by ulterior motives, officeholding by journalists was an indescribable abomination.

It was almost inevitable that Cobbett and the *Edinburgh Review* would clash. Cobbett thought even less of the Scots than had Dr. Johnson, and like most radical reformers, he hated the Whigs who boasted of their liberal principles yet did nothing to demonstrate that they meant them. It was also inevitable after Horner and Brougham became active politicians, that the *Edinburgh Review* would become involved in politics. The change took place with the issue of July 1807, an issue that, according to Lord Holland, first irrevocably stamped the review's character as a political publication.[9] Specifically, the issue of July 1807 contained a thirty-six page article on Cobbett's *Political Register*. It was written by Francis Jeffrey at the instigation of Henry Brougham.[10] It began with these words: "We are induced to take some notice of this Journal, because we are pursuaded that it has more influence with the most important and most independent class of society, which stands just above the lowest, than was ever possessed before by any similar publication." At a later point came the assertion that Cobbett himself "has more influence . . . than all the other journalists put together." This eulogistic preamble was offered as an explanation as to why Cobbett's wrong thinking (i.e., his attacks on the Tory and Whig ruling class) needed to be exposed.

The exposure fell mainly into two parts: a twelve-page demonstration of Cobbett's inconsistencies — principally his shift from conservative to radical — and a twenty-page essay on what Jeffrey called Cobbett's "pernicious and reprehensible" doctrines, chiefly Cobbett's claim that Parliament did not represent the people and should be reformed. Despite the widespread recognition that seats in the House of Commons were bought and sold and that a few hundred individuals controlled a working majority of the vote in the Commons, Jeffrey stoutly contended that the lower house as then constituted adequately represented "all the different opinions" in the country and reflected what he called the "balance of the constitution" since it contained persons who had obtained the influence of the "peers and the great families" and those chosen "in the consequence of their reputation or popularity with the majority of their electors."

The final few pages of Jeffrey's article consisted of a strange reversal of the middle section. It contained a long list of dangers that concerned Jeffrey, dangers almost identical to those Cobbett had been complaining of, and ended with the admission that the legislature had "recently exhibited some strange and alarming appearances."

One month after this "dead-set," as Hazlitt called it, appeared in the *Edinburgh Review, Cobbett's Weekly Political Register* (August 29) contained an article on Samuel Whitbread's bill to provide schools for children of the poor, a proposal based on the theory that education would reduce the numbers on poor relief.[11] Whitbread supported his proposal by pointing to the schooling provided in Scotland. Any claimed good coming from the Scots was sure to raise Cobbett's hackles. He hotly denied that the English could learn anything from them: "This notion about Scotch example," he wrote

seems to have come up amongst us with the juvenile economists, whom the late ministers drafted from the office of the Edinburgh Review, which is a sort of depot for speculators in politics, who go off, each in his turn, as he can make shift to write himself into place.

Cobbett claimed that Whitbread's reference to the Scottish example was "an outrage upon the orderly and honest and laborious . . . people of England . . . who, though pressed down with poverty, can, at their return from their daily labour, spend the twilight in works of neatness round their cottages," which he contrasted with the "garden-less and floorless and chimney-less cabbins [sic] of Scotland, where the master of the mansion nestles in at night in company with his pig or his cow."

Hazlitt assumed that this language, which was Cobbett's reply to Whitbread's education proposal, was Cobbett's response to the attack that had been made on him by the *Edinburgh Review*. But there is nothing in Cobbett's August article to suggest that he had ever read the July issue of the *Edinburgh Review*. It was common enough in those days for quarterlies to come out long after scheduled publication dates, and we know that Cobbett did not subscribe to the *Edinburgh Review,* which had a far smaller circulation than his *Political Register*. Whenever Cobbett wanted to see the *Edinburgh Review,* he borrowed a copy from someone.

Although Hazlitt's mistake may have been due to self-interest (he had contributed to the *Edinburgh Review* since 1815), it is more likely that it was due to his carelessness. Cobbett's reply to Jeffrey did not appear until October 17. The week before he gave notice of the impending tongue-lashing, adding:

I cannot say but I have a sneaking kindness for [them]. They have done a great deal of good in lashing the boobies and bastards that are fastened upon the public; but, what has long appeared to me evident, is, that they want to supplant them, and to fasten *themselves* upon us; rather than which I, for my part, who being somewhat gorged already, are likely to suck our blood less unmercifully than those northern leeches would. All I want to do, with respect to them, is to keep them *out of place.* If we can keep them from pocketing the public money, they will be, to use the obituary phrase, most "valuable members of society." This Review, with all their partiality, is, even now, worth all the other things, called Reviews, put together.[12]

In the following week, in the issue of October 17, Cobbett, as promised, dealt directly with the attack that had been made on him.[13] No one who reads this article could contend that Cobbett turned tail or slunk out of the controversy. To Jeffrey's claim of his inconsistency, Cobbett pointed out that he had already publicly explained on more than one occasion why he had left the Tories and became a radical. The *Edinburgh Review* itself had been guilty of inconsistency, but its inconsistency, unlike Cobbett's, had been due to selfish motives. In 1804 the *Edinburgh*

Review had condemned a proposal to conciliate the Irish Catholics, and three years later, when the party allegiance of its principal authors had shifted, it endorsed a similar proposal. The April 1807 issue of the *Edinburgh Review* criticized the system of parliamentary patronage, and three months later, it condoned it. The editors of the Scottish journal were accused of cowardice, of "selfish motives, and . . . profligate principles," of being hunters "after the public money," and of willful misrepresentation, phrases hardly calculated to avoid further dispute.[14]

There is no indication in Cobbett's conduct after 1807 that he was endeavoring to avoid a continued controversy. He ran one article after another from correspondents attacking the *Edinburgh Review*.[15] Nor was he personally idle; he kept up a continuous flow of invective directed at the contributors and the editors of the journal. He did on occasion have a nice word to say about the *Review*, but, as in the example already quoted, he often coupled the praise with condemnation.[16] In his weekly articles he called them from time to time "parasites and place-hunters," "arrogant and stupid place-hunters," "shoeless Scotch hirelings," "toad eaters," "conceited, arrogant and ignorant," "spiteful and stupid" and "Scotch blood-hounds."[17] He also accused them of "shallowness"; of a desire to pocket "the public money, to live upon the labour of the people . . . to fatten upon the cowardice and the credulity of the nation"; of "vulgar notions"; of the "most profound ignorance that ever disgraced the human mind"[18] As to the magazine itself, Cobbett claimed that it was the "very basest of the periodical publications" and a "depot for speculators in politics."[19] None of which, to me at least, sounds as though he was running from an argument.

If either of the parties can be said to have turned tail, it was the *Edinburgh Review*. In 1807 Cobbett was for parliamentary reform and the *Edinburgh Review* was opposed. Cobbett remained an advocate throughout his life, while during that period the

Edinburgh Review was converted from opponent to supporter. Indeed, the process began within eighteen months after the 1807 episode, when the *Edinburgh Review* ran two articles disavowing the very principles that were at the core of Jeffrey's argument: the position that the crown and nobility should be represented in the House of Commons in order to provide "constitutional balance" and the position that there was no need for a reform of the House of Commons.[20]

During the fifteen years following the 1807 attack on him, Cobbett kept up his assaults on the *Edinburgh Review,* as the long list of quotations suggests. The *Review,* in return, maintained a policy of discreet nonbelligerence,[21] impelling Cobbett in 1822 to announce that the editors of the journal "are not quite dead, though sinking fast to the grave." A week later he threw an additional goad in their direction when he mentioned the *Review* followed by the comment "if their book be yet alive."[22]

In 1823 the lamented Scots proved their continued existence in a surprising manner. The year before Cobbett had published one of his most charming and useful books, *Cottage Economy,* in which he showed how a farm laborer could get the most out of his small income. The February 1823 issue of the *Edinburgh Review* included a twenty-one page commentary on *Cottage Economy,* finding it "an excellent little book—written not only with admirable clearness and good sense, but in a very earnest and entertaining manner—and abounding with kind and good feelings as well as with most valuable information." It urged "all persons in easy circumstances, who live in the country," to distribute "these little books" to the neighboring poor.[23]

Cottage Economy is an excellent book, and Cobbett knew it without being told. He wrote that "every person, ought, upon pain of loss of ears, to present [a copy] to every girl he marries, rich or poor."[24] Hence Cobbett probably found nothing strange in the nice things the *Edinburgh Review* said about it. What was surprising was that it was reviewed at all since after Cobbett had turned reformer, the polite press almost uniformly refused to recognize the existence of any of his books.

The review of *Cottage Economy* was followed three months later by another remarkable article in the *Edinburgh Review* that referred to Cobbett. Entitled "The Periodical Press," this is what it said about him:

Of the Weekly Journalists, Cobbett stands first in power and popularity. Certainly he has earned the latter; would that he abused the former less! We once tried to cast this Antaeus to the ground; but the earth-born rose again, and still staggers on, blind or one-eyed, to his remorseless, restless purpose—sometimes running upon posts and pitfalls—sometimes shaking a country to its centre. It is best to say little about him, and keep out of his way; for he crushes, by his ponderous weight, whomsoever he falls upon; and what is worse, drags to cureless ruin whatever cause he lays his hands upon to support.[25]

This was written, it must be noted, before Cobbett's great victories on behalf of Catholic Emancipation and parliamentary reform. Cobbett might reasonably have found the article more objectionable than the "dead-set" of 1807, but he took no notice of it for three years. He may not have known of it, or, more likely, he knew of it but decided to bide his time. In the intervening period he regularly condemned the *Edinburgh Review* for its views on various subjects, intermingled with an occasional patronizing pat on the back. He even coined some new names for the editors of the magazine, "old shuffle-breeches" and "hireling hacks" and some new descriptions of their work: "Dark and deep heeps of rubbish" and "prime piece of Scotch humbug."[26]

In 1826 Cobbett wrote his reply to the Antaeus article. The occasion was the notorious failure of Archibald Constable & Co., publishers of the *Edinburgh Review*. Although, as it turned out, the journal managed to find another publisher and continue for another 103 years, Cobbett saw the Constable failure as a serious blow, perhaps even a mortal blow, to the quarterly publication. His article was headed "Scotch Humbug Blown to the Devil."[27]

Whereas the *Edinburgh Review* had claimed three years before that Cobbett had brought to ruin every "cause he lays his hands upon to support," Cobbett now suggested that the magazine had brought to ruin Constable and repeated many of the charges he had previously leveled against the publication: They had never been right on any issue; they were "conceited, pert, arrogant, impudent and insolent coxcombs"; they were adventurers who "look upon the mass of the people *as cattle,* to be used for the *benefit of some master,* with whom the adventurers constantly endeavour [to] *come in for a share."* As for the classical reference, Cobbett denied the Antaeus label, claiming that it belonged to the *Edinburgh Review* and that he was Hercules, the destroyer of Antaeus.

Following this exchange, matters returned to their former status. Cobbett coined some new gibes, such as "pertinacious, stupid, perverse brutes," "base old hacks," "batch of fools," and "conceited Scotch fellows."[28] The *Review* itself was given a splendid new name: "Old Mother Mange."[29] It was not a review at all, declared Cobbett, but a "periodical set of essays the object of which is to get public money into the pockets of the writers." Cobbett claimed that after Pitt's death "truly frightful" Scots had flooded London: "crowds of gaunt and impudent fellows, strutting about, with red hair, freckled skins and high cheek bones."[30]

The last quoted comment was in 1830, five years before Cobbett's death. More than seventy years were to pass before the old quarrel was revived. In 1907, the hundredth anniversary of the 1807 article, long after all the individuals originally involved had left the scene, the *Edinburgh Review* ran a long article on Cobbett, which endeavored to do justice to the man. The author was J. L. Hammond, writing four years before the publication of his book *The Village Labourer.*[31]

The first paragraph of Hammond's article harked back to the quarterly's attack of 1807:

Exactly a century ago, in July 1807, the *Edinburgh Review* devoted an article to an analysis of the political past of William Cobbett. That fact alone was an important compliment to his position . . . if the *Edinburgh Review* thought that Cobbett's vicissitudes and changes were worth attention and study, it was not merely because these changes had been unusually violent and unusually conspicuous. It was rather because Cobbett had forced his way by the sheer power of his character into a position where everything that he did or said was of moment and importance to the nation.

And the objectivity gained through the passage of a century enabled the journal, which had once severely chided Cobbett for his inconsistency, to discover that there had been after all some "essential unity" in Cobbett's conduct.:

Quarrelsome and contentious as he was, changeable and arbitrary as he seemed, he had throughout a public and disinterested object; and that object was constant and real. What distinguished Cobbett was that he saw more vividly than anybody else what was happening in England: how the England in which he had been born . . . was changing all its features . . . how the new England which was springing up was an England unkind and inhospitable to the poor.

The final paragraph of this final word in the century-old contest contains a summary of Cobbett's place in history. It ends with these words:

He was a great tribune of the Poor, and in spite of his wild excesses, his bitter and often unjust maledictions, his rancour, his brawls, his raw judgements, his crude dogmatism, he had a great and spacious conception of the politics of his country. In everything that he did and wrote he set himself, by every means that could bring him into touch with the imagination of the people, to arrest the impoverishment of a race and to dethrone the fatal doctrine that the rich could be trusted to act for the poor.

Not a bad summary for a man whose complicated character cannot be fully encompassed within a two-volume biography.

NOTES

1. George Spater, *William Cobbett: The Poor Man's Friend,* 2 volumes (Cambridge: Cambridge University Press, 1982).

2. Articles signed "A.O.," 11 PR 397, 883, 935; article signed "The Author of a Reply to the Essay on Population," 18 PR 1014.

3. *An Essay on the Principle of Population,* Bk. 4, ch. 7.

4. James Sambrook, *William Cobbett* (London: Routledge and Kegan Paul, 1973), p. 191.

5. *The Spirit of the Age* (1825), pp. 223, 234-235. The essay had been published four years earlier in *Table Talk.*

6. John Clive, *Scotch Reviewers: The "Edinburgh Review," 1802-1815* (London: Faber and Faber, 1957), p. 66 n. 3.

7. Horner, who had gone to London in 1803, was appointed to the board of commissioners dealing with the claims of the creditors of the nabob of Arcot in February 1806; Brougham settled in London in 1805 and became secretary to a mission to Portugal in 1806.

8. PR 368.

9. Clive, *Scotch Reviewers,* p. 104.

10. *Edinburgh Review* 386-421, July 1807; Cobbett claimed (12 PR 577-578) that the attack on him was motivated by his article of March 21, 1807 (11 PR 440), in which he referred to the "increasing brood of 'young friends' " of Lord Henry Petty, drawing their nourishment from the "paps" of the country. Petty, chancellor of the Exchequer in the short-lived Ministry of all the Talents, was a friend of the principle *Edinburgh Review* authors. Cobbett attacked Petty's young friends again in 12 PR 335.

11. 12 PR 327-328.

12. 12 PR 556; Cobbett's attention had been called to the *Edinburgh Review* attack by letters from correspondents, one published September 5 and another dated September 28 (12 PR 373, 600). At least one regular reader of the *Edinburgh Review,* Leveson-Gower, did not read the article in the July *Edinburgh Review* until September 25 (Clive, *Scotch Reviewers,* p. 106 n.4).

13. 12 PR 577-594.

14. 12 PR 577, 581, 588.

15. 12 PR 600, 722, 824, 982; 16 PR 444, 449, 547; 17 PR 529, 631.

16. See 12 PR 556, 684; 14 PR 906; 15 PR 179-180; 16 PR 770; 19 PR 1193; 29 PR 391.

17. 12 PR 684; 13 PR 169; 19 PR 718; 27 PR 739; 37 PR 1679; 38 PR 130; 40 PR 209, 702. Also "poor hungry lads," "cunning loons," "dull," "hired writers," "hungry and mercilous band." 13 PR 903; 19 PR 718; 27 PR 739; 37 PR 608; 41 PR 187.

18. 19 PR 965, 1193; 29 PR 398; 37 PR 1638. See also 41 PR 81.

19. 19 PR 1193 and 39 PR 618. Other criticism by Cobbett of the *Edinburgh Review* appears in 12 PR 688; 13 PR 395; 14 PR 322; 16 PR 758, 798; 18 PR 104, 177, 197; 19 PR 902; 29 PR 363; 36 PR 759; 39 PR 508; 40 PR 962, 974.

20. 13 *Edinburgh Review* 185-205, 215-234, October 1808; Clive, *Scotch Reviewers*, pp. 110ff.; for Cobbett's reaction to the turnabout, see 14 PR 906.

21. After the 1807 attack, the *Edinburgh Review's* comments on Cobbett were few and restrained: 14 *Edinburgh Review* 302-303, July 1809; 15 *Edinburgh Review* 509, January 1810; 20 *Edinburgh Review* 320, 449, November 1812. Little or nothing appeared in the *Edinburgh Review* between 1812 and 1822.

22. 43 PR 89, 154.

23. 38 *Edinburgh Review*, 105-125, February 1823.

24. 71 PR 173.

25. 38 *Edinburgh Review* 368, May 1823.

26. 57 PR 68, 260-261.

27. 57 PR 257-284. Until Constable's failure, the *Edinburgh Review* was published by Constable in conjunction with Longman of London. Afterwards it was published by Longman, Hurst, Rees, Orme, Brown and Green, and Adam Black of Edinburgh.

28. 61 PR 78; 66 PR 16; 67 PR 640.

29. 67 PR 639, 800.

30. 70 PR 388.

31. 206 *Edinburgh Review* 128-148. Mr. Ian Dyck, University of Sussex, has called my attention to the article by Martin Wiener, "The Changing Image of William Cobbett," *Journal of British Studies* 13 (1974): 143 n.27, in which the author of the *Edinburgh Review* essay is identified as J. L. Hammond.

Bibliographical Essay

In recent years Victorian journalism has become something of a growth industry in the academic world. A professional organization, the Research Society for Victorian Periodicals (RSVP), was founded in 1969 for the purpose of promoting research in this area. It has sponsored a number of important activities, including the preparation of several bibliographies. At present it is coordinating the publication of a major reference work that will describe several hundred nineteenth-century serials. RSVP's journal, the *Victorian Periodicals Review,* edited at Southern Illinois University, is published quarterly and includes many articles on aspects of Victorian journalism. Academic conferences have been held in both Great Britain and North America on the theme of the press. Likewise, the annual "Victorian Bibliography," compiled by *Victorian Studies,* with its many references to work being done on the press, attests to the increasing importance of this subject.

Much of this work on the Victorian press contains useful information about editors. *The Wellesley Index to Victorian Periodicals, 1824-1900,* edited by Walter E. Houghton, 3 volumes (Toronto: University of Toronto Press, 1966, 1972, 1979), which has undertaken the task of identifying the authors of articles in leading journals, contains a great deal of fascinating information about the editors of these journals in its excellent introductions. It is a starting point for work on Victorian editors. Back issues of the *Victorian Periodicals Review* (formerly the *Victorian Periodicals Newsletter*) and *Victorian Studies* should be perused carefully. Two significant bibliographical projects contain helpful references to editors: J. Don Vann and Rosemary T. VanArsdel, eds., *Victorian Periodicals: A Guide to Research* (New York: The Modern Language Association of America, 1978), and Lionel Madden and Diana Dixon, *The Nineteenth-Century Periodical Press in Britain: A Bibliography of Modern Studies* (Toronto: Victorian Periodicals Newsletter, 1975). The former volume consists of miscellaneous essays on aspects of Victorian periodicals research; the latter is an impressive listing of books, articles, and unpublished theses dealing with the Victorian press. Its section entitled "Studies and Memoirs of Proprietors, Editors, Journalists and Contributors" is particularly helpful. The most comprehensive source for biographical information about editors is the *Dictionary of National Biography,* though it is dated and generally limited only to better known journalists. A similar reservation applies to Frederic Boase, *Modern English Biography,* 6 volumes (1892-1921), and to other standard biographical sources such as *Men and Women of the Time: A Dictionary of Contemporaries* (1852-1901, then incorporated into *Who's Who*) and *Chambers's Biographical Dictionary* (1897, subsequently reprinted and expanded several times). William H. Scheuerle's essay on "Biographical Resources" in Vann and VanArsdel, *Victorian Periodicals,* pp. 64-80, provides guidelines for using such research tools. Not covered by Scheuerle are several recent biographical projects in related areas that include material about editors. The best of these are the *Biographical Dictionary of Modern British Radicals: Volume I: 1770-1830*, ed. Joseph O. Baylen and Norbert J. Gossman (Hassocks, Sussex: Harvester Press, 1979); the *Dictionary of Labour Biography*, ed. John Saville and Joyce Bellamy, 6 volumes (London: Macmillan, 1972-1982); and the *Encyclopaedia of Unbelief*, ed. Gordon Stein (Buffalo, New York: Prometheus Books, 1985).

There is no up-to-date general history of the British press, and so one must turn to older works for information about editors. Of these, Henry R. Fox Bourne, *English Newspapers: Chapters in the History of Journalism*, 2 volumes (London: Chatto and Windus, 1887), is the best. It includes a considerable amount of information about editors as well as balanced judgments about developments in the press. However, because it was published in the 1880s, it lacks perspective on such an important phenomenon as the rise of a new journalism. James Grant, *The Newspaper Press: Its Origin – Progress – and Present Opinion*, 3 volumes (London: Tinsley Brothers, 1871-1872), though more complete than Bourne in its accounts of individual newspapers, was published almost two decades earlier and is difficult to use because it lacks an index. T. H. S. Escott, *Masters of English Journalism: A Study of Personal Forces* (London: T. Fisher Unwin, 1911), is by a journalist who had almost unrivaled knowledge of the late nineteenth-century press. Its emphasis on the personal element in journalism is particularly relevant for a study of editors. Other general press histories that contain information about editors include Joseph Hatton, *Journalistic London: Being a Series of Sketches of Famous Pens and Papers of the Day* (London: Sampson Low, Marston, Searle, and Rivington, 1882), an impressionistic study that concentrates on the late Victorian scene; H. Simonis, *The Street of Ink: An Intimate History of*

Journalism (London: Cassell and Company, 1917), an anecdotal history of individual newspapers, which emphasizes the increasing division between editing and other branches of journalism; and William Hunt, *Then and Now; or, Fifty Years of Newspaper Work* (Hull, 1887), a useful personal account of the provincial press by a newspaperman who worked extensively in the West Country.

Of more recent general books dealing with journalism, the late Stephen Koss's magisterial two-volume *The Rise and Fall of the Political Press in Britain* (London: Hamish Hamilton, 1981, 1984) is indispensable for an understanding of political editing, particularly the relationship between editors and politicians. John Gross, *The Rise and Fall of the Man of Letters: Aspects of English Literary Life Since 1800* (London: Weidenfeld and Nicolson, 1969), though not a work of original scholarship, includes some brilliant analyses of the editors of leading literary magazines, including George Henry Lewes, Walter Bagehot, and Robert Holt Hutton. Joanne Shattock and Michael Wolff, eds., *The Victorian Periodical Press: Samplings and Soundings* (Leicester: Leicester University Press, 1982), has suggestive general references to editing in its introduction as well as two important essays that deal specifically with editors: Sheila Rosenberg, "The Financing of Radical Opinion: John Chapman and the *Westminster Review,*" which is concerned not only with Chapman (an often overlooked editor) but also with the texture and the shape of editing, and Donald Gray, "Early Victorian Scandalous Journalism: Renton Nicholson's *The Town,*" which examines the unsavory practices of several editors. Similarly, a few of the essays in George Boyce, James Curran, and Pauline Wingate, eds., *Newspaper History: From the Seventeenth Century to the Present Day* (London: Constable, 1978), provide insights into the role of editors, especially Anthony Smith, "The Long Road to Objectivity and Back Again: The Kinds of Truth We Get in Journalism," and

Virginia Berridge, "Popular Sunday Papers and Mid-Victorian Society." Alan J. Lee's *The Origins of the Popular Press in England, 1855-1914* (London: Croom Helm, 1976) is an important book that is concerned primarily with the interaction between economic change and a liberal vision of the press. Its chapter on "The Old Journalism and the New" is illuminating about the evolving professionalism of editors.

Several writers have attempted to place the editor in a journalistic context. The most interesting is by Leslie Stephen, "The Evolution of Editors," in his *Studies of a Biographer* (New York: G. P. Putnam's Sons, 1898), vol. 1, pp. 37-73, which examines the history of editing in the late eighteenth century and documents the increasing separation between proprietors and editors. "E. T. Raymond" (Edward Raymond Thompson), *Portraits of the Nineties* (London: T. Fisher Unwin, 1921), shows how the function of editors became transformed again in the late nineteenth century, this time as between independent editors and management. Lucy Maynard Salmon's chapter, "The Editor and the Editorial," in her book *The Newspaper and the Historian* (London: Oxford University Press, 1923), though based on secondary sources, includes information about leader writing and the impersonality of modern editing. In addition to his *Masters of English Journalism,* T. H. S. Escott has written about editors. An essay by him entitled "Literature and Journalism," *Fortnightly Review,* n.s. vol. 91 (1912): 115-130, analyzes how late-Victorian editors absorbed and incorporated literary influences into popular journalism. Two chapters in his book *Platform, Press, Politics and Play: Being Pen and Ink Sketches of Contemporary Celebrities* (Bristol: J. W. Arrowsmith, 1894) deal with bohemian journalism, an underestimated aspect of the history of the press that nurtured many fine editors.

A considerable number of influential editors have not yet been the subject of full-sized biographies. But some good biographies have been published and a few more are in the pipeline. The two great editors of *The Times,* Thomas Barnes and John Thaddeus Delane, have been extensively written about. Derek Hudson, *Thomas Barnes of "The Times"* (Cambridge: Cambridge University Press, 1943), is a well-written study that attempts to make the case for Barnes as "the first truly responsible and independent editor in English journalism." There are two biographies of Delane that are worth reading: Arthur I. Dasent, *John Thaddeus Delane, Editor of "The Times": His Life and Correspondence,* 2 volumes (London: John Murray, 1908), a massive work that draws heavily on his letters, and Sir Edward Cook, *Delane of "The Times"* (London: Constable and Company, 1915), a shorter study that concludes with a judicious chapter on "The Influence of Delane." James A. Davies, *John Forster: A Literary Life* (Leicester: Leicester University Press, 1983), deals primarily with Forster's literary friendships and helps pinpoint his creative abilities as the editor of the *Daily News* and the *Examiner.* Priscilla Metcalf, *James Knowles: Victorian Editor and Architect* (Oxford: Clarendon Press, 1980), is an intelligent biography of a leading Victorian who combined the professions of architect and editor *(Contemporary Review, Nineteenth Century).* J. Saxon Mill, *Sir Edward Cook, K.B.E.: A Biography* (London: Constable and Company, 1921), is a somewhat dated account of one of the key editors of the late-Victorian period, a man who helped shape the history of the *Daily News,* the *Pall Mall Gazette,* and the *Westminster Gazette.*

Among other biographies of editors, Arthur A. Adrian, *Mark Lemon: First Editor of "Punch"* (London: Oxford University Press, 1966), is a work of careful analysis and scholarship. It is considerably better than George Somes Layard's account of Lemon's successor as the editor of the humor magazine, *A Great "Punch" Editor: Being the Life, Letters, and Diaries of Shirley Brooks* (London: Sir Isaac Pitman and Sons, 1907). A fine recent biography is Stephen Koss, *Fleet Street Radical: A. G. Gardiner and the "Daily News"* (Hamden, Connecticut: Archon Books, 1973). Gardiner's career stretched well into the twentieth century, but he began work as a journalist in the late-Victorian years, and there is much of interest about this period in Koss's book. H. W. Massingham, an important contemporary of Gardiner who edited the *Star*, the *Daily Chronicle*, and the *Nation*, is less well served in Alfred F. Havighurst, *Radical Journalist: H. W. Massingham (1860-1924)*, a somewhat prolix account of his life. W. T. Stead, a pioneer of the new journalism, is not yet the recipient of the detailed biography he deserves. But Joseph O. Baylen, "W. T. Stead and the 'New Journalism' ", *Emory University Quarterly* 21 (1965): 196-206, is a perspicuous analysis of his contribution to a popular press; Raymond L. Schults, *Crusader in Babylon: W. T. Stead and the "Pall Mall Gazette"* (Norman, Oklahoma: University of Oklahoma Press, 1972), though not based on archival research, is a balanced account of an important aspect of his career. Joel H. Wiener, *Radicalism and Freethought in Victorian Britain: The Life of Richard Carlile* (Westport, Connecticut: Greenwood Press, 1983), analyzes the contribution to journalism of an early nineteenth-century radical editor. George Spater does likewise in his monumental, two-volume study, *William Cobbett: The Poor Man's Friend* (Cambridge: Cambridge University Press, 1982). Algar Labouchere Thorold, *The Life of Henry Labouchere* (London: G. P. Putnam's Sons, 1913), concentrates on his subject's political career and contains useful information about Labouchere's editorship of *Truth*. Reginald Lucas, *Lord Glenesk and the "Morning Post"* (London: Alston Rivers, 1910), is a lightweight study that adds little to an understanding of Algernon Borthwick's significant achievements as a journalist. Similarly lacking a scholarly base is Leonard E. Naylor, *The Irrepressible Victorian: The Story of Thomas Gibson Bowles, Journalist, Parliamentarian and Founder Editor of the Original "Vanity Fair"* (London: MacDonald, 1965).

Studies of individual newspapers and journals shed some light on the role of editors. *The History of "The Times"*, 5 volumes (London: *The Times*, 1935-84), is a narrative account that draws extensively on archival material in the possession of the newspaper. It is enlightening not only about the paper's well-known editors but also about a large number of subeditors and assistant editors. David Ayerst, *The "Manchester Guardian": Biography of a Newspaper* (Ithaca, New York: Cornell University Press, 1971), though not as imposing in scope, is almost as good, especially in its treatment of the paper's three nineteenth-century editors, Jeremiah Garnett, Edward Taylor, and C. P. Scott. Lord Burnham, *Peterborough Court: The Story of the "Daily Telegraph"* (London: Cassell and Company, 1955), is a gossipy history of this famous newspaper, which has only cursory references to its editors. J. W. Robertson Scott, *The Story of the "Pall Mall Gazette," of its First Editor, Frederick Greenwood, and of its Founder, George Murray Smith* (London: Oxford University Press, 1950), though somewhat rambling, is a useful study of the paper under the editorship of Greenwood (1865-1880).

Histories of magazines are more abundant and, on the whole, better than those of newspapers. M. H. Spielmann, *The History of "Punch"* (London: Cassell and Company, 1895), is a detailed account of this great comic journal, which contains an enormous amount of information about its editors. Leslie A. Marchand, *The "Athenaeum": A Mirror of Victorian Culture* (Chapel Hill, North Carolina: The University of North Carolina Press, 1941), is strongest in its analysis of the career of Sir Charles Dilke, one of its outstanding editors. Merle M. Bevington, *The "Saturday Review," 1855-1868: Representative Educated Opinion in Victorian England* (New York: Columbia University Press, 1941), is primarily concerned with the journal as an index of leading critical opinion and is insightful about its first and greatest editor,

John Douglas Cook. Edwin Mallard Everett, *The Party of Humanity: The "Fortnightly Review" and Its Contributors, 1865-1874* (Chapel Hill, North Carolina: The University of North Carolina Press, 1939), emphasizes the magazine's intellectual strengths during the editorship of John Morley. Janet Courtney, *The Making of an Editor: W. L. Courtney, 1850-1918* (London: Macmillan and Company, 1930), is basically the story of the *Fortnightly Review* and of its distinguished editor Leonard Courtney at a later stage in its history.

Joseph L. Altholz, *The Liberal Catholic Movement in England: The "Rambler" and Its Contributors, 1848-1864* (London: Burns and Oates, 1962), is an excellent study of the *Rambler* and its two notable editors, Richard Simpson and Sir John Acton. Alan Willard Brown, *The Metaphysical Society: Victorian Minds in Crisis, 1869-1880* (New York: Columbia University Press, 1947), documents the history of the *Contemporary Review* in its early years and of its editor, James Knowles. William Beach Thomas, *The Story of the "Spectator," 1828-1928* (London: Methuen, 1928), is a worthwile centennial volume; its accounts of its two great Victorian editors, Robert Stephen Rintoul and Richard Holt Hutton, are enlightening. Richmond P. Bond, *The "Tatler": The Making of a Literary Journal* (Cambridge, Massachusetts: Harvard University Press, 1972), is a scholarly study of this literary magazine and its editors. Also worth reading is *"The Economist," 1843-1943: A Centenary Volume* (London: Oxford University Press, 1943), which includes two essays on Walter Bagehot, who edited the magazine from 1860 to 1877.

There are many memoirs by and about Victorian editors. Among the best are those by two editors discussed in this book: Samuel Carter Hall, *Retrospect of a Long Life: From 1815 to 1883,* 2 volumes (London: Bentley and Son, 1883), and Edmund Yates, *His Recollections and Experiences,* 2 volumes (London: Richard Bentley and Son, 1884). Anthony Trollope, *An*

Autobiography (London: Oxford University Press, 1950, first published in 1883), is a deservedly classic work, although it is none too revealing about his work as an editor. *Fifty Years of Fleet Street: Being the Life and Recollections of Sir John R. Robinson,* ed. Frederick Moy Thomas (London: Macmillan and Company, 1904), is based on diaries and is first rate on the inner workings of the *Daily News,* which Robinson managed for several decades. Another important account by an editor who was primarily a manager is Thomas Catling, *My Life's Pilgrimage* (London: John Murray, 1911). Catling wrote "fillers" for *Lloyd's Weekly Newspaper* for more than fifty years (his first idea was accepted after thirty-six years on the paper), and he provides a great deal of information about journalism. Sir Joseph Crowe, *Reminiscences of Thirty-Five Years of My Life* (London: John Murray, 1895), by a foreign correspondent for the *Daily News,* the *Illustrated London News,* and *The Times,* has some interesting recollections of editors.

Henry Vizetelly, *Glances Back Through Seventy Years: Autobiographical and Other Reminiscences,* 2 volumes (London: Kegan Paul, Trench, Trubner and Company, 1893), is among the best journalistic memoirs. It is especially good on the earlier phase of Vizetelly's career when he edited the *Illustrated Times.* Less useful is Charles Mackay, *Forty Years' Recollections of Life, Literature, and Public Affairs from 1830 to 1870,* 2 volumes (London: Chapman and Hall, 1877). Mackay was a minor journalist who worked as a subeditor on the *Morning Chronicle* and as the managing editor of the *Illustrated London News* in the 1850s. *The Life and Adventures of George Augustus Sala, Written by Himself,* 2 volumes (London: Cassell and Company, 1895), though somewhat unreliable about factual matters, is a major account by a great Victorian journalist who never actually became an editor. William Edwin Adams, *Memoirs of a Social Atom,* 2 volumes (London, 1903; reprinted New York: Augustus Kelley,

1967), is by a freethinker who edited the *Newcastle Weekly Chronicle* for thirty-six years. Frank Harris, *My Life and Loves* (New York: Grove Press, 1963; first published in 1923), is less revealing about Harris's career as the editor of the *Evening News, the Fortnightly Review,* and the *Saturday Review* than it is about his alleged sexual escapades. The five volumes of reminiscences by the political journalist Henry W. Lucy—*Sixty Years in the Wilderness* (London: John Murray, 1909, 1912, 1916) and *The Diary of a Journalist* (London: John Murray, 1920, 1922)—are informative about editors he knew as well as about changes in journalism. Other volumes of memoirs that contain interesting references to Victorian editors are Percy Fitzgerald, *Memoirs of an Author,* 2 volumes (London: Richard Bentley and Son, 1894); W. P. Frith, *My Autobiography and Reminiscences* (London: Richard Bentley and Son, 1888); William Tinsley, *Random Recollections of an Old Publisher* (London: Simpkin, Marshall, Kent and Company, 1900); Sir Francis C. Burnand, *Records and Reminiscences: Personal and General,* 2 volumes (London: Methuen, 1904); *Autobiography of Sir Walter Besant* (New York: Dodd, Mead and Company, 1902); and George Hodder, *Memories of My Time: Including Personal Reminiscences of Eminent Men* (London: Tinsley Brothers, 1870).

Some interesting volumes have been published that deal with the relationship between publishers and editors. John C. Francis, *John Francis, Publisher of the Athenaeum: A Literary Chronicle of Half a Century,* 2 volumes (London: Richard Bentley and Son, 1888), contains material about Francis's relationships with several editors, including Dilke. Samuel Smiles, *A Publisher and His Friends: Memoir and Correspondence of the Late John Murray, with an Account of the Origin and Progress of the House, 1768-1843,* 2 volumes (London: John Murray, 1891), is informative about John Murray, an interventionist publisher who was a part-owner of *Blackwood's Edinburgh Magazine* and for a time the owner of the *Quarterly Review.* Murray was frequently embroiled in disputes with his editors. Mrs. Oliphant, *Annals of a Publishing House: William Blackwood and His Sons, Their Magazine and Friends,* 3 volumes (Edinburgh: William Blackwood and Sons, 1897), is a monumental work that is chock-full of letters about literary and editorial entanglements. Leonard Huxley, *The House of Smith Elder* (London, 1923), has material on the *Cornhill Magazine* and, specifically, on James Payn's editorship from 1883 to 1896. Royal A. Gettmann, *A Victorian Publisher: A Study of the Bentley Papers* (Cambridge: Cambridge University Press, 1960), deals with the firm's publication of *Bentley's Miscellany* and *Temple Bar.* Charles Morgan, *The House of Macmillan (1843-1943)* (London: The Macmillan Company, 1943), sheds light on the contacts between the publishing house and those who edited its famous journal, *Macmillan's Magazine.*

The development of editing as a profession is a subject that has not attracted much attention. A. Aspinall, "The Social Status of Journalists at the Beginning of the Nineteenth Century," *The Review of English Studies* 21 (1945): 216-232, is a somewhat exaggerated account of the disreputable standing of journalists in the pre-Victorian years. A more balanced analysis is found in Lenore O'Boyle, "The Image of the Journalist in France, Germany, and England, 1815-1848," *Comparative Studies in Society and History* 10 (1968): 290-317. Christopher Kent, "Higher Journalism and the Mid-Victorian Clerisy," *Victorian Studies* 8 (1969): 181-198, is a brilliant account of arguments for and against anonymous journalism, which was defended by many editors for reasons of professionalism. A. S. Collins, *The Profession of Letters: A Study of the Relation of Author to Patron, Publisher, and Public, 1780-1832* (New York: E. P. Dutton and Company, 1929), makes a persuasive case for journalism as "the great avenue to success in the profession of letters."

Finally, there have been a number of books and articles in recent years that deal with editing as an offshoot of a larger study. Both Joel H. Wiener, *The War of the Unstamped: The Movement to Repeal the British Newspaper Tax, 1830-1836* (Ithaca, New York: Cornell University Press, 1969), and Patricia Hollis, *The Pauper Press: A Study in Working-Class Radicalism of the 1830s* (London: Oxford University Press, 1970), contain a great deal of information about the editors of radical unstamped papers. Brian Harrison, *Drink and the Victorians: The Temperance Question in England, 1815-1872* (London: Faber and Faber, 1971), is perceptive on the subject of temperance editing. Dorothy Thompson, *The Chartists: Popular Politics in the Industrial Revolution* (London: Maurice Temple Smith, 1984), has an interesting chapter on "The Chartist Press." Both David Roberts, *Paternalism in Early Victorian England* (New Brunswick, New Jersey: Rutgers University Press, 1979), and Gertrude Himmelfarb, *The Idea of Poverty: England in the Early Industrial Age* (New York: Alfred A. Knopf, 1984), draw heavily on the writings of editors for illustrative material.

Index

Notes on Contributors

JOSEF L. ALTHOLZ is professor of history at the University of Minnesota. He is the author of *The Liberal Catholic Movement in England* (1962), *The Churches in the Nineteenth Century* (1967), and a bibliographical handbook, *Victorian England, 1837-1901*. He has also edited *The Mind and Art of Victorian England* (1976) and is a coeditor of *The Correspondence of Lord Acton and Richard Simpson*, 3 vols. (1971-75). At present he is working on a general history of the religious periodical press in nineteenth-century Britain.

MARY BOSTETTER is an American historian who has been working on Victorian medical history in London for the last ten years. She has recently completed her biography of Dr. Thomas Wakley and is presently writing a history of the medical reform movement in Britain for the four-volume history of the American and British medical professions.

ROBERT A. COLBY, professor of library and information studies at Queen College, has for a long time been a student of the Victorian reading public. His principal publications are *Fiction with a Purpose* (1967), *Thackeray's Canvas of Humanity: An Author and His Public* (1979), and *The Equivocal Virtue: Mrs. Oliphant and the Victorian Literary Marketplace* (1966, with Vineta Colby). His essay in this volume will eventually be incorporated in a book in progress on the relationship between fiction and didactic literary forms in the nineteenth century.

STEPHEN ELWELL is an independent scholar living and working in Cincinnati, Ohio. He completed a dissertation on "Victorian Middle-Class Culture and the English Popular Magazine" at Indiana University-Bloomington in 1981.

DEREK FRASER, recently professor of history at UCLA, was formerly profesor of modern history at the University of Bradford. He is the author of several books and many articles on Victorian England, including *Urban Politics in Victorian England* (1976) and *Power and Authority in the Victorian City* (1979). He is currently working on a study of the making of social policy during the 1940s.

SHEILA R. HERSTEIN is associate professor of library science at City College. She has published articles on aspects of Victorian history and is the author of *Barbara Leigh Smith Bodichon (1827-1891): Mid-Victorian Feminist,* to be published by Yale University Press in 1985.

ANNE HUMPHERYS is professor of English at Lehman College. She has published *Travels into the Poor Man's Country: the Work of Henry Mayhew* (1977) and articles on Dickens, G. W. M. Reynolds, and Mayhew. She is currently working on a study of popular literature in the Victorian period, particularly as seen in the work of G. W. M. Reynolds.

CHRISTOPHER KENT, professor of history at the University of Saskatchewan, was the editor of the *Canadian Journal of History*, 1977-1983. He has written several articles on Victorian periodicals, most recently the introduction to Alvin Sullivan, ed., *British Literary Magazines of the Victorian and Edwardian Age.* He is the author of *Brains and Numbers: Comtism, Elitism and Democracy in Mid-Victorian England* (1978) and is currently working on two books, one on the relationship between the novel and social history, the other on the anatomy of bohemia in Victorian London.

ANN P. ROBSON, associate professor of history at the University of Toronto and a member of the Editorial Committee of the *Collected Works of J. S. Mill,* is currently editing Mill's newspaper writings for that edition. She is also working on a biography of Helen Taylor.

JOHN M. ROBSON, professor of English, Victoria College, University of Toronto, and general and textual editor of the *Collected Works of J. S. Mill,* has most recently edited *Essays on French History and Historians* and *Essays on Equality, Law, and Education,* respectively vols. XX and XXI. He is working with Ann P. Robson and Bruce Kinzer on a study of Mill's parliamentary career.

BARBARA QUINN SCHMIDT is associate professor of English at Southern Illinois University at Edwardsville and vice president of the Research Society for Victorian Periodicals. She has published a number of articles on aspects of Victorian publishing and journalism.

JOANNE SHATTOCK is bibliographer at the Victorian Studies Centre and lecturer in English at the University of Leicester. She has edited, with Michael Wolff, *The Victorian Periodicals Press: Samplings and Soundings* (1982) and has published articles on literary reviewing, the quarterlies, nineteenth-century publishing, and the novel. She is currently working on a book on the Victorian quarterlies.

GEORGE A. SPATER, a former chairman of American Airlines, retired to England in the 1970s to undertake scholarly research on the Victorian era. He published *A Marriage of True Minds: An Intimate Portrait of Leonard and Virginia Wolff*, with Ian Parsons, in 1978 and *William Cobbett: The Poor Man's Friend*, two volumes, in 1982. He was working on a life of Thomas Paine at the time of his death in June 1984.

HARTLEY S. SPATT teaches in the Department of Humanities, State University of New York, Maritime College. He has published many articles on Victorian literature and art, including studies of Conrad, Morris, and Mary Shelley. He is currently writing a book on *The Narrative Impulse in Nineteenth-Century English Poetry*.

CHARLOTTE C. WATKINS is professor emeritus of English, Howard University. She is the author of numerous articles on eighteenth-century and Victorian literature.

JOEL H. WIENER, professor of history at City College, has published widely on nineteenth-century British history. His books include *The War of the Unstamped* (1969), *A Descriptive Finding List of Unstamped British Periodicals* (1970), and *Radicalism and Freethought in Victorian Britain* (1983). He has edited two multivolume collections of documents: *Great Britain: Foreign Policy and the Span of Empire* (1972) and *Great Britain: The Lion at Home* (1974). He is currently writing a biography of William Lovett.

About the Editor

JOEL H. WIENER is Professor of History and Chairman of the Department at the City College of New York. He is the author of *Radicalism and Freethought in Victorian Britain* (Greenwood Press, 1983), *Great Britain: Foreign Policy and the Span of Empire, A Descriptive Finding List of Unstamped Periodicals, The War of the Unstamped* and essays in *Victorian Periodicals: A Guide to Research* and *Censorship: 500 Years of Conflict.*